This volume makes available for the first time in English the most important of Hans-Georg Gadamer's extensive writings on art and literature. The principal text included is "The Relevance of the Beautiful," Gadamer's most sustained treatment of philosophical aesthetics. The eleven other essays focus particularly on the challenge issued by modern painting and literature to our customary ideas of art, and use that challenge to revitalize our understanding of it. Gadamer demonstrates the continuing importance of such concepts as imitation, truth, symbol, and play for our appreciation of contemporary art, and thereby establishes its continuity with the Western tradition.

The essays here are not technical and are readily accessible to the beginning student and the general reader. The collection as a whole serves to illustrate the practice of hermeneutics and to introduce Gadamer's thought. Robert Bernasconi provides an introduction clarifying the central aims of the essays and their relations to Gadamer's major work, *Truth and Method*, and to the philosophy of art since Kant. A bibliography of Gadamer's writings available in English is also included.

THE RELEVANCE OF THE BEAUTIFUL
AND OTHER ESSAYS

THE RELEVANCE
OF THE
BEAUTIFUL AND
OTHER ESSAYS

Hans-Georg Gadamer

Translated by Nicholas Walker

Edited with an Introduction by
Robert Bernasconi

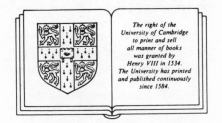

The right of the
University of Cambridge
to print and sell
all manner of books
was granted by
Henry VIII in 1534.
The University has printed
and published continuously
since 1584.

Cambridge University Press

CAMBRIDGE

NEW YORK   PORT CHESTER

MELBOURNE   SYDNEY

Published by the Press Syndicate of the University of Cambridge
The Pitt Building, Trumpington Street, Cambridge CB2 1RP
40 West 20th Street, New York, NY 10011, USA
10 Stamford Road, Oakleigh, Melbourne 3166, Australia

Part I published in German as *Die Aktualität des Schönen,*
© Phillip Reclam Jr., Stuttgart, 1977.

Part II published in German in *Kleine Schriften, Band II, IV*
© J.C.B. Mohr (Paul Siebeck). Tübingen, 1967 and 1977.

Appendix published in German as "Anschauung und Anschaulichkeit" in
Anschauung als ästhetische Kategorie, ed. R. Bubner et al.,
© Vandenhoeck & Ruprecht, Gottingen, 1980.

English translation © Cambridge University Press 1986

First published 1986
Reprinted 1987, 1988, 1989, 1991

Printed in the United States of America

Library of Congress Cataloging-in-Publication Data

Gadamer, Hans-Georg, 1900–
The relevance of the beautiful and other essays.
Bibliography: p.
Includes index.
1. Aesthetics. I. Bernasconi, Robert. II. Title.
B3248.G34G33 1986 111'.85   86-12947

British Library Cataloguing in Publication Data

Gadamer, Hans-Georg
The relevance of the beautiful and other essays.
1. Aesthetics
I. Title II. Bernasconi, Robert
700'.1 BH39

ISBN 0 521 24178 2 hardback
ISBN 0 521 33953 7 paperback

Contents

vi   *Contents*

Foreword

This book contains a selection of previously untranslated essays by the German philosopher Hans-Georg Gadamer on the hermeneutics of art and literature. Gadamer's extensive influence on English speaking literary critics, philosophers, and theologians, both through his major work *Truth and Method* and his frequent visits to the United States, has made such a collection long overdue. The main item in the collection is the lecture series "The Relevance of the Beautiful," Gadamer's most sustained work devoted specifically to the question of art. Together with the other essays included here, all but one of which postdates *Truth and Method*, the reader should be able to construct a balanced impression of the range and development of Gadamer's thinking on art over the last twenty-five years or so. This volume does not include any of Gadamer's numerous interpretative essays on specific poets, such as Goethe, Hölderlin, George, Rilke, or Celan, although many of these also warrant translation.

With the exception of a more technical essay on Kant's concept of intuition, which has for that reason been placed in an appendix, all of the pieces included here are readily accessible to the general reader. This is something that might be regarded as unusual for a work by a major contemporary European philosopher. Nevertheless Gadamer's apparent straightforwardness bears with it the corresponding danger that some of the underlying issues of these essays might be overlooked. Ease of assimilation can, like over-familiarity, be more obstructive than helpful to the hermeneutical process, precisely because it appears to render a hermeneutic understanding unnecessary. In my introduction I have sought to confront that obstacle by concentrating on those issues that will in the first instance be most foreign to many readers of this volume but that, once discovered, will prove the most challenging. This is why I have focused on the issues I have – Gadamer's relation to Heidegger, his interpretation of Kant's *Critique of Judgment*, the question of the so called "death of art," the relation of these essays to *Truth and Method* – and not out of a belief that writers should be read in terms of their original context.

Gadamer's questions are, like his whole approach, quite different from those of contemporary Anglo-American aesthetics, and yet he more than anyone would want to find points of contact that would allow for a genuine dialogue. These points of contact are in my view best sought in the tradition of philosophical reflection on art that we in the West hold in common. The renewed interest in the history of aesthetics on the part of Anglo-American writers gives this collection a certain timeliness. It will not, however, take the reader long to discover that the essays in this volume do not belong to the genre of the academic paper that has come to dominate the practice of philosophy in the English-speaking world. Such papers are written to be defended. That is not Gadamer's way, and philosophers brought up in this mold may find themselves puzzled by the way Gadamer sometimes overstates his case without protecting himself through the obvious qualifications. Art historians and literary critics will no doubt be more generous, but being unused to philosophers trespassing on their respective fields, they might wish that Gadamer had gone into more detail with his examples, while at the same time challenging him whenever he does. But if Gadamer sometimes scorns exactness and specificity, I trust his generalizations may be found more suggestive and provocative than confusing and irritating. It would be a mistake to regard as dogmatic or as final assertions statements that are only meant to have the status of interventions in a continuing dialogue.

I believe that the light touch Gadamer displays, as well as the thematic unity of the book, will make this book a suitable one for introductory courses in aesthetics. With this in mind, I have greatly extended the number of references given, while trying – I hope not too unsuccessfully – to avoid giving students too little credit for what they might already know or their teachers too much credit for what they would want their students to know. These editorial additions have all been indicated so that they can be readily distinguished from Gadamer's own references, except in the case of "Intuition and Vividness," where references to Kant's *Critique of*

Judgment are to be found in the main body of the text. When Gadamer revised "The Relevance of the Beautiful" for republication as an inexpensive paperback in the popular Reclam series, the main alteration he made was to multiply the number of references. I have tried to complete the process of identifying all quotations in this and the other essays in the volume, although I have on occasion been defeated. Where Gadamer has made an error in transcribing a quotation or a reference, the correction has usually been made silently, unless there was some special reason for drawing attention to it. References have been given to the standard English translations, although those translations have not always been followed in the main body of the text.

In the course of translating Gadamer's essays, an attempt has been made to reduce the use of words with a linguistic bias toward the male sex. On many occasions, however, this could only have been accomplished by complicating or rewriting Gadamer's sentences. In such instances, male nouns and pronouns have reluctantly been maintained.

In my introduction, I try to explain why I believe that, although the first part of *Truth and Method* remains quite indispensable for an understanding of Gadamer's approach to art, it cannot be regarded as Gadamer's definitive discussion of art and the aesthetic consciousness. One reason is that the discussion of art there remained subordinated to the theme of truth in the human sciences. One can mourn the fact that Gadamer has not chosen to write an extended monograph on the arts, but in the absence of such a book, we must make do with the essays collected in this volume. In fact they afford the not inconsiderable compensation of showing Gadamer in his true colors as an essayist and a teacher. It has to be admitted that the essays collected here prove more repetitive than would have been the case had Gadamer indeed written a single systematic treatise devoted to the question of art. Gadamer is not a system builder, a fact that lies very much at the heart of his conception of philosophy. To see Gadamer repeatedly approaching the same issue from different angles, always looking for new ways to illuminate the problems that preoccupy him, is to witness the real Gadamer.

Readers will readily observe for themselves the development of Gadamer's views. To assist them, the essays that accompany "The Relevance of the Beautiful" have been presented in chronological order. The list of sources at the front of this volume shows that chronologically, "The Relevance of the Beautiful" would stand ninth.

Nick Walker and I would like to share in thanking David Krell for coming to our rescue when on a couple of occasions our best efforts could still not penetrate Gadamer's idiom. Krell proved always so helpful that we might justly be blamed for not turning to him more often. I myself would in turn like to thank Nick Walker for his careful work on the translation and for his patience during the many hours we spent discussing it. I am particularly grateful to him for his help in bringing Dan Tate's version of "Intuition and Vividness" into uniformity with the other translations in this collection. Finally, I would like to thank Dan Tate for allowing us to include in an appendix his translation of "Intuition and Vividness," in which Gadamer gives his most sustained reading of Kant's *Critique of Judgment* so far, thereby illuminating the remarks made by Gadamer on Kant in other essays in the volume, as I try to show in my introduction.

Robert Bernasconi

Editor's introduction

Although Edmund Husserl, the founder of phenomenology, had relatively little to say about the question of art, many of the thinkers aligned with the phenomenological movement have given a central place to painting, architecture, and, above all, poetry. They have not regarded the arts as just one more sphere in which philosophical concepts might be applied and tested. Rather they have sought to learn from individual poems and paintings. And insofar as they have also engaged in more general discussions of art, these have tended in consequence to explore how it is that we might learn from a poet or an artist. In other words, they have been preoccupied with the sense in which we might speak of the truth of a work of art.

So, for example, Heidegger's influential lecture of 1936, "The Origin of the Work of Art," raises the question of the epochal nature of truth in the context of a discussion of art.[1] Art is of course for Heidegger only one way in which truth occurs, but it was through a reading of Hölderlin's poems that Heidegger came to pose the question in the way he did, and this brought a pronounced urgency to the question of the relation of art and truth. The development of Heidegger's understanding of the task of thinking is impossible to follow if one does not take into account Hölderlin's self-interpretation as a poet in "unpropitious times."[2] To take another example, Merleau-Ponty's study of perception is much indebted to what he had learned from the painter Cézanne. Like Heidegger, Merleau-Ponty came to reflect on how it is that painters and sculptors can instruct us about a world upon which science depends but about which it finds itself unable to speak. Taking Klee and Rodin as his principal examples, Merleau-Ponty pursued this question in the essay "Eye and Mind."[3]

Phenomenology's turn to the arts is in sharp contrast with the dominant role that science has played throughout the whole modern period by providing a model for philosophy and the human sciences generally. Nor should it be forgotten that phenomenology as understood by Husserl very much reflected this tendency, a tendency that has essentially meant the dominance of method. In Nietzsche's phrase, "it is not the victory of science that distinguishes our nineteenth century, but the victory of scientific method over science."[4] When in *Truth and Method,* his magnum opus of 1960, Gadamer sought to show the drawbacks of methodology's rule within the human sciences, it was inevitable, given his background in the phenomenological school, that he would turn first to our experience of the work of art.[5] Essentially Gadamer's point was that we gain access through the arts to an irresistible truth that the dogmatic application of method overlooks. Method is not presented by Gadamer in crude antithesis to truth, but Gadamer's reader is left in no doubt that concentration on method can conceal much that art and history has to teach us.

To a certain extent, Gadamer's treatment of art in *Truth and Method* is one-sided precisely because he uses the example of art to make a point of more general significance.[6] All but one of the lectures and essays collected here were written after *Truth and Method* and in them we see Gadamer extending and refining the concepts that he had first introduced in that book. We also see him trying, for example in "The Play of Art," to develop his description of what actually happens when we undergo an experience with a work of art, believing that this will prove more instructive than an analysis of the logical status of aesthetic judgments. He is more concerned with what our experience of art actually is than with what it thinks it is (*TM,* 89), just as *Truth and Method* was generally more concerned with what takes place in the human sciences than with what practitioners of the human sciences would have take place there (*TM,* xvi). The issue of the truth of art remains particularly prominent. But a new question emerges, one that remained undeveloped in *Truth and Method,* although, as I shall try to show, it is of fundamental significance for that book. This question is best introduced with reference to Heidegger, who as Gadamer's teacher in Marburg during the 1920s had a decisive influence on him. Any assessment of Gadamer inevitably turns on his relation to Heidegger and he himself explicitly asks that his efforts be measured against Heidegger's own thorough penetration of both Husserl's descriptive rigor and Dilthey's historical breadth (*TM*, xv).

When Heidegger poses the question of the origin of the work of art, he deliberately raises it in such a way as to invite the conventional answers that refer art to the genius of the artist or the taste of the observer and the conditions under which the work is seen. But in the course of Heidegger's questioning he instructs us to think not in these terms, but rather to conceive of art as an origin announcing and enshrining the ultimate truths of an epoch. When Heidegger says that art is historical, he makes it clear that he means that art plays a founding role in history, and that this founding is an "overflowing" that cannot be explained in terms of anything else, not even retrospectively (*PLT*, 75). Indeed, the primary sense of history is no longer that of a continuing sequence through time, but of rare founding events that break with what went before. Heidegger would not deny the unity of Western art, but great art can never be confined to this unity because it always disrupts and begins anew.

There is much in Gadamer that is directly reminiscent of Heidegger's discussion. For example, the notion of excess or superabundance (*Überschuss*), which is sometimes introduced when Gadamer is discussing art as play, recalls the sense in which for Heidegger art is an "overflowing" (*Überfluss*). Gadamer even talks of the work of art as being its own origin (*TM*, 108), but by that he means that the work is to be understood in terms of itself and not from outside, so that the word no longer bears the sense of founding an epoch as in Heidegger. These examples are indicative of an important shift in focus that has occurred in the course of Gadamer's assimilation of Heidegger's account of the truth of the work of art. The latter is explicitly confined to "great art" (*PLT*, 40), whereas Gadamer attempts to transform Heidegger's concepts so that they become generally applicable to the broader range of art. Indeed, he is also concerned to show the continuity of what we call art and, for example, ritual dance and other religious rites. It could not, except in a very loose sense, be said of everything we call art that it institutes a world, but Gadamer does take from Heidegger the idea that the work brings its own world with it, so that there is in our encounter with it what he calls elsewhere "a fusion of horizons" (*TM*, 273). In this way the work of art issues us a challenge, or as

Gadamer would prefer to say, makes a claim on us, thereby appealing to a concept with theological as well as Heideggerian overtones.[7] He means by this that the experience of the work of art does not conform to the model of an adventure. Art is not to be understood as a magical, fantastic realm to which we can escape. We do not encounter the work of art without being transformed in the process.

Gadamer makes this point in German by means of the distinction between *Erfahrung* and *Erlebnis* (*TM*, 62–63, 316–320). When we say of a play, a novel, or a film that it introduces us to an unfamiliar world, we are referring to what is no doubt an impressive technical achievement. But if we were to base our assessment of its excellence on that alone we would have succumbed to the aesthetic conception of art as *Erlebnis*. For if we do not take anything from that world, if we are unchanged when we leave it, then for Gadamer we will not have heard the claim art makes on us. We will have reduced it to a mere entertainment, an interlude. However, if we undergo an experience of art in the sense of *Erfahrung*, a word that Gadamer borrows from Hegel and Heidegger, then we will find that we have been transformed. It is in these terms that Gadamer tries to extend the range of application of Heidegger's notion of the truth of a work of art, although it should be noted that there is with Gadamer also a narrowing of the range of application of the notion of art. For we find that we have no basis for discussing art except where we have had this experience, and the range and occurrence of such experiences will presumably be different for everyone.

There is no doubt that this imposes its own limitations on Gadamer's discussion, which are often overlooked or misunderstood. But rather than rehearse these, I shall here limit myself to the question of whether Heidegger's concepts can be taken up and extended in the way suggested by Gadamer, because I believe that this question is the source of the difficulties that Gadamer confronts in his recent essays on art. Gadamer conceives of his own work as engaged, like Heidegger's, in the "overcoming of aesthetics," but the phrase does not mean the same for both thinkers. For Heidegger, aesthetics began with Plato and Aristotle at the very time when "the great art and also the great philosophy which flourished along with it comes to an end."[8] Heidegger is not here passing an aesthetic judgment; he is concerned with elucidating art's role "of representing the absolute, that is, of establishing the absolute definitively as such in the realm of historical man" (*Nietzsche,* 84). The criterion is Hegel's and it formed the basis for Hegel's claim that "art is and remains for us, with regard to its highest determination something past."[9] Heidegger accepts this judgment even though, as I shall try to show later, he transforms its meaning in the process.

Gadamer understands the overcoming of aesthetics somewhat differently. For him the notion of aesthetics is often used in a technical sense to characterize a specific consciousness of art which, though prepared for earlier, only becomes clearly apparent from the late eighteenth century onward. Philosophically it takes the form of a one-sided reading of Kant, but it also has an institutional reality as, for example, in the way the institution of the museum has developed (*TM,* 78). Gadamer's initial point against aesthetics is that the description that aesthetic consciousness provides of its encounter with art is inadequate: aesthetic consciousness is more than it knows itself to be. The fault lies in the abstraction – sometimes referred to as "disinterestedness," though not as Kant uses the term – that engulfs aesthetic consciousness. Gadamer also gives to it the name "aesthetic differentiation," by which he means abstraction from all the conditions of the work's accessibility, including the religious or secular function that gives it significance. This of course is what is at issue for him in his description of the transformation that we undergo in our encounter with art. By understanding art as a realm divorced from everyday life, aesthetics comes to be viewed as separated from the truth. Indeed, insofar as our notion of art is a product of this aesthetic consciousness, the very concept of art becomes questionable (*TM,* 73). The breadth of the notion of art we usually employ is sustained only by a kind of abstraction whereby we deprive many religious or even secular artifacts of their original significance.[10] The specific determination by which our concept of art includes painting, sculpture, architecture, music, and poetry but excludes much else, has its source only as far back as the eighteenth century. Gadamer's notion of art is by contrast sustained not by abstraction but by reference to a form of experience. Gadamer's model is not so much "great art" as the relation of art that he regards as characteristic of "the great ages in the history of art" (*TM,* 73).

The challenge that Gadamer issues to the idea of art as a special magical realm is carried through by showing the continuity between the world of art and our everyday world. "We sublate (*aufheben*) the discontinuous punctuality of experience (*Erlebnis*) in the continuity

of our existence (*Dasein*)" (*TM*, 86). This conjunction in the same
sentence of Hegel's word *aufheben* and Heidegger's conception of
the temporality of *Dasein* (*TM*, 109) is not accidental, for these two
thinkers provide the decisive theoretical underpinning for Gadamer's notion of continuity at this point. Gadamer finds in ancient
tragedy an illustration of how art contributes to our self-understanding only on the basis of such continuity (*TM*,113). Tragedy is
dependent on the spectators acknowledging that the actions on the
stage take place in a world continuous with their own. This is why
he believes that tragedy is possible only insofar as the spectators
recognize themselves and their finiteness in the power of a fate that
affects everyone (*TM*, 117).[11] At this juncture the discussion is concerned with the continuity of an individual's life. Only in the second
part of *Truth and Method* does Gadamer makes the transition to historical continuity. Indeed, his account of Dilthey focuses on the latter's inability to make this transition, in part because of his
dependence on the notion of *Erlebnis* (*TM*, 97). Gadamer believes
that Hegel and Heidegger will also provide him with the resources
for making the transition to historical continuity.

Nevertheless Gadamer fails in *Truth and Method* to integrate this
discussion of historical continuity with his own earlier discussion of
art. He does not there fulfill his undertaking to "absorb aesthetics
into hermeneutics" (*TM*, 146) and so his subsequent essays on art
which are now collected in this volume can properly be seen as
attempting to do this.[12] The difficulty is that whereas Gadamer can
confront aesthetics with the theme of the continuity of life and art
by reference to Hegel and Heidegger, it is less obvious that the question of the historical continuity of art can be dealt with in the same
way. It is sufficient in this regard to refer to the theme of the "past
character of art" as maintained by Hegel and adopted from him by
Heidegger to indicate the difficulties involved. Gadamer's attempt
to establish the idea of the general continuity of the tradition by
drawing on both Hegel and Heidegger is a complex matter that I
have tried to deal with elsewhere.[13] Here I shall confine myself to
the question as it arises in respect of art.

Hegel's idea that art is something past is not to be confused with
popular representations of the so-called death of art. Hegel is not
asking us to believe that art will come to a halt. His point is rather
that the time of its highest vocation is over and that the role once
played by art is now fulfilled by philosophy. What occupies

Heidegger, on the other hand, is the thought that philosophy might also be "past" in the same sense as art, thereby transforming the meaning of Hegel's claim. And again in contrast to Hegel, Heidegger invites us to await "another beginning" of thinking and of art. The importance of the poet Hölderlin is that he is, as it were, the prophet of this possibility. In the opening pages of "The Relevance of the Beautiful," Gadamer reexamines Hegel's claim in an effort to establish the continuing relevance of art. In the process he concedes a great deal about contemporary alienation and the break in tradition that takes place in twentieth-century painting, just as in "Art and Imitation" he will acknowledge the sense in which mass production has deprived the modern industrial world of good honest "things." But whether Gadamer succeeds in assimilating Hegel's position or not, the greater difficulties arise in respect to Heidegger – and these difficulties constitute the hidden agenda of Gadamer's essays on art. For in the context of the question of the historical continuity of art, it is no longer legitimate to say that Gadamer extends the application of Heidegger's notion of the truth of the work of art. The conception of art as an historical origin and an overflowing conflicts with a conception of its overriding continuity. So far as Gadamer is concerned, "It is precisely continuity that every understanding of time has to achieve, even when it is a question of the temporality of the work of art" (*TM*, 109). Gadamer can draw on Hegel's retrospective gaze which shows that where the new claimed to replace the old, the old was taken up and preserved along with the new in the process of negation. That is *Aufhebung*. But there is in Heidegger no such standpoint from which we might make that retrospective gaze. That is one major difference between Heidegger's history of Being and Hegel's history of Spirit, and it opens the way to Heidegger's conception of a tradition that speaks to us only in a fragmentary and ambiguous way.

Gadamer denies epochal discontinuity while at the same time maintaining the truth of the work of art, two claims that were inseparable in Heidegger's discussion of art. The history of art has for Heidegger, like the history of philosophy, a certain unity even if it cannot be told as a continuous story. The decisive break therefore is found in the modern period, and so inevitably Gadamer must turn to the discussion of modern art and literature in order to justify his recasting of Heidegger's concepts. This serves to explain the frequent references in this volume to the question of pure poetry.[14]

Gadamer introduces it as a possible counter-example to his insistence on continuity. Its renunciation of linguistic content might seem to amount to a renunciation of one of the more obvious ways in which continuity is secured; its refusal to acknowledge the non-artistic values of truth and morality would seem to exemplify aesthetics. And yet no one would deny that what goes under the name of "pure poetry" is genuinely art. Gadamer's strategy here, as with non-objective painting, is to show that, properly understood, the ancient idea of *mimesis* can still be applied.[15] In fact, throughout these essays, Gadamer appeals to such notions as imitation, participation, play, symbol, and festival with the aim of showing their relevance to modern as much as to traditional art. Gadamer does not give these concepts a normative status; he is simply offering their resilience as evidence of the way the art of modernity stands united with the great art of the past. In this way Gadamer strives to bring his reflections on art into conformity with his account of historical consciousness.

Gadamer's discussion of the continuing relevance of the Greek experience of the religious festival and the Greek conception of mimesis illustrate his hermeneutic practice. We find ourselves in a situation where, although at first we seem unequipped to understand the present condition of art, the resources for such an understanding are indeed available to us if we but return to the tradition, a tradition that we grossly underestimate if we regard it as in some way "past". Modern writers and artists may frequently have understood themselves as in revolt against previous forms of art, but their revolt has often had as its real target only the aesthetic definition of art developed in the late eighteenth and nineteenth centuries. Once the philosopher is able to show that the aesthetic definition of art is only a limited and distorted conception of art, then the self-understanding of the contemporary artist as someone in revolt against the tradition is itself open to challenge. It is only by way of the past that we have access to the present, and yet it is in the present and by way of what is most new and unforeseeable in it that we discover the resources of the past.

Gadamer's reading of Kant's *Critique of Judgment* as given in the essays in this volume, particularly "Intuition and Vividness" offers a further illustration of this process and one that again shows how Gadamer's position has developed since the publication of *Truth and Method*. There has been some controversy as to the degree to which we find in Kant's *Critique of Judgment* a genuine basis for a philosophy of art and whether, if such a basis is there, it is to be found in the concept of genius, which is how many of Kant's immediate successors read him. Gadamer's discussion of the relation of taste to genius in 1960 was by no means unambiguous, although this was perhaps only a reflection of the ambiguity of Kant's text itself. Gadamer is insistent that "there is no shift in Kant's standpoint from taste to genius" (*TM*, 43) and that "there is no question of the position of genius ousting that of taste" (*TM*, 50). At the same time he concedes that there is "some justification in Kant for this reversal of values" once Kant introduces the idea of a perfection of taste (*TM*, 51–52). Indeed, he goes so far as to suggest that Kant's grounding of aesthetics in the concept of taste was "not wholly satisfactory" and that it would have been more appropriate for him to use the concept of genius than that of taste, although in saying this he would appear to be vindicating the reading of Kant provided by German idealism and by Schiller (*TM*, 53).

All of this is in stark contrast to Gadamer's direct assertion in "The Relevance of the Beautiful" that in Kant "the overcoming of the standpoint of taste in favor of the standpoint of genius" took place (see p. 21 below). This formulation – which Gadamer had earlier used with reference to Schiller in direct opposition to Kant (*TM*, 73) – might be dismissed as a passing simplification rather than a revision of Gadamer's position, but in the essay "Art and Imitation" Gadamer says similarly that the concept of genius rather than the free beauty of ornament forms the basis of Kant's theory of art (see p. 97). These restatements of Gadamer's position would allow us to conclude that even though Gadamer remains convinced that the notion of genius is suspect, we would also be ill-advised to look, as has sometimes been done, to Kant's discussion of decorative beauty in an effort to escape its influence.

But the essay "Intuition and Vividness" draws the map somewhat differently. Gadamer no longer feels the need to resist the concept of genius that accomplishes the transition from natural beauty to artistic beauty. The point is rather to insure that "genius" is not understood according to a theoretical paradigm that distorts its proper role in the elucidation of our experience of art (see p. 165). Once this has been done – and it is wholly in keeping with Gadamer's overall project to insure that the model of scientific knowledge remains within its proper bounds – then we may formulate an aesthetics of the sublime, an aesthetics that surpasses both the standpoint of taste and that of genius, an aesthetics that is no longer "aesthetics" in the contested sense. The focus of the 1980 essay on intuition, therefore, does not lie so much in the transition to genius as in Kant's account of the sublime. In *Truth and Method* Gadamer presented Kant as occupying "an intermediate" position (*TM*, 52). The complexity of Gadamer's discussion is adequate testimony to the difficulty of maintaining the appropriate balance. But much of the complexity arose no doubt because of the role Kant was made to play in the book as a whole. Gadamer's presentation of Kant had the negative purpose of showing how the use of Kant as a basis for the philosophy of art proves inadequate, whether it be by way of an aesthetics of taste, of genius, or of ornament. On that occasion Gadamer's focus was on the aesthetics of genius, because he believes that it provided the basis for the subjectivization and abstraction or "differentiation" of aesthetics in the narrower and contested sense, and because he would go on in the second part of *Truth and Method* (*TM*, 169) to show that aesthetics was responsible for the limitations of Schleiermacher's hermeneutics.

In "Intuition and Vividness" the focus has shifted and, as in the other essays, Gadamer makes an attempt to find within the tradition the resources for an understanding of nonobjective painting. There is no doubt that there is much in Kant's discussion of "dependent beauty" that ill fits nonobjective painting and "pure poetry." And yet one hardly does justice to nonobjective painting by placing it within the alternative sphere of "free beauty" along with carpets and wallpaper. Gadamer's proposal is that we should look to the free play of understanding and imagination in the aesthetic ideas in order to situate this tendency in modern art. Gadamer is clear that he is not offering a rigorous or complete interpretation of Kant: the question governing the interpretation is too one-sided for that. But he is, as it were, highlighting a resource in Kant upon which we may draw in our efforts to understand the situation of art today. In other words, Gadamer here gives us an exemplification of how the continuity of tradition is maintained within change. We can find in Kant another route which avoids making either taste or genius the ultimate standpoint. This alternative route is by way of Hegel's lectures on art, whose proper significance has, Gadamer believes, suffered in consequence of its neo-Kantian interpretation. For it is Hegel whom Gadamer has in mind when he writes here of an art where "humanity encounters itself" (see p. 167) or indeed whenever the theme of self-recognition arises in these essays, as it so frequently does.

In Gadamer's account, modern art does not so much break with tradition as extend our awareness of the depth and versatility of our heritage. But it has to be asked whether the freedom and openness of Gadamer's interpretations of the tradition are not themselves symptomatic of a greater fragmentation than Gadamer could afford to allow. This is particularly apparent in the plurality of readings that emerges as Gadamer reflects on the history of Kant's text and at the same time suggests still further possibilities for its development. Gadamer has himself offered an elegant account of the position in which we find ourselves. "We accept that the matter at hand presents itself historically in different ways at different times or when approached from a different standpoint. We accept that those ways are not simply cancelled (*aufheben*) in the continuity of progressive research, but are like mutually exclusive conditions that persist by themselves and are only united in us. Our historical consciousness is always filled with a multiplicity of voices that echo the past" (*TM*, 252). But with this description, as also with his description of the alienation of the modern world and the loss of thinghood there, the echoes take on a Heideggerian rather than a Hegelian resonance and Gadamer's privileging of continuity over rupture remains in question. This is what makes the issues discussed in this volume so pressing and the assessment Gadamer offers of them so important to confront.

Sources

PART I

Die Aktualität des Schönen (Stuttgart:Philipp Reclam, 1977). A revised version of a lecture delivered under the title "Art as Play, Symbol, and Festival" during the Salzburger Hochschulwochen from 29 July to 10 August 1974. The original version was published in *Kunst Heute,* ed. Ansgar Paus (Graz, Austria: Styria, 1975), pp. 25–84.

PART II

"Über die Festlichkeit des Theaters." Text of a lecture delivered on the occasion of the 175th anniversary of the founding of the National Theater of Mannheim. Originally appeared in *Mannheimer Hefte,* III (1954), pp. 26–30. Reprinted in *Kleine Schriften* Vol. II (Tübingen: J.C.B. Mohr, 1967), pp. 170–177. On its original publication it was dedicated to Walter F. Otto for his eightieth birthday.

"Dichten und Deuten." Lecture given at the Darmstädter Akademie für Sprache und Dichtung in Tübingen in 1961. First publication in the *Jahrbuch für Sprache und Dichtung* (1961), pp. 13–21. Reprinted in *Kleine Schriften* Vol. II, pp. 9–15.

"Bild und Gebärde." The text is a reworking of a lecture given in 1964 in Leverkusen as an introduction to Werner Scholz' exhibition, "The Mythology of the Greeks." First published in *Kleine Schriften* Vol. II, pp. 210–217.

"Vom Verstummen des Bildes." Text of a lecture given in 1965 at the opening of an exhibition in Heidelberg of the Rhein-Neckar Art Association. First published in the *Neue Zürcher Zeitung* of 21/22 August 1965. Reprinted in *Kleine Schriften* Vol. II, pp. 227–234.

"Kunst und Nachahmung." Text of a lecture given in 1966 at the Mannheimer Kunstverein. First published in *Kleine Schriften* Vol. II, pp. 16–26.

"Über den Beitrag der Dichtkunst bei der Suche nach der Wahrheit." First published in *Zeitwende Die neue Furche*, XLII (1971), pp. 402–410, under the title "Wahrheit und Dichtung." Reprinted in *Kleine Schriften* Vol. IV, (Tübingen:J. C.B.Mohr, 1977), pp. 218–227.

"Dichtung und Mimesis." First published in the *Neue Zürcher Zeitung* of 9 July 1972 under the title "Dichtung und Nachahmung." Reprinted in *Kleine Schriften* Vol. IV, pp. 228–233.

"Das Spiel der Kunst." Text of a radio talk given in 1973 and published in *Kleine Schriften* Vol. IV, pp. 234–240.

"Philosophie und Poesie." First published in *Geist und Zeichen, Festschrift für Arthur Henkel zu seinem 60. Geburtstag,* edited by H. Anton, B. Gajek, and P. Pfaff (Heidelberg: 1977), pp. 121–126. Reprinted in *Kleine Schriften* Vol. IV, pp. 241–248.

"Ästhetische und religiöse Erfahrung." *Nederlands Theologisch Tijdschrift,* XXXII (1978), pp. 218–230.

APPENDIX

"Anschauung und Anschaulichkeit" in *Anschauung als ästhetische Kategorie,* ed. by R. Bubner, K. Cramer, and R. Wiehl, *Neue Hefte für Philosophie.* XVIII-XIX (Göttingen:Vandenhoeck & Ruprecht, 1980), pp. 1–13.

It would appear from the prospectus that with only two exceptions, all the above pieces will be reprinted in Volume 8 of Gadamer's *Gesammelte Werke* to be published by J.C.B.Mohr. "Image and Gesture" will appear in Volume 9 and "Aesthetic and Religious Experience" in Volume 2. It is not entirely clear from the prospectus where the essays "The Play of Art" and "Art and Imitation" will reappear, if at all, but it seems most likely that they will also be in Volume 8. Gadamer is supervising the republication of these essays and he has indicated that he may take the opportunity to introduce revisions and additions to the previously published versions.

PART I

The relevance of
the beautiful
Art as play, symbol, and festival

I think it is most significant that the question of how art can be justified is not simply a modern problem, but one that has been with us
from the very earliest times. My first efforts as a scholar were
dedicated to this question when in 1934 I published an essay entitled
"Plato and the Poets."[1] In fact, as far as we know, it was in the context of the new philosophical outlook and the new claim to
knowledge raised by Socratic thought that art was required to justify
itself for the first time in the history of the West. Here, for the first
time, it ceased to be self-evident that the diffuse reception and interpretation of traditional subject matter handed down in pictorial or
narrative form did possess the right to truth that it had claimed.
Indeed, this ancient and serious problem always arises when a new
claim to truth sets itself up against the tradition that continues to
express itself through poetic invention or in the language of art. We
have only to consider the culture of late antiquity and its often
lamented hostility to pictorial representation. At a time when walls
were covered with incrustation, mosaics, and decoration, the artists
of the age bemoaned the passing of *their* time. A similar situation
arose with the restriction and final extinction of freedom of speech
and poetic expression imposed by the Roman Empire over the
world of late antiquity, and which Tacitus lamented in his famous
dialogue on the decline of rhetoric, the *Dialogue on Oratory*. But
above all, and here we approach our own time more closely than we
might at first realize, we should consider the position that Christianity adopted toward the artistic tradition in which it found itself.
The rejection of iconoclasm, a movement that had arisen in the
Christian Church during the sixth and seventh centuries, was a decision of incalculable significance. For the Church then gave a new
meaning to the visual language of art and later to the forms of poetry

and narrative. This provided art with a new form of legitimation. The decision was justified because only the new content of the Christian message was able to legitimate once again the traditional language of art. One of the crucial factors in the justification of art in the West was the *Biblia Pauperum,* a pictorial narration of the Bible designed for the poor, who could not read or knew no Latin and who consequently were unable to receive the Christian message with complete understanding.

The great history of Western art is the consequence of this decision which still largely determines our own cultural consciousness. A common language for the common content of our self-understanding has been developed through the Christian art of the Middle Ages and the humanistic revival of Greek and Roman art and literature, right up until the close of the eighteenth century and the great social transformations and political and religious changes with which the nineteenth century began.

In Austria and Southern Germany, for example, it is hardly necessary to describe the synthesis of classical and Christian subjects that overwhelms us with such vitality in the great surging waves of Baroque art. Certainly this age of Christian art and the whole Christian–classical, Christian–humanist tradition did not go un-challenged and underwent major changes, not least under the influence of the Reformation. It in turn brought a new kind of art into prominence, a kind of music based on the participation of the congregation, as in the work of Heinrich Schutz and Johann Sebastian Bach, for example. This new style revitalized the language of music through the text, thereby continuing in a quite new way the great unbroken tradition of Christian music that had begun with the chorale, which was itself the unity of Latin hymns and Gregorian melody bequeathed by Pope Gregory the Great.

It is against this background that the question of the justification of art first acquires a specific direction. We can seek help here from those who have already considered this question. This is not to deny that the new artistic situation experienced in our own century really does signify a break in a tradition still unified until its last great representatives in the nineteenth century. When Hegel, the great teacher of speculative idealism, gave his lectures on aesthetics first in Heidelberg and later in Berlin, one of his opening themes was the doctrine that art was for us "a thing of the past."[2] If we reconstruct Hegel's approach to the question and think it through afresh, we shall be amazed to discover how much it anticipates the question that we ourselves address to art. I should like to show this briefly by way of introduction so that we understand why it is necessary in the further course of our investigation to go beyond the self-evident character of the dominant concept of art and lay bare the anthropological foundation upon which the phenomenon of art rests and from the perspective of which we must work out a new legitimation for art.

Hegel's remark about art as "a thing of the past" represents a radical and extreme formulation of philosophy's claim to make the process through which we come to know the truth an object of our knowledge and to know this knowledge of the truth in its own right. In Hegel's eyes, this task and this claim, which philosophy has always made, are only fulfilled when philosophy comprehends and gathers up into itself the totality of truth as it has been unfolded in its historical development. Consequently Hegelian philosophy also claimed above all to have comprehended the truth of the Christian message in conceptual form. This included even the deepest mystery of Christian doctrine, the mystery of the trinity. I personally believe that this doctrine has constantly stimulated the course of thought in the West as a challenge and invitation to try and think that which continually transcends the limits of human understanding.

In fact Hegel made the bold claim to have incorporated into his philosophy this most profound mystery – which had developed, sharpened, refined, and deepened the thinking of theologians and philosophers for centuries – and to have gathered the full truth of this Christian doctrine into conceptual form. I do not want to expound here this dialectical synthesis whereby the trinity is understood philosophically, in the Hegelian manner, as a constant resurrection of the spirit. Nevertheless, I must mention it so that we are in a position to understand Hegel's attitude to art and his statement that it is for us a thing of the past. Hegel is not primarily referring to the end of the Christian tradition of pictorial imagery in the West, which, as we believe today, was actually reached then. He did not have the feeling of being plunged into a challenging world of alienation in his time, as we do today when confronted by the production of abstract and nonobjective art. Hegel's own reaction would certainly have been quite different from that of any visitor to the Louvre today who, as soon he enters this marvelous collection of the great fruits of Western painting, is overwhelmed by the

revolutionary subjects and coronation scenes depicted by the
revolutionary art of the late eighteenth and early nineteenth
centuries.

Hegel certainly did not mean – how could he? – that with the
Baroque and its later development in the Rococo, the last Western
artistic style had made its appearance on the stage of human history.
He did not know, as we know in retrospect, that the century of his-
toricism had begun. Nor could he suspect that in the twentieth century a daring liberation from the historical shackles of the
nineteenth century would succeed in making all previous art appear
as something belonging to the past in a different and more radical
sense. When Hegel spoke of art as a thing of the past he meant that
art was no longer understood as a presentation of the divine in the
self-evident and unproblematical way in which it had been understood in the Greek world. There the divine was manifest in the temple, which in the southern light stood out against the natural
background, open to the eternal powers of nature, and was visibly
represented in great sculpture, in human forms shaped by human
hands. Hegel's real thesis was that while for the Greeks the god or
the divine was principally and properly revealed in their own artistic
forms of expression, this became impossible with the arrival of
Christianity. The truth of Christianity with its new and more profound insight into the transcendence of God could no longer be adequately expressed within the visual language of art or the imagery of
poetic language. For us the work of art is no longer the presence of
the divine that we revere. The claim that art is a thing of the past
implies that with the close of antiquity, art inevitably appeared to
require justification. I have already suggested that what we call the
Christian art of the West represents the impressive way in which this
legitimation was accomplished over the centuries by the Church and
fused with the classical tradition by the humanists.

So long as art occupied a legitimate place in the world, it was
clearly able to effect an integration between community, society,
and the Church on the one hand and the self-understanding of the
creative artist on the other. Our problem, however, is precisely the
fact that this self-evident integration, and the universally shared
understanding of the artist's role that accompanies it, no longer
exists – and indeed no longer existed in the nineteenth century. It is
this fact that finds expression in Hegel's thesis. Even then, great
artists were beginning to find themselves to a greater or lesser

degree displaced in an increasingly industrialized and commercialized society, so that the modern artist found the old reputation of the itinerant artist of former days confirmed by his own bohemian fate. In the nineteenth century, every artist lived with the knowledge that he could no longer presuppose the former unproblematic communication between himself and those among whom he lived and for whom he created. The nineteenth-century artist does not live within a community, but creates for himself a community as is appropriate to his pluralistic situation. Openly admitted competition combined with the claim that his own particular form of creative expression and his own particular artistic message is the only true one, necessarily gives rise to heightened expectations. This is in fact the messianic consciousness of the nineteenth-century artist, who feels himself to be a "new savior" (Immermann) with a claim on mankind.[3] He proclaims a new message of reconciliation and as a social outsider pays the price for this claim, since with all his artistry he is only an artist for the sake of art.

But what is all this compared to the alienation and shock with which the more recent forms of artistic expression in our century tax our self-understanding as a public?

I should like to maintain a tactful silence about the extreme difficulty faced by performing artists when they bring modern music to the concert hall. It can usually only be performed as the middle item in a program – otherwise the listeners will arrive later or leave early. This fact is symptomatic of a situation that could not have existed previously and its significance requires consideration. It expresses the conflict between art as a "religion of culture" on the one hand and art as a provocation by the modern artist on the other. It is an easy matter to trace the beginnings of this conflict and its gradual radicalization in the history of nineteenth-century painting. The new provocation was heralded in the second half of the nineteenth century by the breakdown of the status of linear perspective, which was one of the fundamental presuppositions of the self-understanding of the visual arts as practised in recent centuries.[4]

This can be observed for the first time in the pictures of Hans von Marées. It was later developed by the great revolutionary movement that achieved worldwide recognition through the genius of Paul Cézanne. Certainly linear perspective is not a self-evident fact of artistic vision and expression, since it did not exist at all during the Christian Middle Ages. It was during the Renaissance, a time of a

vigorous upsurge of enthusiasm for all scientific and mathematical
construction, that linear perspective became the norm for painting
as one of the great wonders of artistic and scientific progress. It is
only as we have gradually ceased to expect linear perspective and
stopped taking it for granted that our eyes have been opened to the
great art of the High Middle Ages. At that time paintings did not
recede like views from a window with the immediate foreground
passing into the distant horizon. They were clearly to be read like a
text written in pictorial symbols, thus combining spiritual instruc-
tion with spiritual elevation.

Thus linear perspective simply represented a historical and temporary form of artistic expression. Yet its rejection anticipated more
far-reaching developments in modern art, which would take us even
further from the previous tradition of artistic form. Here I would
draw attention to the destruction of traditional form by Cubism
around 1910, a movement in which almost all the great painters of
the time participated, at least for some time; and to the further
transformation of the Cubist break with tradition, which led to the
total elimination of any reference to an external object of the process of artistic creation. It remains an open question whether or not
this denial of our realistic expectations is ever really total. But one
thing is quite certain: the naive assumption that the picture is a view
– like that which we have daily in our experience of nature or of
nature shaped by man – has clearly been fundamentally destroyed.
We can no longer see a Cubist picture or a nonobjective painting at a
glance, with a merely passive gaze. We must make an active contribution of our own and make an effort to synthesize the outlines of
the various planes as they appear on the canvas. Only then, perhaps,
can we be seized and uplifted by the profound harmony and right-
ness of a work, in the same way as readily happened in earlier times
on the basis of a pictorial content common to all. We shall have to
ask what that means for our investigation. Or, again, let me mention
modern music and the completely new vocabulary of harmony and
dissonance that it employs, or the peculiar complexity it has
achieved by breaking the older rules of composition and the principles of musical construction that were characteristic of the classical
period. We can no more avoid this than we can avoid the fact that
when we visit a museum and enter the rooms devoted to the most
recent artistic developments, we really do leave something behind
us. If we have been open to the new, we cannot help noticing a

peculiar weakening of our receptiveness when we return to the old. This reaction is clearly only a question of contrast, rather than a lasting experience of a permanent loss, but it brings out the acute difference between these new forms of art and the old.

I would also mention hermetic poetry, which has always been of particular interest to philosophers. For, where no one else can understand, it seems that the philosopher is called for. In fact, the poetry of our time has reached the limits of intelligible meaning and perhaps the greatest achievements of the greatest writers are themselves marked by tragic speechlessness in the face of the unsayable.[5] Then there is modern drama, which treats the Classical doctrine of the unity of time and action as a relic of the past and consciously and emphatically denies the unity of dramatic character, even making this denial into a formal principle of drama, as in Bertolt Brecht, for example. Then there is the case of modern architecture: what a liberation – or temptation, perhaps – it has been to defy the traditional principles of structural engineering with the help of modern materials and to create something totally new that has no resemblance to the traditional methods of erecting buildings brick upon brick. These buildings seem to teeter upon their slender delicate columns, while the walls, the whole protective outer structure, are replaced by tentlike coverings and canopies. This cursory overview is only intended to bring out what has actually happened and why art today poses a new question. Why does the understanding of what art is today present a task for thinking?

I would like to develop this on various levels. I shall proceed initially from the basic principle that our thinking in this matter must be able to cover the great traditional art of the past, as well as the art of modern times. For although modern art is opposed to traditional art, it is also true that it has been stimulated and nourished by it. We must first presuppose that both are really forms of art and that they do belong together. It is not simply that no contemporary artist could have possibly developed his own daring innovations without being familiar with the traditional language of art. Nor is it simply a matter of saying that we who experience art constantly face the coexistence of past and present. This is not simply the situation in which we find ourselves when we pass from one room to another in a museum or when we are confronted, perhaps reluctantly, with modern music on a concert program or with modern plays in the theater or even with modern reproductions of

Classical art. We are always in this position. In our daily life we proceed constantly through the coexistence of past and future. The essence of what is called spirit lies in the ability to move within the horizon of an open future and an unrepeatable past. Mnemosyne, the muse of memory and recollective appropriation, rules here as the muse of spiritual freedom. The same activity of spirit finds expression in memory and recollection, which incorporates the art of the past along with our own artistic tradition, as well as in recent daring experiments with their unprecedented deformation of form. We shall have to ask ourselves what follows from this unity of what is past and what is present.

But this unity is not only a question of our aesthetic understanding. Our task is not only to recognize the profound continuity that connects the formal language of the past with the contemporary revolution of artistic form. A new social force is at work in the claim of the modern artist. The confrontation with the bourgeois religion of culture and its ritualistic enjoyment of art leads the contemporary artist to try and involve us actively in this claim in various ways. For example, the viewer of a Cubist or a nonobjective painting has to construct it for himself by synthesizing the facets of the different aspects step by step. The claim of the artist is that the new attitude to art that inspires him establishes at the same time a new form of solidarity or universal communication. By this I do not simply mean that the great creative achievements of art are absorbed, or rather diffused, in countless ways into the practical world or the world of decorative design all around us, and so come to produce a certain stylistic unity in the world of human labor. This has always been the case and there is no doubt that the constructivist tendency that we observe in contemporary art and architecture exerts a profound influence on the design of all the appliances we encounter daily in the kitchen, the home, in transport, and in public life. It is no accident that the artist comes to terms with a tension in his work between the expectations harbored by custom and the introduction of new ways of doing things. Our situation of extreme modernity, as exhibited by this kind of conflict and tension, is so striking that it poses a problem for thought.

Two things seem to meet here: our historical consciousness and the self-conscious reflection of modern man and the artist. We should not think of historical awareness in terms of rather scholarly ideas or in terms of world-views. We should simply think of what we take for granted when confronted with any artistic work of the past. We are not even aware that we approach such things with historical consciousness. We recognize the dress of a bygone age as historical, we accept traditional pictorial subjects presented in various kinds of costume, and we are not surprised when Altdorfer as a matter of course depicts medieval soldiers marching in "modern" troop formations in his painting "The Battle of Issus" –as if Alexander the Great had actually defeated the Persians dressed as we see him there.[6] This is self-evident to us because our sensibility is historically attuned. I would even go so far as to say that without this historical sensibility we would probably be unable to perceive the precise compositional mastery displayed by earlier art. Perhaps only a person completely ignorant of history, a very rare thing today, would allow himself to be really disturbed by things that are strange in this way. Such a person would be unable to experience in an immediate way that unity of form and content that clearly belongs to the essence of all true artistic creation.

Historical consciousness, then, is not a particularly scholarly method of approach, nor one that is determined by a particular world-view. It is simply the fact that our senses are spiritually organized in such a way as to determine in advance our perception and experience of art. Clearly connected with this is the fact – and this too is a form of self-conscious reflection – that we do not require a naive recognition in which our own world is merely reproduced for us in a timelessly valid form. On the contrary, we are self-consciously aware of both our own great historical tradition as a whole and, in their otherness, even the traditions and forms of quite different cultural worlds that have not fundamentally affected Western history. And we can thereby appropriate them for ourselves. This high level of self-conscious reflection which we all bring with us helps the contemporary artist in his creative activity. Clearly it is the task of the philosopher to investigate the revolutionary manner in which this has come about and to ask why historical consciousness and the new self-conscious reflection arising from it combine with a claim that we cannot renounce: namely, the fact that everything we see stands there before us and addresses us directly as if it showed us ourselves. Consequently I regard the development of the appropriate concepts for the question as the first step in our investigation. First, I shall introduce in relation to philosophical aesthetics the conceptual apparatus with which we intend to tackle the subject in question. Then I shall show how the three concepts announced in the title will play a leading role in what follows: the appeal to play, the explication of the concept of the symbol (that is, of the possibility of self-recognition), and finally, the festival as the inclusive concept for regaining the idea of universal communication.

It is the task of philosophy to discover what is common even in what is different. According to Plato, the task of the philosophical dialectician is "to learn to see things together in respect of the one."[7] What means does the philosophical tradition offer us to solve this problem or to bring it to a clearer understanding of itself? The problem that we have posed is that of bridging the enormous gap between the traditional form and content of Western art and the ideals of contemporary artists. The word *art* itself gives us a first orientation. We should never underestimate what a word can tell us, for language represents the previous accomplishment of thought. Thus we should take the word *art* as our point of departure. Anyone with the slightest historical knowledge is aware that this word has had the exclusive and characteristic meaning that we ascribe to it today for less than two hundred years. In the eighteenth century it was still natural to say "the fine arts" where we today would say "art." For alongside the fine arts were the mechanical arts, and the art in the technical sense of handicrafts and industrial production, which constituted by far the larger part of human skills. Therefore we shall not find our concept of art in the philosophical tradition. But what we can learn from the Greeks, the fathers of Western thought, is precisely the fact that art belongs in the realm of what Aristotle called *poietike episteme*, the knowledge and facility appropriate to production.[8] What is common to the craftsman's producing and the artist's creating, and what distinguishes such knowing from theory or from practical knowing and deciding is that a work becomes separated from the activity. This is the essence of production and must be borne in mind if we wish to understand and evaluate the limits of the modern critique of the concept of the work, which has been directed against traditional art and the bourgeois cultivation of enjoyment associated with it. The common feature here is clearly the emergence of the work as the intended goal of regulated effort. The work is set free as such and released from the process of production because it is by definition destined for use. Plato always emphasized that the knowledge and skill of the producer are subordinate to considerations of use and depend upon the knowledge of the user of the product.[9] In the familiar Platonic example, it is the ship's master who determines what the shipbuilder is to build.[10] Thus the concept of the work points toward the sphere of common use and common understanding as the realm of intelligible communication. But the real question now is how to distinguish "art" from the mechanical arts within this general concept of productive knowledge. The answer supplied by antiquity, which we shall have to consider further, is that here we are concerned with imitative activity. Imitation is thereby brought into relation with the total horizon of *phusis* or nature. Art is only "possible" because the formative activity of nature leaves an open domain which can be filled by the productions of the human spirit. What we call art compared with the formative activity of production in general is mysterious in several respects, inasmuch as the work is not real in the same way as what it represents. On the contrary, the work functions as an imitation and thus raises a host of extremely subtle philosophical problems, including above all the problem of the ontological status of appearance. What is the significance of the fact that nothing "real" is produced here? The work has no real "use" as such, but finds its characteristic fulfillment when our gaze dwells upon the appearance itself. We shall have more to say about this later. But it was clear from the first that we cannot expect any direct help from the Greeks, if they understood what we call art as at best a kind of imitation of nature. Of course, such imitation has nothing to do with the naturalistic or realistic misconceptions of modern art theory. As Aristotle's famous remark in the *Poetics* confirms, "Poetry is more philosophical than history."[11] For history only relates how things actually happened, whereas poetry tells us how things may happen and teaches us to recognize the universal in all human action and suffering. Since the universal is obviously the topic of philosophy, art is more philosophical than history precisely because it too intends the universal. This is the first pointer that the tradition of antiquity provides.

A second, more far-reaching point in our considerations of the word *art* leads us beyond the limits of contemporary aesthetics. "Fine art" is in German *die schöne Kunst*, literally "beautiful art." But what is the beautiful?

Even today we can encounter the *concept of the beautiful* in various expressions that still preserve something of the old, original Greek meaning of the word *kalon*. Under certain circumstances, we too connect the concept of the beautiful with the fact that, by established custom, there is open recognition that some things are worth seeing or are made to be seen. The expression *die schöne Sittlichkeit* – literally "beautiful ethical life" – still preserves the memory of the Greek ethico-political world which German idealism contrasted with the soulless mechanism of the modern state (Schiller, Hegel). This phrase does not mean that their ethical customs were full of beauty in the sense of being filled with pomp and ostentatious splendor. It means that the ethical life of the people found expression in all forms of communal life, giving shape to the whole and so allowing men to recognize themselves in their own world. Even for us the beautiful is convincingly defined as something that enjoys universal recognition and assent. Thus it belongs to our natural sense of the beautiful that we cannot ask why it pleases us. We cannot expect any advantage from the beautiful since it serves no purpose. The beautiful fulfills itself in a kind of self-determination and enjoys its own self-representation. So much for the word.

Where do we encounter the most convincing self-fulfillment of the essence of the beautiful? In order to understand the effective background of the problem of the beautiful, and perhaps of art as well, we must remember that for the Greeks it was the heavenly order of the cosmos that presented the true vision of the beautiful. This was a Pythagorean element in the Greek idea of the beautiful. We possess in the regular movements of the heavens one of the greatest intuitions of order to be found anywhere. The periodic cycle of the year and of the months, the alternation of day and night, provide the most reliable constants for the experience of order and stand in marked contrast with the ambiguity and instability of human affairs.

From this perspective, the concept of the beautiful, particularly in Plato's thought, sheds a great deal of light on the problem with which we are concerned. In the *Phaedrus* Plato offers us a great mythological description of man's destiny, his limitations compared with the divine, and his attachment to the earthly burden of the sensuous life of the body.[12] Then he describes the marvelous procession of souls that reflects the heavenly movement of the stars by night. There is a chariot race to the vault of the heavens led by the Olympian gods. The human souls also drive their chariots and follow the daily processions of the gods. At the vault of the heavens, the true world is revealed to view. There, in place of the disorder and inconstancy that characterize our so-called experience of the world down here on earth, we perceive the true constants and unchanging patterns of being. But while the gods surrender themselves totally to the vision of the true world in this encounter, our human souls are distracted because of their unruly natures. They can only cast a momentary and passing glance at the eternal orders, since their vision is clouded by sensuous desire. Then they plunge back toward the earth and leave the truth behind them, retaining only the vaguest remembrance of it. Then we come to the point that I wish to emphasize. These souls who, so to speak, have lost their wings, are weighed down by earthly cares, unable to scale the heights of the truth. There is one experience that causes their wings to grow once again and that allows them to ascend once more. This is the experience of love and the beautiful, the love of the beautiful. Plato describes this experience of growing love in a wonderful and elaborate fashion and relates it to the spiritual perception of the beautiful and the true orders of the world. It is by virtue of the beautiful that we are able to acquire a lasting remembrance of the true world. This is the way of philosophy. Plato describes the beautiful as that which shines forth most clearly and draws us to itself, as the very visibility of the ideal.[13] In the beautiful presented in nature and art, we experience this convincing illumination of truth and harmony, which compels the admission: "This is true."

The important message that this story has to teach is that the essence of the beautiful does not lie in some realm simply opposed to reality. On the contrary, we learn that however unexpected our encounter with beauty may be, it gives us an assurance that the truth does not lie far off and inaccessible to us, but can be encountered in the disorder of reality with all its imperfections, evils, errors, extremes, and fateful confusions. The ontological function of the beautiful is to bridge the chasm between the ideal and the real. Thus the qualification of art as "beautiful" or "fine" provides a second essential clue for our consideration.

A third step leads us directly to *aesthetics* as it is called in the history of philosophy. As a late development aesthetics coincided, significantly enough, with the process by which art proper was detached from the sphere of technical facility; and with this emancipation it came to acquire the quasi-religious function that it possesses for us now, both in theory and practice.

As a philosophical discipline, aesthetics only emerged during the

age of rationalism in the eighteenth century. It was obviously
stimulated by modern rationalism itself, which was based upon the
development of the constructive sciences of nature in the seventeenth century, sciences which, by their breathtakingly rapid
transformation into technology, have in turn come to shape the face
of our world.

What led philosophy to turn its attention to the beautiful? The
experience of art and beauty seems to be a realm of utterly subjective caprice compared with the rationalist's exclusive orientation
toward the mathematical regularities of nature and its significance
for the control of natural forces. For this was the great breakthrough
of the seventeenth century. What claims can the phenomenon of the
beautiful have in this context? Our recourse to ancient thought helps
us to see that in art and the beautiful we encounter a significance that
transcends all conceptual thought. How do we grasp this truth?
Alexander Baumgarten, the founder of philosophical aesthetics,
spoke of a *cognitio sensitiva* or "sensuous knowledge."[14] This idea is a
paradoxical one for the traditional conception of knowledge as it has
been developed since the Greeks. We can only speak of knowledge
proper when we have ceased to be determined by the subjective and
the sensible and have come to grasp the universal, the regularity in
things. Then the sensible in all its particularity only enters the scene
as a particular case of a universal law. Now clearly in our experience
of the beautiful, in nature and in art, we neither verify our expectations, nor record what we encounter as a particular case of the
universal. An enchanting sunset does not represent a case of sunsets
in general. It is rather a unique sunset displaying the "tragedy of the
heavens." And in the realm of art above all, it is self-evident that the
work of art is not experienced in its own right if it is only ac-
knowledged as a link in a chain that leads elsewhere. The "truth"
that is possesses for us does not consist in some universal regularity
that merely presents itself through the work. Rather, *cognitio sensitiva*
means that in the apparent particularity of sensuous experience,
which we always attempt to relate to the universal, there is something in our experience of the beautiful that arrests us and compels
us to dwell upon the individual appearance itself.

What is the relevance of this fact? What do we learn from this?
What is the importance and significance of this particular experience
which claims truth for itself, thereby denying that the universal
expressed by the mathematical formulation of the laws of nature is

the only kind of truth? It is the task of philosophical aesthetics to supply an answer to this question.[15] And it is useful to ask which of the arts is likely to provide the best answer. We recognize the great variety and range of artistic activities that stretches from the transitory arts of music and spoken language to the static arts like painting and sculpture and architecture. The different media in which human art finds expression allow its products to appear in a different light, but we can suggest an answer to this question if it is approached from a historical point of view. Baumgarten once defined aesthetics as the *ars pulchre cogitandi* or the "art of thinking beautifully."[16] Anyone with a sensitive ear will immediately notice that this expression has been formed on analogy with the definition of rhetoric as the *ars bene dicendi* or the "art of speaking well." This relationship is not accidental, for rhetoric and poetics have belonged together since antiquity, and in a sense, rhetoric took precedence over poetics. Rhetoric is the universal form of human communication, which even today determines our social life in an incomparably more profound fashion than does science. The classic definition of rhetoric as the "art of speaking well" carries immediate conviction. Baumgarten clearly based his definition of aesthetics as the "art of thinking beautifully" on this definition. There is an important suggestion here that the arts of language may well play a special part in solving the problems that we have set ourselves. This is all the more important since the leading concepts that govern our aesthetic considerations usually start from the opposite direction. Our reflection is almost always oriented toward the visual arts, and it is in that realm that our aesthetic concepts are most readily applied. There are good reasons for this. It is not simply on account of the visible presence of static art, in contrast to the transitory nature of drama, music, or poetry, which present themselves only fleetingly. It is surely because the Platonic heritage permeates all our reflections upon the beautiful. Plato conceived true being as the original image, and the world of appearance as the reflected image, of this exemplary original.[17] There is something convincing about this as far as art is concerned, as long as we do not trivialize it. In order to understand our experience of art, we are tempted to search the depths of mystical language for daring new words like the German *Anbild* – an expression that captures both the image and the viewing of it.[18] For it is true that we both elicit the image from things and imaginatively project the image into things in one and the same process. Thus aesthetic reflection is oriented above all toward the power of imagination as the human capacity of image building.

It is here that Kant's great achievement is to be found. He far surpassed Baumgarten, the rationalist pre-Kantian founder of aesthetics, and recognized for the first time the experience of art and beauty as a philosophical question in its own right. He sought an answer to the question of how the experience in which we "find something beautiful" could be binding in such a way that it does not simply express a subjective reaction of taste. Here we find no universality comparable to that of the laws of nature, which serve to explain individual sensuous experience as a particular case. What is this truth that is encountered in the beautiful and can come to be shared? Certainly not the sort of truth or universality to which we apply the conceptual universality of the understanding. Despite this, the kind of truth that we encounter in the experience of the beautiful does unambiguously make a claim to more than merely subjective validity. Otherwise it would have no binding truth for us. When I find something beautiful, I do not simply mean that it pleases me in the same sense that I find a meal to my taste. When I find something beautiful, I think that it "is" beautiful. Or, to adapt a Kantian expression, I "demand everyone's agreement."[19] This presumption that everyone should agree with me does not, however, imply that I could convince them by argument. That is not the way in which good taste may become universal. On the contrary, each individual has to develop his sense for the beautiful in such a way that he comes to discriminate between what is beautiful to a greater or lesser degree. It does not come about by producing good reasons or conclusive proofs for one's taste. The realm of art criticism that tries to develop taste hovers between "scientific" demonstration and the sense of quality that determines judgment without becoming purely scientific. "Criticism" as the discrimination of degrees of beauty is not really a subsequent judgment by means of which we could subsume the "beautiful" scientifically under concepts or produce a comparative assessment of quality. Rather it is the experience of the beautiful itself. It is significant that Kant uses primarily natural beauty rather than the work of art to illustrate the "judgment of taste" in which the perception of beauty is elicited from appearances and demanded of everyone. It is this "nonsignificant beauty" that cautions us against applying concepts to the beautiful in art.[20]

I shall here simply draw upon the philosophical tradition of aesthetics to help us with the question that we have posed: how can we find an all-embracing concept to cover both what art is today and what it has been in the past? The problem is that we cannot talk about great art as simply belonging to the past, any more than we can talk about modern art only becoming "pure" art through the rejection of all significant content. This is a remarkable state of affairs. If we reflect for a moment and try to consider what it is that we mean when we talk about art, then we come up against a paradox. As far as so-called classical art is concerned, we are talking about the production of works which in themselves were not primarily understood as art. On the contrary, these forms were encountered within a religious or secular context as an adornment of the life-world and of special moments like worship, the representation of a ruler, and things of that kind. As soon as the concept of art took on those features to which we have become accustomed and the work of art began to stand on its own, divorced from its original context of life, only then did art become simply "art" in the "museum without walls" of Malraux.[21] The great artistic revolution of modern times, which has finally led to the emancipation of art from all of its traditional subject-matters and to the rejection of intelligible communication itself, began to assert itself when art wished to be art and nothing else. Art has now become doubly problematic: is it still art, and does it even wish to be considered art? What lies behind this paradoxical situation? Is art always art and nothing but art?

Kant's definition of the autonomy of the aesthetic, in relation to practical reason on the one hand and theoretical reason on the other, provided an orientation for further advances in this respect. This is the point of Kant's famous expression according to which the joy we take in the beautiful is a "disinterested delight."[22] Naturally, "disinterested delight" means that we are not interested in what appears or in what is "represented" from a practical point of view. Disinterestedness simply signifies that characteristic feature of aesthetic behavior that forbids us to inquire after the purpose served by art. We cannot ask, "What purpose is served by enjoyment?"

It is true that the approach to art through the experience of aesthetic taste is a relatively external one and, as everyone knows, somewhat diminishing. Nevertheless Kant rightly characterizes such taste as *sensus communis* or common sense.[23] Taste is communicative; it represents something that we all possess to a greater or lesser

degree. It is clearly meaningless to talk about a purely individual and
subjective taste in the field of aesthetics. To this extent it is to Kant
that we owe our initial understanding of the validity of aesthetic
claims, even though nothing is subsumed under the concept of a
purpose. But what then are the experiences that best fulfill the ideal
of "free" and disinterested delight? Kant is thinking of "natural
beauty," as in a beautiful drawing of a flower or of something like
the decorative design on a tapestry which intensifies our feeling for
life by the play of its pattern.[24] The function of decorative art is to
play this ancillary role. The only things that can simply be called
beautiful without qualification are either things of nature, which
have not been endowed with meaning by man, or things of human
art, which deliberately eschew any imposition of meaning and
merely represent a play of form and color. We are not meant to
learn or recognize anything here. There is nothing worse than an
obtrusive wallpaper that draws attention to its individual motifs as
pictorial representations in their own right, as the feverish dreams of
childhood can confirm. The point about this description is precisely
that the dynamic of aesthetic delight comes into play without a process of conceptualization, that is, without our seeing or understanding something "as something." But this is an accurate description
only of an extreme case. It serves to show that when we take
aesthetic satisfaction in something, we do not relate it to a meaning
which could ultimately be communicated in conceptual terms.

But this is not the question at issue. Our question concerns what
art is. And certainly we are not primarily thinking here of the
secondary forms of the decorative arts and crafts. Of course,
designers can be significant artists, but as designers they perform a
service. Now Kant defined beauty proper as "free beauty," which in
his language means a beauty free from concept and significant content.[25] Naturally he did not mean that the creation of such beauty
free from significant content represents the ideal of art. In the case
of art, it is true that we always find ourselves held between the pure
aspect of visibility presented to the viewer by the "in-sight"
(*Anbild*), as we called it, and the meaning that our understanding
dimly senses in the work of art. And we recognize this meaning
through the import that every encounter has for us. Where does this
meaning come from? What is this additional something by virtue of
which art clearly becomes what it is for the first time? Kant did not
want to define this additional something as a content. And indeed, as

we shall see, there are good reasons why it is actually impossible to do so. Kant's great achievement, however, lay in his advance over the mere formalism of the "pure judgment of taste" and the overcoming of the "standpoint of taste" in favor of the "standpoint of genius."[26] It was in terms of genius that the eighteenth century experienced Shakespeare's work and its violation of the accepted rules of taste, which had been established by French classicism. Lessing, for example, opposed the classicist aesthetic of rules derived from French tragedy, although in a very one-sided fashion, and he celebrated Shakespeare as the voice of nature realizing its own creative spirit through genius.[27] And in fact, Kant too understood genius as a natural power. He described the genius as a "favorite of nature" who thereby, like nature, creates something that seems as though it were made in accordance with rules, although without conscious attention to them.[28] Furthermore, the work seems like something unprecedented, which has been produced according to still unformulated rules. Art is the creation of something exemplary which is not simply produced by following rules. Clearly this definition of art as the creation of genius can never really be divorced from the con-geniality of the one who experiences it. A kind of free play is at work in both cases.

Taste was also characterized as a similar play of the imagination and the understanding. It is, with a different emphasis, the same free play as that encountered in the creation of the work of art. Only here the significant content is articulated through the creative activity of the imagination, so that it dawns on the understanding, or, as Kant puts it, allows us "to go on to think much that cannot be said."[29] Naturally this does not mean that we simply project concepts onto the artistic representation before us. For then we would be subsuming the perceptually given under the universal as a particular case of it. That is not the nature of aesthetic experience. On the contrary, it is only in the presence of the particular individual work that concepts "come to reverberate,"[30] as Kant says. This fine phrase originated in the musical language of the eighteenth century, with particular reference to the favorite instrument of the time, the clavichord, which created a special effect of suspended reverberation as the note continued to vibrate long after being struck. Kant obviously means that the concept functions as a kind of sounding board capable of articulating the free play of the imagination. So far, so good. German idealism in general also recognized the appearance of meaning or the idea – or whatever else one chooses to call it – without thereby making the concept the real focal point of aesthetic experience. But is this sufficient to solve our problem concerning the unity that binds together the classical artistic tradition and modern art? How can we understand the innovative forms of modern art as they play around with the content so that our expectations are constantly frustrated? How are we to understand what contemporary artists, or certain trends of contemporary art, even describe as "happenings" or anti-art? How are we to understand what Duchamp is doing when he suddenly exhibits some everyday object on its own and thereby produces a sort of aesthetic shock reaction? We cannot simply dismiss this as so much nonsense, for Duchamp actually revealed something about the conditions of aesthetic experience. In view of the experimental practice of art today, how can we expect help from classical aesthetics? Obviously we must have recourse to more fundamental human experiences to help us here. What is the anthropological basis of our experience of art? I should like to develop this question with the help of the concepts of play, symbol, and festival.

I

The concept of play is of particular significance in this regard. The first thing we must make clear to ourselves is that play is so elementary a function of human life that culture is quite inconceivable without this element. Thinkers like Huizinga and Guardini, among others, have stressed for a long time that the element of play is included in man's religious and cultic practices.[31] It is worth looking more closely at the fundamental givenness of human play and its structures in order to reveal the element of play as free impulse and not simply negatively as freedom from particular ends. When do we speak of play and what is implied when we do? Surely the first thing is the to and fro of constantly repeated movement – we only have to think of certain expressions like "the play of light" and "the play of the waves" where we have such a constant coming and going, back and forth, a movement that is not tied down to any goal. Clearly what characterizes this movement back and forth is that neither pole of the movement represents the goal in which it would come to rest. Furthermore, a certain leeway clearly belongs to such a movement. This gives us a great deal to think about for the question of art. This freedom of movement is such that it must have the form of self-movement. Expressing the thought of the Greeks in general, Aristotle had already described self-movement as the most fundamental characteristic of living beings.[32] Whatever is alive has its source of movement within itself and has the form of self-movement. Now play appears as a self-movement that does not pursue any particular end or purpose so much as movement *as* movement, exhibiting so to speak a phenomenon of excess, of living self-representation. And in fact that is just what we perceive in nature – the play of gnats, for example, or all the lively dramatic forms of play we observe in the animal world, expecially among their young. All this arises from the basic character of excess striving to express itself in the living being. Now the distinctive thing about human play is its ability to involve our reason, that uniquely human capacity which allows us to set ourselves aims and pursue them consciously, and to outplay this capacity for purposive rationality. For the specifically human quality in our play is the self-discipline and order that we impose on our movements when playing, as if particular purposes were involved – just like a child, for example, who counts how often he can bounce the ball on the ground before losing control of it.

In this form of nonpurposive activity, it is reason itself that sets the rules. The child is unhappy if he loses control on the tenth bounce and proud of himself if he can keep it going to the thirtieth. This nonpurposive rationality in human play is a characteristic feature of the phenomenon which will be of further help to us. It is clear here, especially in the phenomenon of repetition itself, that identity or self-sameness is intended. The end pursued is certainly a nonpurposive activity, but this activity is itself intended. It is what the play intends. In this fashion we actually intend something with effort, ambition, and profound commitment. This is one step on the road to human communication; if something is represented here – if only the movement of play itself – it is also true to say that the onlooker "intends" it, just as in the act of play I stand over against myself as an onlooker. The function of the representation of play is ultimately to establish, not just any movement whatsoever, but rather the movement of play determined in a specific way. In the end, play is thus the self-representation of its own movement.

I should add straightaway: such a definition of the movement of play means further that the act of playing always requires a "playing along with." Even the onlooker watching the child at play cannot possibly do otherwise. If he really does "go along with it," that is nothing but a *participatio,* an inner sharing in this repetitive movement. This is often very clear in more developed forms of play: for example, we have only to observe on television the spectators at a tennis match cricking their necks. No one can avoid playing along with the game. Another important aspect of play as a communicative activity, so it seems to me, is that it does not really acknowledge the distance separating the one who plays and the one who watches the play. The spectator is manifestly more than just an observer who sees what is happening in front of him, but rather one who is a part of it insofar as he literally "takes part." Of course, in these simple forms of play we have not yet arrived at the play of art. But I hope to have shown that it is only a step from ritual dance to ritual observances taking the form of representation. And from there, to the liberation of representation in the theater, for example, which emerged from this ritual context. Or to the visual arts, whose decorative and expressive function arose out of the context of religious life. All the forms merge with one another. This continuity is confirmed by the common element in play as we discussed it earlier: namely, the fact that something is *intended as something,* even if it is not something conceptual, useful, or purposive, but only the pure autonomous regulation of movement.

I think this point is enormously significant for the contemporary discussion of modern art. What ultimately concerns us here is the question of the work. One of the basic impulses of modern art has been the desire to break down the distance separating the audience, the "consumers," and the public from the work of art. There is no doubt that the most important creative artists of the last fifty years have concentrated all their efforts on breaking down just this distance. We need only to think of the theory of epic theater in Brecht, who specifically fought against our being absorbed in a theatrical dream-world as a feeble substitute for human and social consciousness of solidarity. He deliberately destroyed scenic realism, the normal requirements of characterization, in short, the identity of everything usually expected of a play. But this desire to transform the distance of the onlooker into the involvement of the participant can be discerned in every form of modern experimentation in the arts.

Does this mean that the work itself no longer exists? That is indeed how many contemporary artists see the situation – and so too the aesthetic theorists who follow them – as if it were a question of renouncing the unity of the work. But if we just think back to our conclusions about human play, we discovered even there a primary experience of rationality in the observance of self-prescribed rules, for example, in the very identity of whatever we try to repeat. Something like a hermeneutic identity was already at play here – something absolutely inviolable in the play of art. It is quite wrong to think that the unity of the work implies that the work is closed off from the person who turns to it or is affected by it. The hermeneutic identity of the work is much more deeply grounded. Even the most fleeting and unique of experiences is intended in its self-identity when it appears or is valued as an aesthetic experience. Let us take the case of an organ improvisation. This unique improvisation will never be heard again. The organist himself hardly knows afterwards just how he played, and no one transcribed it. Nevertheless, everyone says, "That was a brilliant interpretation or improvisation," or on another occasion, "That was rather dull today." What do we mean when we say such things? Obviously we are referring back to the improvisation. Something "stands" before us; it is like a work and not just an organist's finger exercise. Otherwise we should never pass judgment on its quality or lack of it. So it is the hermeneutic identity that establishes the unity of the work. To understand something, I must be able to identify it. For there was something there that I passed judgment upon and understood. I identify something as it was or as it is, and this identity alone constitutes the meaning of the work.

If that is true – and I think everything is in favor of it – there cannot be any kind of artistic production that does not similarly *intend* what it produces to be what it is. This is confirmed by even the most extreme example of an everyday object – like a bottle-rack – when suddenly exhibited as a work of art to such great effect. It has its determinate character in the effect it once produced. In all likelihood, it will not remain a lasting work in the sense of a permanent classic, but it is certainly a "work" in terms of its hermeneutic identity.

The concept of a work is in no way tied to a classical ideal of harmony. Even if the forms in which some positive identification is made are quite different, we still have to ask how it actually comes about that the work addresses us. But there is yet another aspect here. If the identity of the work is as we have said, then the genuine reception and experience of a work of art can exist only for one who "plays along," that is, one who performs in an active way himself. Now how does that actually happen? Certainly not simply through retention of something in memory. In that case there would still be identification, but without that particular assent by virtue of which the work means something to us. What gives the work its identity as work? What makes this what we call a hermeneutic identity? Obviously, this further formulation means that its identity consists precisely in there being something to "understand," that it asks to be understood in what it "says" or "intends." The work issues a challenge which expects to be met. It requires an answer – an answer that can only be given by someone who accepted the challenge. And that answer must be his own, and given actively. The participant belongs to the play.

We all know from our own experience that visiting a museum, for example, or listening to a concert, sets a task requiring profound intellectual and spiritual activity. What do we do in such situations? Certainly there are differences here: in the one case we are dealing with a reproductive art, and in the other nothing is reproduced – the originals hang on the wall immediately in front of us. And yet after going through a museum, we do not leave it with exactly the same feeling about life that we had when we went in. If we really have had a genuine experience of art, then the world has become both brighter and less burdensome.

This definition of the work as the focal point of recognition and understanding also means that such an identity is bound up with variation and difference. Every work leaves the person who responds to it a certain leeway, a space to be filled in by himself. I can show this even with the most classical theoretical concepts. Kant, for example, has a remarkable doctrine. He defended the view that in painting, form is the vehicle of beauty. Color, on the other hand, is supposed to be simply a stimulus, a matter of sensuous affection that remains subjective and thus has nothing to do with its genuine artistic or aesthetic formation.[33] Anyone who knows anything of neoclassical art – that of Thorvaldsen, for example – will indeed admit that as far as such marmoreally pale neoclassical art is concerned, line, configuration, and form stand in the foreground. Kant's view is obviously historically conditioned. We should never admit that colors affect us merely as stimuli. We know perfectly well that it is quite possible to construct with colors, and that artistic composition is not necessarily restricted to line and contour as used in drawing. We are not interested here in the one-sidedness of such historically conditioned taste. The interesting thing is what Kant is clearly aiming at. What is it that is so distinctive about form? The answer is that we must trace it out as we see it because we must construct it actively – something required by every composition, graphic or musical, in drama or in reading. There is constant cooperative activity here. And obviously, it is precisely the identity of the work that invites us to this activity. The activity is not arbitrary, but directed, and all possible realizations are drawn into a specific schema.

Let us consider the case of literature. It was the merit of the great Polish phenomenologist Roman Ingarden to have been the first to explore this.[34] What, for example, is the evocative function of a story? I shall take a famous example: *The Brothers Karamazov*.[35] I can see the stairs down which Smerdjakov tumbles. Dostoevsky gives us a certain description. As a result, I know exactly what this staircase looks like. I know where it starts, how it gets darker and then turns to the left. All this is clear to me in the most concrete way and yet I also know that no one else "sees" the staircase the way I do. But anyone who is receptive to this masterly narrative will "see" the staircase in a most specific way and be convinced that he sees it as it really is. This is the open space creative language gives us and which we fill out by following what the writer evokes. And similarly in the visual arts. A synthetic act is required in which we must unite and bring together many different aspects. We "read" a picture, as we say, like a text. We start to "decipher" a picture like a text. It was not Cubist painting that first set us this task, though it did so in a drastically radical manner by demanding that we successively superimpose upon one another the various facets or aspects of the same thing, to produce finally on the canvas the thing depicted in all its facets and thus in a new colorful plasticity. It is not only when confronted by Picasso and Braque and all the other Cubists of the period that we have to "read" the picture. It is always like this. Someone who, on admiring a famous Titian or Velazquez depicting some mounted Habsburg ruler or other, thinks, "Oh, yes, that's Charles V," has not really seen anything of the picture at all. Rather, it is a question of constructing it, reading it word for word as it were, so that after this necessary construction it comes together as a picture resonant with meaning. It portrays a world ruler upon whose empire the sun never sets.

So what I should basically like to say is this: there is always some reflective and intellectual accomplishment involved, whether I am concerned with the traditional forms of art handed down to us or whether I am challenged by modern forms of art. The challenge of the work brings the constructive accomplishment of the intellect into play.

For this reason, it seems a false antithesis to believe that there is an art of the past that can be enjoyed and an art of the present that supposedly forces us to participate in it by the subtle use of artistic technique. The concept of play was introduced precisely to show that everyone involved in play is a participant. It should also be true of the play of art that there is in principle no radical separation between the work of art and the person who experiences it. This is what I meant in claiming emphatically that we must also learn how to read the more familiar classical works of art laden as they are with traditional meaning. However, reading is not just scrutinizing or taking one word after another, but means above all performing a constant hermeneutic movement guided by the anticipation of the whole, and finally fulfilled by the individual in the realization of the total sense. We have only to think what it is like when someone reads aloud a text that he has not understood. No one else can really understand what is being read either.

The identity of the work is not guaranteed by any classical or formalist criteria, but is secured by the way in which we take the construction of the work upon ourselves as a task. If this is the meaning of artistic experience, we might recall Kant's achievement when he demonstrated that there is no question here of bringing or subsuming a work in all its sensuous particularity under a concept. The art historian and aesthetic theorist Richard Hamann expressed this once when he said that it is a question of the "autonomous significance of the perceptual content."[36] By this he meant that perception here is no longer simply embedded within the pragmatic contexts of everyday life in which it functions, but expresses and presents itself in its own significance. Naturally we must be clear about what perception means if we are to realize the full and proper meaning of this formulation. Perception must not be understood as if the "sensible skin of things" were all that counted aesthetically – a view still natural to Hamann in the final period of Impressionism. To perceive something is not to collect together utterly separate sensory impressions, but is rather, as the marvelous German word *wahrnehmen* itself says, "to take something as true." But that means that what is presented to the senses is seen and taken as something. In the belief that we generally employ an inadequate and dogmatic concept of sensory perception as an aesthetic criterion, I have chosen in my own investigations the rather elaborate expression "aesthetic nondifferentiation" to bring out the deep structure of perception.[37] By that I mean it is a secondary procedure if we abstract from whatever meaningfully addresses us in the work of art and wholly restrict ourselves to a "purely aesthetic" evaluation.

That would be like a critic at the theater who exclusively took issue with the way the production was directed, the quality of the individual performances, and so on. Of course, it is quite right that he should do so – but the work itself and the meaning it acquired for us in the actual performance does not come to light in this way. The artistic experience is constituted precisely by the fact that we do not distinguish between the particular way the work is realized and the identity of the work itself. That is not only true of the performing arts and the mediation or reproduction that they imply. It is always true that the work as such still speaks to us in an individual way as the same work, even in repeated and different encounters with it. Where the performing arts are concerned, of course this identity in variation must be realized in a twofold manner insofar as the reproduction is as much exposed to identity and variation as the original. What I described as aesthetic nondifferentiation clearly constitutes the real meaning of that cooperative play between imagination and understanding which Kant discovered in the "judgment of taste." It is invariably true that when we see something, we must think something in order to see anything. But here it is a *free* play and not directed towards a concept. This cooperative interaction forces us to face the question about what is actually built up in this process of free play between the faculties of imagination and conceptual understanding. What is the nature of this significance whereby something can be experienced meaningfully and is so experienced? It is obvious that any pure theory of imitation or reproduction, any naturalistic copy theory, completely misses the point. The essence of a great work of art has certainly never consisted in the accurate and total imitation or counterfeit of "Nature."

As I showed with reference to Titian's "Charles V," it is doubtless always the case that a specific stylization is accomplished in the construction of a picture.[38] The horse has that particular quality that always recalls the rockinghorse of one's childhood; then, too, the resplendent background and the watchful gaze of the military commander and emperor of this great kingdom: we see how it all interacts, how the autonomous significance of perception arises here precisely out of this cooperative play. Obviously anyone who asked, for example, "Is the horse a success?" or even "Has he caught this ruler, Charles V, and his particular physiognomy?" would be overlooking the real work of art. Perhaps this example will show that this problem is extraordinarily complex. What then do we really understand? How does the work speak and what does it tell us? Here we should do well to remember, as a first defense against all theories of imitation, that it is not only in the face of art that we enjoy this aesthetic experience, but in the presence of nature as well. This is the problem of "natural beauty."

Kant, who worked out most clearly the autonomy of aesthetics, was primarily oriented toward natural beauty. It is certainly not without significance that we find nature beautiful, for it is an ethical experience bordering on the miraculous that beauty should manifest itself in all the fecund power of nature as if she displayed her beauties for us.[39] In Kant a creationist theology stands behind this unique human capacity to encounter natural beauty, and forms the self-evident basis from which he represents the production of the genius and the artist as an extreme intensification of the power that nature, as divinely created, possesses. But it is obvious that what natural beauty expresses is peculiarly indeterminate. In contrast to the work of art, in which we invariably seek to recognize or to interpret something *as something* – even if perhaps we are compelled to give up the attempt – nature speaks meaningfully to us in a kind of indeterminate feeling of solitude. A deeper analysis of this aesthetic experience of natural beauty teaches us that, in a certain sense, this is an illusion and that in fact we can only see nature with the eyes of men experienced and educated in art. We remember, for example, how the Alps were still described in travel diaries of the eighteenth century as terrifying mountains whose ugly and fearful wildness was experienced as a denial of beauty, humanity, and the familiar security of human existence.[40] Today, on the other hand, everyone is convinced that our great mountain ranges represent not only the sublimity, but also the exemplary beauty of nature.

It is obvious what has happened here. In the eighteenth century, we saw through the eyes of an imagination educated in the school of rational order. Before the English garden style introduced a new kind of truth to nature or naturalness, the eighteenth-century garden was constructed geometrically as an extension into nature of domestic architectural construction. Thus in fact we see nature, as the example shows, with sight schooled by art. Hegel rightly grasped that natural beauty is a reflection of artistic beauty,[41] so that we learn how to perceive beauty in nature under the guidance of the artist's eye and his works. The question of course remains how that helps us today in the critical situation of modern art. Under the guidance of modern art, it would be extremely difficult to recognize natural beauty in a landscape with any success. In fact, today we must experience natural beauty almost as a corrective against the claims of a perception educated by art. Natural beauty reminds us once again that what we acknowledge in a work of art is not at all that in which the language of art speaks. It is precisely indeterminacy of reference that addresses us in modern art and that compels us to be fully conscious of the significance of the exemplary meaning of what we see before us.[42] What is the point of this indeterminate reference? I shall describe it in terms of the "symbol," a word whose meaning has been decisively influenced by Goethe, Schiller, and the tradition of German classicism.

I I

What does the word "*symbol*" mean? Originally it was a technical term in Greek for a token of remembrance. The host presented his guest with the so-called *tessera hospitalis* by breaking some object in two. He kept one half for himself and gave the other half to his guest. If in thirty or fifty years time, a descendant of the guest should ever enter his house, the two pieces could be fitted together again to form a whole in an act of recognition. In its original technical sense, the symbol represented something like a sort of pass used in the ancient world: something in and through which we recognize someone already known to us.

In Plato's *Symposium* there is a beautiful story which I think gives an even more profound indication of the sort of significance that art has for us. In this dialogue, Aristophanes relates a story about the nature of love that has continued to fascinate up to the present day. He tells us that originally all human beings were spherical creatures.

But later, on account of their misbehavior, the gods cut them in two. Thereafter, each of the halves, which originally belonged to one complete living being, seeks to be made whole once again. Thus every individual is a fragment or a *symbolon tou anthropou*.[43] This expectation that there is another half that can complete us and make us whole once more is fulfilled in the experience of love. This profound image for elective affinity and the marriage of minds can be transferred to our experience of the beautiful in art. Clearly it is also the case here that the significance that attaches to the beautiful work of art refers to something that does not simply lie in what we immediately see and understand before us as such. But what sort of reference is this? The proper function of reference is to direct our view toward something else that can be experienced or possessed in an immediate way. If the symbol were referential in this sense, then it would be what has come to be called allegory, at least in the classical use of the term. On this view, "allegory" means that what we actually say is different from what we mean, although we can also say what we mean in an immediate way. As a result of the classicist conception of the symbol, which does not refer to something other than itself in this way, allegory has unfairly come to be regarded as something cold and unartistic. In the case of allegory, the reference must be known in advance. In the case of the symbol, on the other hand, and for our experience of the symbolic in general, the particular represents itself as a fragment of being that promises to complete and make whole whatever corresponds to it. Or, indeed, the symbol is that other fragment that has always been sought in order to complete and make whole our own fragmentary life. The "meaning" of art in this sense does not seem to me to be tied to special social conditions as was the meaning given to art in the later bourgeois religion of culture. On the contrary, the experience of the beautiful, and particularly the beautiful in art, is the invocation of a potentially whole and holy order of things, wherever it may be found.

If we think along these lines for a moment longer, we see that the significant thing is precisely the variety of this experience, which we know as a historical reality as much as a contemporary one. Amidst the variety of art, this same message of the whole addresses us over and over again. Indeed, this seems to provide a more precise answer to our question concerning the significance of art and beauty. This means that in any encounter with art, it is not the particular, but rather the totality of the experienceable world, man's ontological place in it, and above all his finitude before that which transcends him, that is brought to experience. But it does not mean that the indeterminate anticipation of sense that makes a work significant for us can ever be fulfilled so completely that we could appropriate it for knowledge and understanding in all its meaning. This was what Hegel taught when in a profound statement he defined the beautiful in art as "the sensuous showing of the Idea."[44] The Idea, which normally can only be glimpsed from afar, presents itself in the sensuous appearance of the beautiful. Nevertheless, this seems to me to be an idealistic temptation that fails to do justice to the fact that the work speaks to us as a work and not as the bearer of a message. To expect that we can recuperate within the concept the meaningful content that addresses us in art is already to have overtaken art in a very dangerous manner. Yet this was exactly Hegel's guiding conviction, which led him to the problem of art as a thing of the past. We have interpreted this as a fundamental Hegelian claim, since everything that addresses us obscurely and non-conceptually in the particular sensuous language of art was to be recuperated by philosophy in the form of the concept.

However, that is an idealistic temptation which is rejected by all artistic experience. Contemporary art in particular explicitly forbids us to expect from the creative art of our own time any meaningful orientation that could be grasped in the form of the concept. In opposition to this, therefore, I propose that the symbolic in general, and especially the symbolic in art, rests upon an intricate interplay of showing and concealing. In its irreplaceability, the work of art is no mere bearer of meaning – as if the meaning could be transferred to another bearer. Rather the meaning of the work of art lies in the fact that it is there. In order therefore to avoid all false connotations, we should replace the word "work" by the word "creation." This means, for example, that the transitory process in which the flow of speech rushes past comes to stand within the poem in a mysterious fashion and becomes a creation.[45] Above all, this creation is not something that we can imagine being deliberately made by someone (an idea that is still implied in the concept of the work). Someone who has produced a work of art stands before the creation of his hands in just the same way that anyone else does. There is a leap between the planning and the executing on the one hand and the successful achievement on the other. The thing now "stands" and

thereby is "there" once and for all, ready to be encountered by anyone who meets it and to be perceived in its own "quality." This leap
distinguishes the work of art in its uniqueness and irreplaceability.
Walter Benjamin called it the aura of the work of art.[46] We are all
familiar with this from the sense of outrage that we feel over artistic
"sacrilege." The destruction of a work of art always has something
of the feeling of religious sacrilege about it.

These considerations should help us to appreciate the far-
reaching implications of the fact that art achieves more than the
mere manifestation of meaning. We ought rather to say that art is the
containment of sense, so that it does not run away or escape from us,
but is secured and sheltered in the ordered composure of the creation. We owe the possibility of escaping the idealistic conception of
sense to a step taken by Heidegger in our time. He enabled us to
perceive the ontological plenitude or the truth that addresses us in
art through the twofold movement of revealing, unconcealing, and
manifesting, on the one hand, and concealing and sheltering, on the
other. He showed that the Greek concept of concealment (*aletheia*),
only represented one side of man's fundamental experience of the
world.[47] Alongside and inseparable from this unconcealing, there
also stands the shrouding and concealing that belongs to our human
finitude. This philosophical insight, which sets limits to any idealism
claiming a total recovery of meaning, implies that there is more to
the work of art than a meaning that is experienced only in an
indeterminate way. It is the fact that a particular thing such as this
exists that constitutes the "additional something." As Rilke says,
"Such a thing stood among men."[48] This fact that it exists, its fac-
ticity, represents an insurmountable resistance against any superior
presumption that we can make sense of it all. The work of art compels us to recognize this fact. "There is no place which fails to see
you. You must change your life."[49] The peculiar nature of our
experience of art lies in the impact by which it overwhelms us.[50]

Only when we have recognized this can we proceed to an
appropriate conceptual clarification of the question of the proper
significance of art. I should like to pursue more deeply the concept
of the symbolic as taken up by Schiller and Goethe and develop its
own profound truth. The symbolic does not simply point toward a
meaning, but rather allows that meaning to present itself. The symbolic represents meaning. In connection with this concept of representing one should think of the concept of representation in

secular and canon law. Here "representation" does not imply that something merely stands in for something else as if it were a replacement or substitute that enjoyed a less authentic, more indirect kind of existence. On the contrary, what is represented is itself present in the only way available to it. Something of this kind of representative existence applies to art, as when a well-known personality with a high public profile is represented in a portrait. The picture that is displayed in the town hall or the ecclesiastical palace or wherever, is supposed to be a part of that presence. In the representative portrait, the person is actually there in his or her representative role. We consider that the picture is itself representative. Of course, this has nothing to do with idolatry or the cult of images. It means that in the case of art, we are not simply concerned with a memorial token of, reference to, or substitute for the real existence of something.

As a Protestant, I have always found especially significant the controversy over the Last Supper, which raged in the Protestant Church, particularly between Luther and Zwingli. I share with Luther the conviction that Jesus' words "This is my body and this is my blood" do not mean that the bread and wine signify his body and blood. I believe that Luther appreciated this quite clearly, and that, in this respect, he clung to the old Roman Catholic tradition, according to which the bread and wine of the sacrament *are* the flesh and blood of Christ. I am simply making use of this problem of dogma to claim that, if we really want to think about the experience of art, we can, indeed must, think along these lines: the work of art does not simply refer to something, because what it refers to is actually there. We could say that the work of art signifies an increase in being. This is what distinguishes it from all man's productive achievements in the realm of technology and manufacture where the various appliances and devices of our socioeconomic life have been developed. For it is obviously a characteristic of such things that each one we produce merely serves as a means or a tool. When we acquire a household appliance, we do not call an article of this kind a work, for such articles can be produced indefinitely. Since they are conceived in terms of a specific function, they are in principle replaceable.

The work of art, on the other hand, is irreplaceable. This remains true even now in the age of reproduction where we can encounter the greatest works of art in reproductions of exceptionally fine quality. For photography and recording are forms of reproduction rather than of representation. The unique event that characterizes the work of art is not present in the reproduction as such (even if it is a question of a recording of a particular interpretation as a unique event, itself a reproduction). If I find a better reproduction, I shall replace the one I had before, and if I mislay the one I have, I shall obtain a new one. What is this additional something still present in the work of art that distinguishes it from an article that can be indefinitely reproduced at will?

Antiquity gave an answer to this question, and it only needs to be understood once again in its proper meaning. In every work of art we encounter something like mimesis or *imitatio*. Naturally mimesis here has nothing to do with the mere imitation of something that is already familiar to us. Rather, it implies that something is represented in such a way that it is actually present in sensuous abundance. In its original Greek sense, the *mimesis* is derived from the star-dance of the heavens.[51] The stars represent the pure mathematical regularities and proportions that constitute the heavenly order. In this sense I believe the tradition is justified in saying that "art is always mimesis," that is, it represents something. When we say this, however, we must avoid being misunderstood. Whatever comes to speak to us through representation cannot be grasped or even come to be "there" for us in any other way. This is why I consider the debate about objective versus nonobjective painting to be nothing but a spurious and short-sighted dispute within the politics of art. For we must admit that there are very many forms of artistic production in which something is represented in the concentrated form of a particular and unique creation. However different from our everyday experience it may be, this creation presents itself as a pledge of order. The symbolic representation accomplished in art does not have to depend directly on what is already given. On the contrary, it is characteristic of art that what is represented, whether it is rich or poor in connotations or has none whatsoever, calls us to dwell upon it and give our assent in an act of recognition. We shall have to show how this characteristic defines the task that the art of past and present lays upon each of us. And this means learning how to listen to what art has to say. We shall have to acknowledge that learning to listen means rising above the universal leveling process in which we cease to notice anything – a process encouraged by a civilization that dispenses increasingly powerful stimuli.

We have asked what is communicated in the experience of the

beautiful and, in particular, in the experience of art. The decisive and indispensable insight that we gained was that one cannot talk about a simple transference or mediation of meaning there. For this would already be to assimilate the experience of art to the universal anticipation of meaning that is characteristic of theoretical reason. As we have seen, Hegel and the idealists defined the beautiful in art as the sensuous appearance of the Idea, a bold revival of Plato's insight into the unity of the good and the beautiful. However, to go along with this is to presuppose that truth as it appears in art can be transcended by a philosophy that conceives the Idea as the highest and most appropriate form for grasping truth. The weakness of idealist aesthetics lay in its failure to appreciate that we typically encounter art as a unique manifestation of truth whose particularity cannot be surpassed. The significance of the symbol and the symbolic lay in this paradoxical kind of reference that embodies and even vouchsafes its meaning. Art is only encountered in a form that resists pure conceptualization. Great art shakes us because we are always unprepared and defenseless when exposed to the overpowering impact of a compelling work. Thus the essence of the symbolic lies precisely in the fact that it is not related to an ultimate meaning that could be recuperated in intellectual terms. The symbol preserves its meaning within itself.

Thus our exposition of the symbolic character of art returns to our original considerations concerning play. There too we noticed that play is always a kind of self-representation. This fact finds expression in art through the specific nature of *repraesentatio,* that increase in being that something acquires by being represented. If we wish to grasp this aspect of the experience of art in a more appropriate fashion, then I think that idealist aesthetics must be revised accordingly. We have already prepared the ground for the general conclusion to be drawn from this: all art of whatever kind, whether the art of a substantial tradition with which we are familiar or the contemporary art that is unfamiliar because it has no tradition, always demands constructive activity on our part.

I should now like to draw a further conclusion from this which will supply us with a truly comprehensive and universally acceptable structure of art. In the representation that constitutes the work of art, there is no question of the work representing something that it is not, that is, it is not allegory in the sense that it says one thing and gives us to understand something else. On the contrary, what the

work has to say can only be found within itself. This is a universal
claim and not simply a necessary condition of what we call modernity. It is an objectivist prejudice of astonishing naiveté for our first
question to be, "What does this picture represent?" Of course, that
is a part of our understanding of a picture. Insofar as we are able to
recognize what is represented, that recognition is a moment of our
perception of it. Yet we clearly do not regard this as the real goal of
our experience of the work. To convince ourselves of this, we only
have to consider so-called absolute music, for that is a form of nonobjective art. Here it is quite senseless to expect to find a specific
meaning or points of reference, even though the attempt to do so is
occasionally made. We need only think of the hybrid, secondary
forms of program music, opera, and music drama, which precisely as
secondary forms imply the existence of absolute music, that great
achievement of musical abstraction in Western culture which
reached a peak of development in imperial Austria with the classical
Viennese school. Absolute music provides a particularly good illustration of the question that has concerned us all along: What is it
about a piece of music that allows us to say that it is rather shallow
or, in the case of a late Beethoven quartet, that it is truly great and
profound? What is the basis for this? What accounts for the sense of
quality here? Not a determinate relation to anything that we could
identify in terms of meaning. Nor, as the information theory of
aesthetics would have us believe, is it a question of a specific quan-
tity of information. Is it not precisely the difference in quality that is
crucial here? How is it possible to transform a dance-song into a
chorale in a Passion? Is there some obscure relationship with
language at work here? This may well be so, for interpreters of
music have often felt the need to discover such points of reference
and something like traces of conceptual meaning. It is also the case
that when we look at nonobjective art, we can never escape from the
fact that in our everyday experience of the world, our vision is
oriented toward recognizing objects. We also hear the concentrated
expression of music with the same ear with which we otherwise try
to understand language. There remains an ineliminable connection
between what we like to call the wordless language of music and the
verbal language of normal linguistic communication. Perhaps there
is also a similar connection between the objective vision with which
we orient ourselves in the world, and the claim that art makes upon
us both to construct new compositions directly from the elements of

the objective visible world and to participate in the profound tensions that they set up.

These extreme cases help to illuminate how art unites us in its communicative dimension. At the very start I pointed out how the so-called modern age, at least since the beginning of the nineteenth century, had emancipated itself from the shared self-understanding of the humanist – Christian tradition. I also pointed out that the subjects that previously appeared self-evident and binding can now no longer be captured in an artistic form that would allow everyone to recognize them as the familiar language within which new statements are made. This is precisely the new situation as I described it. The artist no longer speaks for the community, but forms his own community insofar as he expresses himself. Nevertheless, he does create a community, and in principle, this truly universal community (*oikumene*) extends to the whole world. In fact, all artistic creation challenges each of us to listen to the language in which the work of art speaks and to make it our own. It remains true in every case that a shared or potentially shared achievement is at issue. This is true irrespective of whether the formation of a work of art is supported in advance by a shared view of the world that can be taken for granted, or whether we must first learn to "read" the script and language of the one who speaks in the creation before us.

III

We have reached the point where I should like to introduce the third element of my title – the festival. If there is one thing that pertains to all festive experiences, then it is surely the fact that they allow no separation between one person and another. A festival is an experience of community and represents community in its most perfect form. A festival is meant for everyone. Therefore, when someone fails to take part, we say that he excludes himself and sets himself apart from the festivities. It is not easy to clarify the characteristic nature of the festival and the structure of temporal experience it entails, and previous research in the area offers us little assistance. Nevertheless, there are some important scholars who have considered the subject, such as the classical philologists Walter F. Otto[52] and the German-Hungarian Karl Kerenyi.[53] And of course, the real nature of the festival and of festive time has always been a theological question.

Perhaps I can begin with the following preliminary observation. We say that a festival is celebrated, and describe the day of the festival as a holiday or day of celebration. But what exactly does it mean to say that we "celebrate a festival?" Is celebration conceived simply negatively as a break from work? And if so, why? Surely because work is something that separates and divides us. For all the cooperation necessitated by joint enterprise and the division of labor in our productive activity, we are still divided as individuals as far as our day-to-day purposes are concerned. Festive celebration, on the other hand, is clearly distinguished by the fact that here we are not primarily separated, but rather are gathered together. It is true, of course, that we now find it hard to realize this unique dimension of festive celebration. Celebrating is an art, and one in which earlier and more primitive cultures were far superior to ourselves. If we ask ourselves what the real nature of this art is, then obviously we must reply that it consists in an experience of community that is difficult to define in precise terms. Furthermore, it is a community in which we are gathered together for something, although no one can say exactly for what it is that we have come together. It is no accident that this experience resembles that of art, since celebration has its own specific kinds of representation. Its established and customary forms have all been hallowed by ancient usage, so that we have become accustomed to doing things in a given way. There is also the specific kind of speech proper to festive celebration which we call the festival address. But perhaps it is quiet, even more than the festival address, that belongs to celebration. Such quiet communicates itself as, for example, when someone chances to encounter a great artistic or religious monument that suddenly strikes him very deeply. I am thinking of the National Museum in Athens, where it seems that every ten years they rescue some miraculous new bronze from the depths of the Aegean and set it up again. On entering the room for the first time, one is overcome by an all-embracing festive quiet and one senses how everyone is gathered together before what they encounter. The celebration of a festival is, in technical terms, an intentional activity. We celebrate inasmuch as we are gathered for something, and this is particularly clear in the case of the experience of art. It is not simply the fact that we are all in the same place, but rather the intention that unites us and prevents us as individuals from falling into private conversations and private, subjective experiences.

Perhaps the question of the temporal structure of the festival will lead us to the festival character of art and the temporal structure of the work of art. Once again, I should like to begin with a linguistic observation. I believe that the only conscientious way to clarify our philosophical ideas is to listen to what is already known by the language that unites us. Let us remember that we speak of "enacting" a celebration. Enacting a celebration is obviously a specific form of behavior. If we wish to think, we must develop an ear for language. The word "enacting" removes all idea of a goal to be attained. To enact is not to set out in order subsequently to arrive somewhere, for when we enact a festival, then the festival is always there from the beginning. The temporal character of the festive celebration that we enact lies in the fact that it does not dissolve into a series of separate moments. Of course, it is quite true that we can organize a program for the celebration, or devise an order of service for a religious festival, perhaps even laying down a timetable of events. But all of this only takes place for the sake of the festival that is being enacted. So although it is perfectly possible to organize the forms of the celebration, the temporal structure of the performance is quite different from the time that simply stands at our disposal.

A certain kind of recurrence belongs to the festival – not in every single case perhaps, although I am inclined to wonder whether in a deeper sense this may not be true. Of course, we distinguish recurrent festivals from unique ones. But the question is whether in fact even the unique festival does not always require repetition as well. We do not describe a festival as a recurring one because we can assign a specific place in time to it, but rather the reverse: the time in which it occurs only arises through the recurrence of the festival itself. The ecclesiastical year is a good example, as are all those cases like Christmas, Easter, or whatever, where we do not calculate time abstractly in terms of weeks and months. Such moments represent the primacy of something that happens in its own time and at the proper time, something that is not subject to the abstract calculation of temporal duration.

Two fundamental ways of experiencing time seem to be in question here.[54] In the context of our normal, pragmatic experience of time, we say that we "have time for something." This time is at our disposal; it is divisible; it is the time that we have or do not have, or at least think we do not have. In its temporal structure, such time is empty and needs to be filled. Boredom is an extreme example of this empty time. When bored, we experience the featureless and repetitive flow of time as an agonizing presence. In contrast to the emptiness of boredom, there is the different emptiness of frantic bustle when we never have enough time for anything and yet constantly have things to do. When we have plans, we experience time as the "right time" for which we have to wait, or as what we need more of in order to get the thing done. These two extremes of bustle and boredom both represent time in the same way: we fill our time with something or we have nothing to do. Either way time is not experienced in its own right, but as something that has to be "spent." There is in addition, however, a totally different experience of time which I think is profoundly related to the kind of time characteristic of both the festival and the work of art. In contrast with the empty time that needs to be filled, I propose to call this "fulfilled" or "autonomous" time. We all know that the festival fulfills every moment of its duration. This fulfillment does not come about because someone has empty time to fill. On the contrary, the time only becomes festive with the arrival of the festival. The manner in which the festival is enacted directly relates to this. We are all familiar with this autonomous time, as we may call it, from our own experience of life: childhood, youth, maturity, old age, and death are all basic forms of such autonomous time. We do not calculate here, nor do we simply add up a gradual sequence of empty moments to arrive at a totality of time. The continuity of the uniform temporal flow that we can observe and measure by the clock tells us nothing about youth or age. The time that allows us to be young or old is not clock time at all, and there is obviously something discontinuous about it. Suddenly we become aware that someone has aged, or that someone is "no longer a child." Here we recognize that everyone has his own time, his autonomous temporality. It is of the nature of the festival that it should proffer time, arresting it and allowing it to tarry. That is what festive celebration means. The calculating way in which we normally manage and dispose of our time is, as it were, brought to a standstill.

It is easy to make a transition from such temporal experiences of life to the work of art. In philosophical thought, art has always appeared in close proximity to life in the fundamental sense of organic structure. Everyone understands when we say that a work of art in some sense maintains an "organic unity." What we mean is readily explained by reference to the fact that every detail or aspect of the picture, text, or whatever it is, is so united with the whole that it does not strike us as something external that has been merely added on; it does not obtrude as if it were some inert element that has simply been imposed in the process of creation. On the contrary, the work seems to possess a kind of center. Similarly, we understand a living organism as a being that bears its center within itself in such a way that the various parts are not subordinated to any particular external purpose, but simply serve the self-preservation of the organism as a living being. This "purposiveness without purpose," as Kant so well described it, is as characteristic a feature of the organism as it clearly is of the work of art.[55] One of the oldest definitions of the beautiful in art corresponds with this. Aristotle says that a thing is beautiful "if nothing can be added and nothing can be taken away."[56] Naturally, this is not to be taken literally, but with a pinch of salt. For we can even put the definition the other way round and say that there is a concentration of the beautiful, which is shown precisely by the fact that we may make a range of possible changes, by altering, replacing, adding, or removing something. Nevertheless, this is only possible on the basis of a central structure which must be left intact if we are not to destroy the living unity of the work. In this respect, the work of art does resemble a living organism with its internally structured unity. In other words, it too displays autonomous temporality.

Obviously this does not mean that it experiences youth, maturity, and old age in the way that a living organism does. But it does mean that the work of art is similarly determined by its own temporal structure rather than by the quantifiable duration of its existence through time. Music may serve as an example. We are all familiar with those vague tempo markings that composers use to describe the individual movements of a piece of music. The instructions are quite indeterminate, but they are not merely technical directions on the composer's part, dependent upon his own decision as to whether a piece is to be taken quickly or slowly. We must find the right time as it is demanded by the work. The tempo markings are only indications that help us to maintain the "correct" tempo or to grasp the work as a whole. The correct tempo can never really be quantified or calculated. One of the major confusions that the technical advances of our age have made possible, and that has even affected artistic practice in certain countries with particularly centralized bureaucracies, is the attempt to regulate performances so that the

authentic version made by the composer or someone authorized by
him becomes canonic along with all the particular tempi of that performance. In fact, the realization of such a thing would spell the
death of artistic reproduction and its substitution by means of some
kind of technical equipment instead. Whenever we try to reproduce
a work by simply copying the original and "authentic" reproduction
of someone else, then we are falling back into a fundamentally non-
creative form of activity which the listener will notice in time – if he
still notices anything at all.

Once again it is a question of articulating that space between
identity and difference with which we are already familiar. One has
to discover the autonomous time proper to a piece of music, the
autonomous time proper to a poetic text, and this can only happen in
one's "inner ear." Every reproduction, every poetic recitation,
every theatrical performance – however great the performers may
be – only succeeds in communicating a genuine artistic experience
of the work itself if with our inner ear we hear something quite different from what actually takes place in front of us. The constituent
elements with which we construct the work are not provided by the
reproduction, the presentation, or the theatrical performance as
such, but by the work that has been raised to ideality in our inner
ear. Anyone who knows a poem particularly well has experienced
this. No one, oneself included, can read it aloud in a totally convincing way. Why is this so? Clearly we encounter once again that
intellectual effort, that spiritual labor, that is rooted in all our so-
called enjoyment of the work. The ideal creation only arises insofar
as we ourselves actively transcend all contingent aspects. If we are to
hear the poem in the completely receptive manner appropriate to it,
then no particular vocal color should characterize the performance
or reading, for there is no such thing given in the text. But since
everyone has a particular vocal color, there is no voice anywhere
that can actually attain the ideality of the poetic text. Each and every
reading will inevitably offend us in a certain sense by virtue of its
contingent qualities. The process by which we liberate ourselves
from such contingency defines the cooperative part we have to play
as participants in the play of art.

The autonomous temporality of the work of art is illustrated particularly well by our experience of rhythm. What a remarkable
phenomenon rhythm is! Psychological research tells us that rhythm

is a factor in our hearing and understanding.[57] If we produce a series of sounds or notes repeated at regular intervals, we find that the listener cannot help introducing rhythm into the series. But where precisely is this rhythm? Is it to be found in the objective and physical temporal relations between the sounds, in the wavelengths, frequencies, and so on? Or is it in the mind of the listener? It is clearly inadequate to conceive the matter in terms of such a crude set of alternatives. It is as true to say that we project the rhythm into the series as it is to say that we perceive it there. Of course, our example of the rhythm to be perceived within a monotonous series is not an example drawn from art. Nevertheless, it shows that we can only hear the rhythm that is immanent within a given form if we ourselves introduce the rhythm into it. That means we must really be actively involved ourselves in order to elicit the rhythm at all.

Every work of art imposes its own temporality upon us, not only the transitory arts of language, music, and dance. When considering the static arts, we should remember that we also construct and read pictures, that we also have to enter into and explore the forms of architecture. These too are temporal processes. One picture may not become accessible to us as quickly as another. And this is especially true of architecture. Our contemporary forms of technical reproduction have so deceived us, that when we actually stand before one of the great architectural monuments of human culture for the first time, we are apt to experience a certain disappointment. They do not look as "painterly" as they seem from the photographic reproductions that are so familiar to us. In fact, this feeling of disappointment only shows that we still have to go beyond the purely artistic quality of the building considered as an image and actually approach it as architectural art in its own right. To do that, we have to go up to the building and wander round it, both inside and out. Only in this way can we acquire a sense of what the work holds in store for us and allow it to enhance our feeling for life.

To sum up the results of these brief reflections: in the experience of art we must learn how to dwell upon the work in a specific way. When we dwell upon the work, there is no tedium involved, for the longer we allow ourselves, the more it displays its manifold riches to us. The essence of our temporal experience of art is in learning how to tarry in this way. And perhaps it is the only way that is granted to us finite beings to relate to what we call eternity.

Let us now summarize the course of our reflections, trying as always to clarify the advances we have made so far. The question posed by contemporary art imposes from the outset the task of bringing together what threatens to fall apart into two antagonistic poles: on the one hand, the art that appears historical, and on the other, the art that seems progressive. The appearance of art as something historical can be described as the delusion of a culture that holds that only what is already familiar to us from our cultural tradition is significant. The appearance of art as something progressive, on the other hand, is sustained by the delusion of the critique of ideology. It claims that history should now begin anew, since we are already thoroughly familiar with the tradition in which we stand and can safely leave it behind. But the riddle that the problem of art sets us is precisely that of the contemporaneity of past and present. There is no question here of anticipation or of degeneration. On the contrary, we have to ask ourselves what it is that maintains the continuity of art and in what sense art represents an overcoming of time. We have attempted to do this in three steps. First, we looked for the anthropological foundations of art in the phenomenon of play as an excess. For it is constitutive of our humanity that our instincts are underdetermined and we therefore have to conceive of ourselves as free and live with the dangers that this freedom implies. This unique characteristic determines all human existence in the most profound fashion. And here I am following the insights of philosophical anthropology developed by Scheler, Plessner, and Gehlen under Nietzsche's inspiration. I have tried to show that the peculiarly human quality of our existence arises in that union of past and present that constitutes the contemporaneity of all ages, styles, races, and classes. For all of this is human. As I said earlier, the penetrating gaze of Mnemosyne, the muse who maintains and retains, marks us out. It was one of the basic intentions of my exposition to show that in our relationship with the world and in all our creative labors – forming or cooperating in the play of form as the case may be – our accomplishment lies in retaining what threatens to pass away.

This activity necessarily reveals the human experience of finitude in a unique way and gives spiritual significance to the immanent transcendence of play as an excess that flows over into the realm of freely chosen possibilities. For us, death is the transcendence of our own mortal stay. The ceremonial burial of the dead and the cult associated with them, the lavishness of burial art and ceremonies of consecration, endow the ephemeral and the transient with a new form of permanence. It seems to me that the advance made now that we have completed our considerations, is that we have seen play's excess to be not only the real ground of our creative production and reception of art, but also the more profound anthropological dimension that bestows permanence. This is the unique character of human play and of the play of art in particular, distinguishing it from all other forms of play in the realm of nature.

That was our first step. We then went on to ask what it is that meaningfully addresses us in the play of form that takes shape and is arrested in the concrete work. I there drew upon the old concept of the symbolic and I should like to take it a step further here. I said that the symbol allows us to recognize something as the host recognised his guest by means of the *tessera hospitalis*. But what is recognition? It is surely not merely a question of seeing something for the second time. Nor does it imply a whole series of encounters. Recognition means knowing something as that with which we are already acquainted. The unique process by which man "makes himself at home in the world," to use a Hegelian phrase, is constituted by the fact that every act of recognition of something has already been liberated from our first contingent apprehension of it and is then raised into ideality. This is something that we are all familiar with. Recognition always implies that we have come to know something more authentically than we were able to do when caught up in our first encounter with it. Recognition elicits the permanent from the transient. It is the proper function of the symbol and of the symbolic content of the language of art in general to accomplish this. Now the question that we are so concerned to answer is precisely this: What is it that we recognize when confronted by an artistic language whose vocabulary, style, and syntax seem so peculiarly empty and alien, or so remote from the great classical traditions of our own culture? Is it not a characteristic of our deeply unsymbolical age that for all our breathless faith in technological, economic, and social progress, we still find recognition impossible to achieve?

I have tried to show that we cannot simply contrast those periods with a rich shared symbolic tradition and those impoverished periods when symbols have lost their meaning. The favorable opportunities of the past and the unfavorable opportunities of the present are not simply facts to be accepted. In fact, recognition of the symbolic is a task that we must take upon ourselves. We have to actualize the possibilities of recognition in the admittedly vast field that confronts us here. It certainly makes a difference whether on the basis of an historical education and a familiarity with modern cultural life we are able to appropriate historically a vocabulary once self-evident to all (acquiring familiarity with it in such a way that it plays its part in our encounter with art), or whether we have to decipher the new and unfamiliar language in order to read it properly.

What is reading? We know that we are able to read something when we cease to notice the letters as such and allow the sense of what is said to emerge. In every case, it is only the constitution of coherent meaning that lets us claim that we have understood what is said. And this alone brings our encounter with the language of art to fruition. It should be obvious that there is an interaction at work here, and we are deceiving ourselves if we really think that we can have one and reject the other. It can hardly be overemphasized that anyone who believes modern art to be degenerate will not be able to understand the great art of the past properly either. We must realize that every work of art only begins to speak when we have already learned to decipher and read it. The case of modern art supplies an effective warning against the idea that we can appreciate the previous language of art without first learning how to read it.

Of course, we must take it upon ourselves to produce this shared community of meaning, which can be neither simply presupposed nor gratefully accepted. André Malraux's famous museum without walls, where all the historical periods of artistic achievement are simultaneously present to consciousness, represents a reluctant recognition of this task in a rather complicated form. It is this collection, brought together in the imagination, that we have to produce for ourselves. The essential thing is that we never possess this collection already or encounter it in the same way as we do when we visit a museum to see what others have collected. Or, to put it another way, as finite beings, we already find ourselves within certain traditions, irrespective of whether we are aware of them or whether we deceive ourselves into believing that we can start anew. For our attitude does nothing to change the power that tradition exercises over us. But it makes a difference whether we face up to the traditions in which we live along with the possibilities they offer for the future, or whether we manage to convince ourselves that we can turn away from the future into which we are already moving and program ourselves afresh. For, of course, tradition means transmission rather than conservation. This transmission does not imply that we simply leave things unchanged and merely conserve them. It means learning how to grasp and express the past anew. It is in this sense that we can say that transmission is equivalent to translation.

In fact, the phenomenon of translation provides a model for the real nature of tradition. The ossified language of literature only becomes art when it becomes part of our own language. The same is true of the figurative arts and architecture as well. We should appreciate the magnitude of the task involved in reconciling in a fruitful and appropriate way the great monuments and buildings of the past with our modern forms of transport, the methods of lighting available to us today, and the different conditions under which we see them. Perhaps I may give an example of what I mean. On a journey in the Iberian peninsula I was deeply moved to discover a cathedral in which the authentic language of these ancient Spanish and Portuguese religious buildings had not yet been obscured, so to speak, by the illumination provided by electric lights. Obviously, the narrow apertures that let us glimpse the sky outside, and the open portal that allows the daylight to flood into the interior represent the only proper way to encounter these mighty citadels of religion. Now I am not suggesting that we can simply disregard the conditions under which we customarily see things. It is no more possible to do this than to disregard all the other aspects of modern life. The task involved in bringing together the petrified remnants of yesterday and the life of today provides a vivid illustration of what tradition always means: not just the careful preservation of monuments, but the constant interaction between our aims in the present and the past to which we still belong.

It is a question, therefore, of allowing what is to be. But this "letting be" does not mean the repetition of something we already know. We let the past be for us as we are now, not by repeated experience of it, but through an encounter with it.

Finally, the third point concerning the festival. I do not want to repeat here how the authentic temporality of art is related to that of the festival, but I should just like to emphasize the single point that a festival unites everyone. It is characteristic of festive celebration that it is meaningful only for those actually taking part. As such, it represents a unique kind of presence that must be fully appreciated. If we keep this in mind, we may be able to question our own cultural

life, which experiences the aesthetic pleasure arising from culture as
a temporary release from all the pressures of everyday existence.
The essence of the beautiful is to have a certain standing in the
public eye. This in turn implies a whole form of life that embraces
all those artistic forms with which we embellish our environment,
including decoration and architecture. If art shares anything with the
festival, then it must transcend the limitations of any cultural definition of art, as well as the limitations associated with its privileged
cultural status. It must also remain immune to the commercial structures of our social life. In saying this, I do not deny that art can be
business too, and that artists may well succumb to the commer-
cialization of their art, but this is not the proper function of art and
never has been. Perhaps I may point out certain facts. Let us recall
the great works of Greek tragedy, which still present problems for
the most perceptive and well-educated of contemporary readers.
We can find certain choral hymns in Sophocles or Aeschylus of
almost hermetic obscurity on account of their intensity and com-
pression. In spite of this, Attic drama united its audience. The success and enormous popularity that Attic drama enjoyed as an integral
part of religious life in the broadest sense, demonstrates that it was
not simply there to represent the ruling class, nor to satisfy the festival committee that awarded prizes for the best piece.

The great Western polyphonic tradition that derives from
Gregorian church music provides us with an analogy. And indeed,
even today we can have an experience like that of the Greeks – and
with those same works of ancient tragedy. The first director of the
Moscow Art Theater was asked immediately after the Revolution
which revolutionary play he would use to open the new revolutionary theater. In fact, *Oedipus Rex* was played with enormous success: ancient tragedy for every society and every period! The
elaborate development of Gregorian chant and the Passion music of
J.S. Bach provide the Christian equivalent to this. In such cases, we
cannot mistake the fact that we are dealing with something quite different from a simple visit to a concert. When we go to a concert, it is
obvious that the audience is different from the congregation that
gathers in a church for the musical performance of the Passion. We
have here a parallel to Greek tragedy. Such works range from the
highest claims of artistic, historical, and musical culture to the openness of the simplest and most heartfelt human needs.

I would insist that the *Threepenny Opera,* or the records of modern songs so popular with the young people of today, are equally legitimate. They too have a capacity to establish comunication in a way that reaches people of every class and educational background. I am not referring here to the contagious and intoxicated enthusiasm that is the object of mass psychology, although that certainly exists and has always accompanied the genuine experience of community. In our world of powerful stimuli and the often irresponsible, commercially motivated love of experimentation for its own sake, there is a great deal that does not establish real communication. For intoxication alone cannot insure lasting communication. Yet it is surely significant that the younger generation feel that they express themselves spontaneously in the obsessive rhythms of modern music, or in very barren forms of abstract art.

We should clearly recognize one thing. The generation gap, which we experience in the home in friendly argument over which program to turn on or which record to play, can also be found within our society as a whole, although we should rather speak of the continuity between the generations – since the older generation also learns something in the process. It is a profound mistake to think that our art is simply that of the ruling class. We can only believe that if we forget all our sports centers, motorways, public libraries, and technical schools, which are frequently more lavishly furnished than the fine old grammar schools, which I myself miss, where chalk dust was almost part of our education. Finally, this is also to forget the mass media and the widespread influence that they have on the whole society. We should recognize that all these things can be used in a rational way. Certainly human culture is greatly endangered by the passivity that is produced when the channels of cultural information are all too instantly available. This is especially true of the mass media. Whether we are talking of the older generation that raises and educates or the younger generation that is raised and educated, we are all as human beings faced with the challenge of teaching and learning for ourselves. What is demanded is precisely the active application of our own thirst for knowledge, and of our powers of discrimination, when we are confronted by art or indeed anything that the mass media make generally available. It is only then that we experience art. The inseparability of form and content is fully realized as the nondifferentiation in which we encounter art as something that both expresses us and speaks to us.

We have only to look at the alternatives to see the nature of this experience. Here I will simply give two extreme examples. First, there is the case when we enjoy something for the sake of some quality or other that is familiar to us. I think that this is the origin of kitsch and all bad art. Here we see only what we already know, not wishing to see anything else. We enjoy the encounter insofar as it simply provides a feeble confirmation of the familiar, instead of changing us. This means that the person who is already prepared for the language of art can sense the intention behind the effect. We notice that such art has designs upon us. All kitsch has something of this forced quality about it. It is often well meant and sincere in intention, but it means the destruction of art. For something can only be called art when it requires that we construe the work by learning to understand the language of form and content so that communication really occurs.

The connoisseur represents the opposite extreme to kitsch. This is particularly common in our attitudes to performing artists. We go to the opera because Callas is singing, rather than because a particular opera is being performed. I recognize this as a fact, but I would claim that such an attitude is incapable of mediating an experience of art in any real sense. When we become aware of an actor or singer or any creative artist as mediator, we exercise a secondary level of reflection. When the complete experience of a work of art is genuine, however, what amazes us is precisely the unobtrusiveness of the performers. They do not display themselves, but succeed in evoking the work and its inner coherence with a kind of unforced self-evidence. Thus we have two extremes here: on the one hand, an artistic intent that manipulates us for a particular purpose and finds expression in kitsch; and on the other, total obliviousness to the real appeal that the work of art addresses to us in favor of a quite secondary level in which we delight in aesthetic taste for its own sake.

The real task seems to lie between these extremes. It consists in accepting and retaining everything that genuine art is capable of communicating to us by virtue of the power in its consummately wrought form. How far it is necessary to bring our culturally mediated historical knowledge to bear upon this task is a secondary question. The art of earlier ages only comes down to us filtered through time and transmitted through a tradition that both preserves it and transforms it in a living way. The nonobjective art of our time – albeit only in its best forms, which we today can hardly distinguish from its imitations – can possess a similar density of composition and a similar capacity for addressing us directly. The work of art transforms our fleeting experience into the stable and lasting form of an independent and internally coherent creation. It does so in such a way that we go beyond ourselves by penetrating deeper into the work. That "something can be held in our hesitant stay"[58] – this is what art has always been and still is today.

PART II

Essays

1. The festive character of theater

We are assembled here to commemorate a long and distinguished period in the history of German theater. Mannheim has had a permanent theater for over 175 years now, and the proud sense of self-confidence associated with this commemoration really belongs to the culture of bourgeois society itself, which originally created and supported the "permanent theater." And this bourgeois spirit still maintains theaters of this kind. And yet, when measured against the larger rhythm of historical change, 175 years is not a very long period of time and offers no guarantee of permanence. The structural transformation of social life that has taken place in this period is so profound and decisive that the social function of theater was and still is bound to register this transformation. In the last 175 years, the face of our world has been transformed more profoundly than during the whole previous period of recorded human history. We have only to consider the eloquent statistics of population growth in the cities and on the continent of Europe as a whole. Modern society is fundamentally shaped by industrial technology, as anyone can easily see for himself if he leaves the ivory towers of Heidelberg for the thriving social and economic life of the busy industrial town of Mannheim. Perhaps the elimination of distance is the most significant sign of this transformation. Everyone travels. Modern society is a democracy of travel. Once it was the members of theatrical troupes visiting the permanent seats of aristocratic and bourgeois culture who were "traveling players." Today it is the audience, friends of theater like ourselves, who have become the travellers, assembling in the festive security of the theater. How can theater remain unchanged under such conditions? How can it retain today an untroubled confidence in its own future?

The products of modern technology have actually already taken hold at the very heart of the theater itself, and it is by no means clear whether it still has any real future at all in our much changed world. Film and radio in particular have developed quite new forms to satisfy our innate pleasure in spectacle and music. Modern sport too has produced a kind of mass spectacle that is festive in character, although it has nothing to do with art. Even in poetry, we can trace the new constructivist tendency of our age, the tendency toward what might be called "montage," a construction on the basis of finished, ready-made components. The person who undertakes this task certainly has an intellectual contribution of his own to make insofar as he still has to foresee the way everything functions as a whole – or, in the case of poetic or theatrical montage, the effect of the work as a whole – but he still belongs to the modern industrial world of labor and is closer to the engineer than to the creative genius. Does this not indicate a fundamental change in the methods of production? And will not the theater, the very center of brilliant improvisation, inevitably lose its place in this new, technologically organized world?

To do justice to this question, thoughtful historians must turn their attention to the festive character that has always been of the essence of theater. Theater is a product of Greece, both in name and nature. It is in essence a play produced to be looked upon, and the unification that it effects – in which we are all onlookers of one and the same event – is a unification at a distance. Greek culture generated this new objective dramatic form, which still has the power to overwhelm us today, from the existing forms of cultic ceremony, dance, and ritual. For there is no doubt that Greek theater had a religious origin as part of [the Greek's] festive celebrations and thus, like all other manifestations of Greek social life, had a fundamentally sacred character. But what precisely is a festival? Festivals are to be celebrated. But what is the festive character of a festival? Naturally, this quality need not always be associated with joy or happiness, since in mourning we also share this festive character together. But a festive occasion is always something uplifting which raises the participants out of their everyday existence and elevates them into a kind of universal communion. Consequently, the festive occasion possesses its own sort of temporality. It is an essentially recurrent phenomenon, and even a unique festival celebration bears the possibility of repetition within itself. The commemoration of a special occasion is itself enacted in a festive fashion.

Enactment is the festival's mode of being, and in the enactment, time becomes the *nunc stans* of an elevated presence in which past and present become one in the act of remembrance. For surely the festival of Christmas is more than a festival of the birth of the Savior who was originally present nearly two thousand years ago. In a mysterious way, every Christmas is contemporary with that distant present. The mystery of festive celebration lies in this suspension of time. In contrast to such festive occasions, we are in our everyday lives constantly bound by particular functions and time-limits. In the festival, the particularity of our purposes gives way to communion in a heightened self-fulfilling moment which does not acquire its significance from any task still to be accomplished and does not gain from any further purpose to be achieved. Clearly, the most original and exemplary manifestation of this self-fulfilling moment lies in the cultic ceremony. Here the manifestation of God is an absolute presence in which the remembrance of the past and the present moment coincide in an instantaneous unity. This explains why the specific character of festive celebration cannot simply be characterized in negative terms. The decisive thing is not just the fact that we are lifted out of everyday life, nor the fact that we do not expect the festival to serve any ulterior purpose. The decisive and characteristic thing is that it presents us with a positive content of its own. In fact, all cultic ceremony is a kind of creation. There is a widespread prejudice among the general public that the essence of all cultic ceremony is to be understood and described in terms of magical practices. This approach is quite natural to an enlightened age in which the increasingly unintelligible ceremonies, practices, and rituals connected with religious celebration are interpreted as a sort of magical supplication undertaken by the community to assure itself of divine favor. But we know from modern research that this account of the nature of cultic ceremony is fundamentally mistaken. It is an account that begins from that extreme form of life that has come to dominate all modern civilization: the deliberate and calculating pursuit of power and material advantage, that tendency toward acquiring and manipulating things to which we owe the principal achievements of our modern civilization. It is an account that fails to perceive that the original and still vital essence of festive celebration is creation and elevation into a transformed state of being.[1]

Anyone who is involved in the regular practice of the particular

forms of worship we have described as cultic celebration knows
what a festival really is. And even the secularized forms of Christian
celebration, like the carnivals still to be seen in Catholic countries,
are not so unrelated to the theater and the festival character belonging to it. For theater, like cultic ceremony, also represents a genuine
creation: something drawn from within ourselves takes shape before
our eyes in a form that we recognize and experience as a more profound presentation of our own reality. This overwhelming truth is
summoned up from hidden depths to address us. In pagan antiquity,
this occurred through the manifestation of the god, and in Christian
ritual, the sacrifice of the Mass has a comparable significance. But
something like this happens in the theater as well, although since the
institution of permanent theaters, it takes place in quite a different
way. The establishment of the permanent theater is not simply an
external change in the way in which contemporary culture preserves
and communicates the old magical festive character of earlier
theater. Rather, it signifies a paradoxical transformation of this festive character. As we saw, it is an intrinsic characteristic of every festival that it enjoys a specific, rhythmical recurrence that elevates it
above the flow of time. In a kind of cosmic rhythm, it assures that
not all times pass by indifferently in the same homogeneous way.
On the contrary, in the course of festive time, the heightened
moment returns. The new permanent theater takes over this festive
character, linking it to works that are performed and enacted there
in ever new ways. The particular nature of modern theater thus rests
upon a paradoxical transformation. I should like to quote something
that Hugo von Hofmannsthal once said about this in one of his prose
sketches – for if anyone has a right to talk about the theater in our
own century, then it must be a Viennese poet. He wrote, "Of all
secular institutions, the theater is the only remaining one of any
power and universal validity that links our love of festival, our joy in
spectacle and laughter, the pleasure that we take in being touched,
excited, and profoundly moved to the ancient instinct for festival
implanted in the human race from time immemorial."[2]

This is what seems to be particularly thoughtworthy when we
consider the enduring function of the theater in this changed society
of ours. The permanent theater brought about by these changes is a
creation of aristocratic and bourgeois circles. But, as I indicated in
my introductory remarks, this function has continued to change in

the context of modern industrial society. On reflection, we can distinguish three great periods in the history of theater.

The first period, which I shall call the age of elevated religious presence, lasted up until the introduction of the permanent theater. Throughout this time, it was taken for granted that dramatic representation was nothing but an ancillary manifestation, an accident, as it were, of the religious festival. It fulfilled the particular function of gathering the religious community for the festival. This form of collective festive celebration has a very long history behind it, and it was particularly characteristic of the cult of Dionysius, from which Greek theater was born. In no other ancient cult was the religious community so closely involved as participants as they were in the orgiastic cult of the god Dionysius. The medieval mystery plays, and even Baroque theater in many of its forms, like the plays of Calderon for example, did not wholly detach themselves from the cultic and courtly focal point of life in the Christian period. It is clearly a decisive characteristic of this chapter in the history of theater that it was still able to serve as a gathering point in which the onlookers were of no less significance than the players. This is still true today, although it is obviously impossible for the onlooker to play this indispensable part along with the players in the most recent forms of cultural life insofar as these have been determined by technology.

This is only possible because it is of the essence of theater to present us with something that is not simply the work of the poet who conceived it or of the producer who gives it visible form. On the contrary, the theatrical presentation calls up something that is at work in all of us even if we are unaware of it. And even the most intimate theatrical occasion of today preserves something of the reality of that age of religious presence when the theatrical festivities were still part of the festive celebration of the whole community.

The second great period in the history of the theater, which is also part of our contemporary cultural heritage, is unmistakably characterized by the permanent theater. The nature of this period is particularly well represented by Schiller, who gave his name to the National Theater of Mannheim. I call this the age of moral transcendence or moral sublimity. What separates this period of theatrical history from the first is the tension that every member of the audience now senses between the prevailing form of real life and the

enchanted world presented on stage. This is the point at which the
onlooker becomes indeed a mere onlooker in the sense we customarily associate with the modern theater audience – although I am
tempted to say that this is no longer the case today. Schiller, and
with him the whole of the nineteenth century, experienced the
theater as a great form of consolation for a world that was becoming
prosaic. The task of drama is as Schiller once expressed it, to
broaden our narrow and restricted "ant like" view of reality, to render the providential governance of things universally transparent by
giving visible form on the dream-world of the stage to the appor-
tionment of guilt and punishment, struggle, and achievement. In
short, drama makes visible the ethical harmony of life that can no
longer be seen in life itself.[3]

Clearly this represents a task of moral transcendence since we all
know that the marvelous events presented on stage show us life as it
really should be. As is well known, Schiller saw the function of the
theater as a moral institution in that it anticipated in the stage play
the transition to a genuinely ethical form of social life.[4] This moral
transcendence returns the onlooker to the innermost recesses of his
being. He is no longer a participant in the sense in which those who
took part in the religious or secular celebration were participants.
He is nothing but an onlooker, and this is reflected by the specific
forms of the stage in front of him. In the darkness, the solitary
onlooker hears from the stage the call of moral transcendence.

In addition, there is something quite new that has arisen since the
permanent theater began to find its place in society. Now, for the
first time in the history of theater, we see the repetition of performances and the revival of previously performed stageworks as standard practice. Now, for the first time, in addition to the newly
created works by contemporary writers, we find a whole classical
repertoire. Now, for the first time, we are faced with the task of
mediating between the contemporaneity of the present and the presence of our historical cultural heritage.

There is no doubt that this alone does not turn the theater into a
museum. Theater does not, indeed cannot ever, simply become
"historical." Whenever a theater performs a piece of merely historical interest, it has already ceased to discharge its proper and preeminent function: to represent presence and nothing but presence.
Indeed we owe to the theater of the last 175 years a whole new
dimension of contemporary awareness: the creative works of Greek,

Spanish, English, classical French and German theater, the highest achievements in the history of dramatic poetry, have all been able to become a new and contemporary possession of every present. However, this does not mean that the purpose of a classical theatrical program is to give authentic performances whose historically accurate style has been established by scholars. On the contrary, the characteristic value of this chapter in the history of theater is precisely the power of fusion that the present possesses as such when it succeeds in elevating past life into presence.

I have thus already suggested that we are about to open up a further chapter in the history of theater. And it is hardly surprising if we begin to sense this today. For the structural transformation in our society is so profound that it would be a miracle if we still entertained the intimate historical museumlike luxury of the kind of theater that fulfilled its specific function in the nineteenth century, when the horse and carriage was the principal form of transport.

What then is the third period? Scholars cannot play the role of prophets here. I will simply sketch certain features of the situation as I see it from the perspective of a grateful friend of contemporary theatrical life. I cannot really think of an adequate name for this as yet unwritten, emerging chapter in the history of the theater. However, I think I sense that this moral tension between reality and the dream world of the stage, the sublime moral call that constituted the greatness of classical theater in the nineteenth century, the distance between the mute onlooker and the distant stage transformed by the lights above it, all these things no longer wholly answer to the way we feel today or correspond to our future possibilities. Today, the unity of onlooker and player is acquiring a new significance. This unity touches us precisely because we feel that the world cannot simply be understood in terms of the tension created by uplifting moral sentiment. On the contrary, we feel that the communal spirit that supports us all and transcends each of us individually represents the real power of theater and brings us back to the ancient religious sources of the cultic festival. There is much in contemporary theater that speaks for such a development. Professionals in the theater will no doubt feel that this has been recognized and practised for a long time now. But the layman only perceives this later as he slowly tries to understand this process.

It is not easy to devise a title for this new chapter so recently begun. It is too early to make out its essential features and much of what the layman notices is possibly quite external. But the whole naturalistic ideal that once succeeded the hollow pathos of the neoclassical stage, the psychological orientation and the atmospheric realistic stage picture – everything that made up the magical world of theater – all this strikes us today as a flight from reality. Even the technical perfection that contributed to this narcotic and hypnotic effect seems to be so much wasted effort.

We should be quite clear what a trap the word "imitation" represents here. For mimesis in the ancient sense and modern forms of mimetic representation are quite different from what we usually understand by imitation. All true imitation is a transformation that does not simply present again something that is already there. It is a kind of transformed reality in which the transformation points back to what has been transformed in and through it. It is a transformed reality because it brings before us intensified possibilities never seen before. Every imitation is an exploration, an intensification of extremes. Modern theater that is bold enough to approach and explore these extremes is not therefore some secondary phenomenon within our society and culture. For it seems to me that the theater has the enormous and lasting advantage, compared with all other possibilities of this kind, that it constantly tries out these bold experiments in transformation in the immediacy of the community constituted by players and onlookers. The player receives back from the onlooker what he has dared to do and inversely we, the onlookers, receive from the daring presentation of the players new possibilities of being that go beyond what we are.

It is the unsettling gaze of the mask that is pure attention, all surface with nothing behind it, and thus pure expression. It is the rigidity of the puppet on a string that nevertheless dances, the alien shock that shakes our comfortable bourgeois self-confidence and puts at risk the reality in which we feel secure. Here we no longer come to self-knowledge within the sovereign realm of our inwardness. We recognize ourselves as the plaything of the mighty, suprapersonal forces that condition our being. Of course, montage and technical skills also help us to make all this visible. But they do not serve to produce a dreamlike mirage of reality. On the contrary, if the theater is to offer us more than psychological depiction, if it is to give a sign that points and a claim that speaks, it requires the same spiritual realization appropriate to language and gesture.

Today we are constantly and intensely aware that the human word and the human gesture have a communicative power in relation to which all the most lavish expenditure of our world-transforming technological culture seems unsure, hesitant, labored, and ephemeral. When a word is well spoken, a knock upon the door well timed, something presents itself that no amount of technical simulation with the most sophisticated methods can ever really achieve. To whom does this present itself and how? Obviously it is not there without us, the onlookers. It is we ourselves who have to redeem what should be there. The truly surprising experience generated by the last few decades of progressive theater is that modern man, constantly submerged in the flood of stimuli and hardly able to protect himself from being helplessly engulfed by the intoxicating currents around him, can still act for himself and succeed in rising up and letting what presents itself to him exist in the elevated form that crowns the festive moment. The theater has become more spiritual than it ever was when the audience was encouraged to sit back and simply enjoy the spectacle. There is an immediacy to theater that we rarely encounter in our thoroughly specialized existence, obscured as it is for us by a thousand different mediations. The genuine experience of the enduring festive character of the theater seems to me to lie in the immediate communal experience of what we are and how things stand with us in the vital interchange between player and onlooker. As Rilke says, "Above, beyond us, the angel plays."[5]

2. Composition
and interpretation

There has long been a tension between the practice of the artist and
that of the interpreter. From the artist's point of view, interpretation
appears arbitrary and capricious, if not actually superfluous. And this
tension becomes all the greater when interpretation is attempted in
the name and spirit of science. The creative artist finds it extremely
difficult to believe that it is possible to overcome all the difficulties
of interpretation by using a scientific approach. The problem of
composition and interpretation actually represents a special case of
the general relationship between the creative artist and the interpreter. As far as poetry and poetic composition are concerned, it is
not uncommon to find the practice of interpretation and artistic
creation united in one and the same individual. This suggests that
poetic composition has a more intimate connection with the practice
of interpretation than the other arts do. Even where we claim scientific status for our interpretation, this practice does not seem as questionable when applied to poetry as is generally believed. The
scientific approach scarcely seems to go beyond what is involved in
any thoughtful engagement with poetry. Nor is this surprising when
we consider just how much philosophical reflection has penetrated
the modern poetry of this century.[1] The relationship between poetic
composition and interpretation does not therefore simply arise
within the context of science or philosophy alone. It also represents
an internal problem of poetic composition itself, for poet and reader
alike.

In discussing the question in this way, I do not wish to become
involved in a dispute between the academic study of literature and
the practice of writing about the claims of interpretation. I shall not
attempt to rival the masterly expression of those who live by the
word and know best how to use it. I should simply like to use my

own craft of philosophical thinking to help people to see what they can all come to understand for themselves.

What explains this proximity between composition and interpretation? It is obvious that they have something in common. Both take place in the medium of language. And yet there is a difference and we need to know how profound it is. Paul Valéry pointed out this difference with great force: everyday language, as well as the language of science and philosophy, points to something beyond itself and disappears behind it. The language of poetry, on the other hand, shows itself even as it points, so that it comes to stand in its own right. Ordinary language resembles a coin that we pass around among ourselves in place of something else, whereas poetic language is like gold itself.[2] Now to begin with, we must recognize that, despite this illuminating comparison, there are transitional cases that stand between poetically articulated language on the one hand and the purely intentional word on the other. And in this century we have become particularly familiar with the intimate fusion of both of these kinds of language.

Let us start with the extreme cases. On the one hand we have lyric poetry (which is no doubt what Valéry had in mind). In our own time we have witnessed a remarkable phenomenon: in Rilke or Gottfried Benn, for example, the language of science has actually invaded the language of poetry in a way that would have seemed quite inconceivable in great poetry only a few generations before. How has it come about that an obviously intentional word, a definition, or even a scientific concept can be integrated with the rhythmic flow of poetic language?

And now let us consider the other extreme of the novel, apparently the most flexible of art forms. Here the language of reflection that relates the things and events around us has always been at home, not merely in the speech of the fictional characters, but also in that of the narrator, whoever it may be. But do we not encounter something new here as well, even when compared with the bold innovations of the romantic novel? We have seen not only the disappearance of the narrative perspective, but the dissolution of the very concept of action itself, and the difference between the language of narration and the language of reflection collapses as a result.

It would appear that even the writer most hostile to the claims of interpretation cannot fail to see the common link between composition and interpretation. This remains true even if he is quite aware of the problematic nature of all interpretation and poetic self-interpretation in particular, believing with Ernst Jünger that "anyone who offers a commentary on his own work demeans himself."[3] What then is interpretation? It is certainly not the same as conceptual explanation. It is much more like understanding or explicating something. And yet there is more to interpretation than this. In its original meaning, interpretation implies pointing in a particular direction. It is important to note that all interpretation points in a direction rather than to some final endpoint, in the sense that it points toward an open realm that can be filled in a variety of ways.

We can distinguish two different senses of interpretation: pointing to something and pointing out the meaning of something. Clearly both of these are connected with one another. "Pointing to something" is a kind of "indicating" that functions as a sign. "Pointing out what something means," on the other hand, always relates back to the kind of sign that interprets itself. Thus when we interpret the meaning of something, we actually interpret an interpretation. The attempt to define and establish the limits of our interpretative activity brings us back to the question concerning the nature of interpretation itself. For what is a sign? Is everything a sign in some sense? Was Goethe right when he made the symbol a fundamental concept for all aesthetics and claimed that "everything points to everything else" and "everything is a symbol"?[4] Or must we qualify this claim? Can we find anything that points like a sign in this way and demands to be taken as such and interpreted accordingly? Certainly we must often try to read the sign character of things. In this way we attempt to interpret that which at the same time conceals itself, as in the expression of gesture, for example.[5] But even there, the interpretation arises within a self-contained totality and clarifies the direction in which the sign points by eliciting that to which it basically points from that which is itself confused, unclear, and indefinite. This interpreting is not a reading in of some meaning, but clearly a revealing of what the thing itself already points to.

This contrast shows us what is at issue here. We do not have to interpret or scrutinize an unambiguous statement or order that simply requires obedience. We have only to interpret something when its meaning is not clearly laid down or when it is ambiguous. Let us recall the classical examples of things that require such interpretation: the flight of birds, oracles, dreams, pictorial images, enigmatic writings. In all these cases there are two sides to interpretation: first, a pointing in a certain direction that itself requires interpretation, but also at the same time a certain holding back on the part of what is to be shown in this way. We have only to interpret that which has a multiplicity of meanings.

We may well ask whether we can interpret such ambiguity except by revealing that ambiguity. This brings us right back to our question concerning the particular connection between composition and interpretation within the overall relationship between the activity of interpretation and the activity of artistic creation. Art demands interpretation because of its inexhaustible ambiguity. It cannot be satisfactorily translated in terms of conceptual knowledge. And this is true of poetry as well. The question concerns the particular relationship between composition and interpretation within the tension between image and concept. The ambiguous meaning of poetry is inseparably bound up with the unambiguous meaning of the intentional word. It is the particular position of language in relation to the other materials of artistic form – stone, color, sound, and even bodily movement in dance – that allows this tension and mutual interference. The elements from which language is constructed and which poetry shapes for its own purposes, are pure signs that can only become elements of poetic form by virtue of their meaing. That is to say, they possess their appropriate mode of being as intentional language. We should especially remember this in our own time when emancipation from an objectively interpreted experience of the world appears to be a basic principle of contemporary art. The poet cannot participate in this process. Language as the medium and material of expression can never fully emancipate itself from meaning. A genuinely nonobjective poetry would simply be gibberish.

Of course, this does not imply that literature is confined merely to intentional language in this sense. On the contrary, it always possesses a kind of identity of meaning and being in the same way that a sacrament combines meaning and being in one. "Song is existence."[6] But what kind of existence is this? All intentional speech points away from itself. Words are not simply complexes of sound, but meaning-gestures that point away from themselves as gestures do. We all know that the sound-quality of poetry only acquires definition through the understanding of meaning. We are only too painfully aware that poetry is language-bound, and realize that the translation of poetry sets an inspiring yet infuriating task that it is impossible to accomplish perfectly.

But that means that the unity of sound-quality and meaning that characterizes every word we speak finds its ultimate fulfillment in poetic speech. Compared with all other art forms, the poetic work of art possesses as language a characteristic indeterminacy. The unity of form that is so characteristic of the poetic work of art, as it is of every other kind, is sensuously present, and to that extent cannot be reduced to the mere intention of meaning. But even this presence still contains an intentional element that points to an indeterminate dimension of possible fulfillments. This is precisely what gives to poetry that priority over the other art forms that has always allowed it to define the tasks of the visual arts. For the linguistic means at the disposal of poetry evoke presence, intuition, and existence. However, in each person who responds to the poetic word, that word is fulfilled in a unique intuitive fashion that cannot be communicated to others. In this way, language summons the visual artist to work. The artist discovers on behalf of all an image that acquires uncontested validity. We call it the dominant style of imagery, and it can only be superseded by a new creative act that produces a new type of imagery. Now the proper function of the poet is a shared saying, a saying that possesses absolute reality simply by virtue of its being said. The Greek word for this is *mythos*. The histories of gods and men recounted in myth only enjoy existence in the recounting of them. They can only be believed as long as they are told and retold. In this very precise sense, all poetry is mythical, for like myth, the credence we give to it depends upon this saying. But it thereby finds itself in the element to which both composition and interpretation belong, and indeed, interpretation is already a part of all composition.

We can confirm this by reference to a poetic device that once possessed unquestioned legitimacy and only lost favor in more modern times with the poetry of subjective experience. I am thinking of allegory, which expresses one thing by means of another. Allegory is only possible for poetry as long as there exists a secure common horizon of interpretation in which it can take its place. If this condition is fulfilled, allegory does not have to appear cold and lifeless. Even when there is a strict correspondence between allegory and meaning, the totality of poetic language in which it is presented can still possess that open dimension of indeterminacy that allows it to be poetic, in the sense of conceptually inexhaustible. I shall try to clarify this with an example. The discussion of Kafka's writings has centered upon the way that he succeeds in constructing an everyday world in an unaccountably detached, lucid, and dispassionate manner. But this apparently familiar world is accompanied by a mysterious feeling of strangeness which creates the impression that everything in it actually points beyond itself to something else. At the same time, we cannot interpret all this as an allegory, precisely because the principal event that this masterly example of narrative art presents to us is the dissolution of any shared horizon of interpretation. The feeling of expectation that everything points toward some decipherable meaning or concept is disappointed. The text evokes poetically the mere semblance of allegory and opens out onto a realm of ambiguity.

Here we have an example of interpretation within composition that yet calls for further interpretation. The question now arises: who is doing the interpreting here, the poet or the interpreter? Or is it the case that both are giving interpretations even while performing their respective functions? Is it the case that in this meaning and this saying, something is intimated but not "intended"? Interpretation seems to be a genuine determination of existence rather than an activity or an intention.

We find something similar when we consider the ambiguity of the oracle. It too belongs more to the realm of intimation than to interpretation. What drives Oedipus to his fate is not a foolish mistake promoted by some malign power. Nor is it some sacrilegious desire to disprove a divine pronouncement that finally leads him to destruction. The meaning of the oracle in this sort of tragedy lies in the fact that the hero provides an exemplary illustration of the ambiguities of fate that hang over every one of us. As human beings, we are essentially caught up in the attempt to interpret the meaning of this ambiguity.

The poetic word shares this ambiguity as well. It is true of poetic language that it is mythical, in the sense that it requires no confirmation from anything beyond itself. The ambiguity of poetic language answers to the ambiguity of human life as a whole, and therein lies its unique value. All interpretation of poetic language only interprets what the poetry has already interpreted. What poetry interprets for us and points to is not of course the same as what the poet intends. What the poet intends is in no way superior to what anyone else intends. Poetry does not consist in intending something else. It consists simply in the fact that what is intended and what is said is there in the poem. The interpretations offered are as much bound up with the existence of the poem as are the ambiguous intimations of the poetry itself. All interpretation comes to share in the being of the poem. Just as the poem suggests a meaning by pointing us in a certain direction, so too the one who interprets the poem points in a given direction. When we read an interpretation, we turn ourselves in a given direction, but we do not intend this particular interpretation as such. Obviously the language of interpretation should not assume the place of that toward which it itself is pointing. An interpretation that attempted to do this would remind us of the dog that, when we try to point something out to it, invariably turns to the pointing hand instead of looking at what we are trying to show it.

The situation seems to be exactly the same when interpretation takes place within composition itself. It belongs to the essence of poetic statement that it too contains a moment that points away from itself. The art and mastery of expression that bestow a level of aesthetic quality upon a poetic statement may be made the object of aesthetic reflection, but such art has its real being in the fact that it points away from itself and lets us see what it is that the poet is speaking about. Neither the poet nor the interpreter possesses any special legitimation as such. Whenever we find ourselves in the presence of real poetry, it always transcends both poet and interpreter. Both of them pursue a meaning that points toward an open realm. Like the interpreter, therefore, the poet must clearly realize that what he himself intends enjoys no special privilege. His own self-conception or conscious intention is guided by many different possibilities of reflective self-understanding and is quite different from what he actually accomplishes if the poem is a success.

Hesiod, who in his famous invocation of the muses was the first to express clearly an awareness of the poet's mission, provides an illustration of what I have been saying. At the beginning of the *Theogony,* the muses appear to him and say, "We know how to say many false things as though they were true, but we also know, when we so wish, how to reveal the truth."[7] Usually these words are understood to reflect a critical attitude to Homer's treatment of the gods, as if the muses had said to him, "We wish you well. Although we could do so, we shall not tell you falsehoods – as with Homer – but only truth." For several reasons, particularly the remarkable symmetry of the two verses, I think that what Hesiod means is this: Whenever the muses have anything to give, they give both truth and falsehood. It is characteristic of the language of poetry that it speaks both truth and untruth and points to the open realm of interpretation. The truth of poetry is not governed by the distinction between true and false as it was understood by the hostile philosophers who claimed that "poets tell many lies."

Thus an answer to my original question now seems to suggest itself. An element of intention and interpretation has always belonged to the ambiguity of poetry. But when the shared horizon of interpretation has collapsed, when there is no longer a shared language, when the remarkable fusion of classical myth and Christian religion still in force two hundred years ago has finally lost its self-evident status, then this breakdown will inevitably be reflected in the language of art. Consequently, we see the element of interpretative reflection assume an ever greater role in the modern novels of Kafka, Thomas Mann, Musil, and Broch, to name only writers who are no longer with us. The common bond between poet and interpreter is becoming increasingly obvious today. In the last analysis, this stems from the fact that we live in a time which, in spite of tireless efforts to discover the definitive word of interpretation, is marked by the renunciation of certainty expressed in Hölderlin's "Mnemosyne": "We are a sign without interpretation."[8]

3. Image and gesture

There is today a great mistrust of all traditional forms of expression. Religious art and portraiture are now problematic. Even landscape, which depicts nature in its familiarity as the field of human activity, has become problematic as a subject of painting. This is even more true of the language of the humanistic tradition, which speaks to us from a remote and alien culture and its now inaccessible religious world. When a modern painter calls upon this symbolic world, laden with cultural meaning, we have to ask whether he has not thereby obscured a harsh reality that we must and do recognize. For surely it is precisely the dearth of symbol, the very renunciation of the symbolic, that characterizes contemporary art in all its forms. This is certainly not the result of arbitrary fashion or some kind of manipulation. On the contrary, it simply reflects the fact that an art that still has anything to say to us today must respond to the needs of the moment.

A symbol is something that facilitates recognition, and the dearth of symbol is a characteristic feature of the historical moment in which we find ourselves. It reflects the growing unfamiliarity and impersonality of the world about us. Recognition is the essence of all symbolic language, and all art of whatever kind will always be a language of recognition. Even the art of our own time, whose mute gaze presents us with such disturbing enigmas, remains a kind of recognition: in such art we encounter the undecipherability of our surroundings. It offers us a pictorial code that we try to read on account of the meaning it expresses, but it is written in an inexplicable and undecipherable sign language. In painting we encounter these signs as the surface elements of point, line, and color, but the meaning inscribed in these signs appears intangible, ineffable, incommensurable with anything we have ever experienced. Nevertheless, we still say that the construction in question stands in its own right, that a dynamic interplay has been captured, or that a solution to a problem has been found. So there is indeed a meaning in all the forms of modern art we see around us, but it is a meaning that cannot be unlocked. Music, perhaps the most sublime of all the arts, has taught us for centuries that such a thing is possible. Every composition of "absolute music" possesses this structure of undecipherable meaning. Even the "absolute painting" of our own time has not simply abandoned the realm of meaning in which we continue to live.

This makes our question more pressing than ever: can art still convincingly evoke the mythical subjects of the Greek world as it found expression in ancient drama and epic poetry, a world that is familiar and revered and yet incredibly remote? Are these symbols adequate for encoding our undecipherable world? It is obvious to anyone who looks back over the developments of the last two hundred years that we cannot possibly employ the recognized forms and familiar symbols for this purpose. We must admit that since the Baroque era and the elevated form of Christian–humanistic expression associated with it, there is no longer a unified symbolic language capable of commanding our acceptance. And I am not thinking here of the feeble efforts of those who attempted a pictorial statement during the age of neoclassicism. One has only to consider the effect produced by looking at the paintings of a master like Feuerbach or the work of the Nazarenes after experiencing the intense use of color and the drive toward abstraction that characterizes the art of our own century. Consequently, we have to ask ourselves whether or not a contemporary artist can still salvage anything from this mythical–humanistic tradition that could become a symbol of our own sense of unfamiliarity.

It is certainly true that we have a profoundly different view of Greece today than Goethe had when in his *Iphigenia* he contrasted the perfect models of humanity with the barbaric customs of the Thracians. Thanks to the efforts of Jacob Burckhardt and Friedrich Nietzsche, it is generally realized just how different the Greeks really were from those noble human beings whom Classicism offered for our emulation. Today the humanistic tradition is vital to us precisely because we are constantly aware of what lay behind the Apollonian splendor of Greek art. The rediscovery of Hölderlin in this century, or rather his discovery for the first time, was a par-

ticularly significant event, since his own work confirmed the new
and more profound view of Greece in which the dark, brooding,
subterranean presence of the Titans took their place alongside the
higher forms of Olympian clarity and splendor.[1]

It is this transformation of our view of the humanistic tradition
that allows it to share in that sense of unfamiliarity that we encounter all around us. For this tradition presents us with the self-
same enigma of human existence: we know and yet do not know
ourselves in the struggle between nature and spirit, animality and
divinity, a dissension that is yet inseparably united in human life. In
a mysterious way, this struggle pervades all our most particular per-
sonal, psychological, and spiritual activities and combines the
unconscious life of natural being with our conscious and freely
chosen existence to produce a unity that is consonant and dissonant
at one and the same time. This is what allows the Greek religion as
we encounter it in epic poetry and drama to speak to us anew: it represents a first attempt to resolve the enigma of our existence.

We can grasp this in an incomparable way in Homer with his
remarkably adventurous but always intimately human account of the
Trojan War and the homecoming of the heroes, and in Hesiod with
his theogony, which has a strange power all its own. Hesiod tells a
terrifying story of the first generation of the old gods, before Zeus
took his place on Olympus to rule men and gods with wisdom and
law. Homer transforms the distant tale of Troy, the homecoming
and the misfortunes that befall the returning heroes and their des-
cendants, into a permanently available source of mythical poetry and
song. If Homer presents his monumental epic tale of the gods and
the sufferings they cause among men in the distanced forms of
narrative, then Greek drama presents us with a unique transformation of this fabled world into the immediate form of religious cult.
However remote they may appear to be, Greek epic and drama are
still present to us, and they still tell us something about ourselves in
proclaiming the deeds of the gods and the heroes who represent
us all.

We owe to the philologist Walter F. Otto the insight that the
Greek gods actually represent aspects of the world itself.[2] That is
why we can still experience their reality despite the fact that their
original, religious, and cultic significance has disappeared. They
remain real for us because we too can still be dismayed by a sudden
transformation in the appearance of things – one event can change

everything at a stroke. We too are familiar with darkness, perplexity, madness, catastrophe, sickness and death, love and hate, jubilation, arrogance and ambition, the whole vast range of human sufferings and passions that the Greeks experienced as the real presence of their gods. Greek myth speaks about this fundamental experience which we all have of the way in which such things befall us.

One may well ask whether this experience of being overwhelmed is all that is involved here. For are we not really agents? What about conflict, decision, error, and guilt? Are not all these to be found in Greek epic and drama as well? This is certainly true, yet one of the most fruitful insights to be gained from the study of antiquity lies in the quite new perspective it offers us upon the nature of "action" in dramatic and particularly in epic literature. And the really astonishing thing here is that such a perspective is not so alien to us. When we find in Homer descriptions in which the gods themselves inspire the decisions of men juxtaposed with other more subjective, more reflective and self-conscious descriptions in which we see the hero making his own decisions in an agony of doubt, we are no longer tempted to refer them to different stages of epic composition, ascribing the passages to authors of a different date, for example. We now realize from a closer observation of reality, and that means also a closer observation of ourselves, that Homer is quite justified in combining both kinds of account in one and the same passage. When a character makes his decision and Athena also inspires him to it, that does not imply two contradictory claims of which only one can be true, so that either the hero makes the decision or the decision was inspired by Athena. On the contrary, we have one and the same event seen from different perspectives. Philologists like Bruno Snell and Albin Lesky[3] in particular have been able to show in connection with the epic and even the drama of antiquity that our concept of action represents an extremely one-sided self-interpretation on the part of modern man. If we are now in a position to see this more clearly, then we owe it less to the advance of scientific knowledge and more to our own experiences, which have forced us to relinquish some of our illusions concerning the nature of human existence and to confront its enigmas in a more sober and less dogmatic way.

The Greeks understood fate in terms of religion. What befell mankind was interpreted in terms of conflict amongst the gods themselves. Here we are not concerned with guilt and atonement, but with fate and sacrifice. The tragic hero resembles, indeed represents, a sacrificial victim. Is there not a profound wisdom in this idea of sacrifice, a participation, a removal of boundaries between the *I,* the *thou,* and the *we* in a unique collective union in which the finitude of fate is transcended? Although all this is characteristic of the Greek world, we do not encounter the idea as something wholly alien to us, separated from us by fathomless stretches of time. On the contrary, it represents the furthest reach of human life, the ambiguous complexity of our own being, presented to us here in Greek form. If I may employ the language of philosophy for a moment, I can clarify this point by recourse to the Hegelian distinction between substance and subject. What Hegel means by "substance," and what I mean by it in this context, is not the category drawn from the Greek philosophy of nature which has come down to us across centuries of metaphysical thought. It is a word that we have all become accustomed to using in its Hegelian sense whenever we speak, for example, about a really substantial individual, or when we say that someone is clever enough but lacks substance. Here "substance" is understood as something that supports us, although it does not emerge into the light of reflective consciousness. It is something that can never fully be articulated, although it is absolutely necessary for the existence of all clarity, consciousness, expression, and communication. Substance is the "spirit which is capable of uniting us."[4] This line of Rilke suggests that spirit is more than the individual knows or could know about himself. Hegel invoked the idea of substance to grasp the nature of the spirit of a people or the spirit of an age: the all-pervasive reality that supports us all and is not fully present in a conscious way in any one particular individual. If Greek religion saw human decision as the result of divine action rather than simply as the exercise of human choice, then it did justice to this truth: we are always other and much more than we know ourselves to be, and what exceeds our knowledge is precisely our real being.

What is the position of contemporary art with respect to this truth which has lost none of its validity? How does it relate to the form in which it appeared among the Greeks? I shall disregard poetry and its specific possibilities, which allow it to present something through the spoken word that captures our attention by its emphatic presence. The investigation of how past and present interpenetrate in the translation of ancient tragedy into new poetic forms is a subject of its own. The visual arts know nothing of the death of a language and its subsequent resurrection in the linguistic medium of the present. They must remain in the field of the visible, must remain visible themselves in a world that by the instruments of modern labor is becoming increasingly faceless through abstraction, construction, reduction, and conformity. How can the anthropomorphic Greek religion of art return in the context of contemporary art? It certainly cannot produce the recognition of the familiar, least of all the recognition of familiar figures like that of Iphigenia as Feuerbach painted her, "her soul still seeking for the land of Greece."[5] The only thing that is universally familiar to us today is unfamiliarity itself, momentarily illuminated by an ephemeral glimmer of meaning. But how can we express that in human form?

I would suggest that this can be done through the language of gesture. What a gesture expresses is "there" in the gesture itself. A gesture is something wholly corporeal and wholly spiritual at one and the same time. The gesture reveals no inner meaning behind itself. The whole being of the gesture lies in what it says. At the same time every gesture is also opaque in an enigmatic fashion. It is a mystery that holds back as much as it reveals. For what the gesture reveals is the being of meaning rather than the knowledge of meaning. Or, to put it in Hegelian terms, the gesture is substantial rather than subjective. Every gesture is human, but not every gesture is exclusively the gesture of a human being. Indeed, no gesture is merely the expression of an individual person. Like language, the gesture always reflects a world of meaning to which it belongs. And the gestures that the artist is able to bring out in his work, the gestures that allow us to interpret our world, are never simply human gestures alone.

These reflections lead me to Werner Scholz's pictures drawn from Greek mythology. In one of the pictures, for example, he depicts three ships that roughly answer to our most basic idea of a sailing ship and yet also contrive to suggest the Mediterranean vessels of antiquity. In this picture, we can make out a red, a green, and a greyish sail. The ships are sailing along one behind the other. When we look at them, we may well remember the Greek homecoming from Troy, the homecoming so often contemplated even before the defeat of the city or their actual catastrophic homecoming after its destruction. On the other hand, we may not even think of the Greeks at all. In any case, the picture is not a depiction of an event that supposedly took place in mythical or in real historical time. What awaits these ships heading for home – and what is home here? – is the uncertainty of the journey itself and the duplicity of fate. These ships present the very gesture of human destiny.

Now consider Werner Scholz's landscapes. What are these landscapes? The coastline and the sea breaking upon the shore before us, the ruins that claw the sky as if to bewail the transience of things, even the flowers, the fishes, the owls, and the butterflies – all these things are gestures.[6] Of course, they represent a special kind of gesture. They speak the silent language of heraldry, a language of symbol that allows us to recognize things that belong together with no need of words. And then finally there are the human gestures as well. These are not simply the gestures of individual human beings in a pictorially represented world. They are themselves pictorial gestures. Nor am I simply thinking of the gesturing human figures whose form can just be recognized here and there. The background against which they stand out and with which they are interwoven is itself no less a gesture in accordance with the principles of surface and color. In one case we are offered an image of Antigone immured, slowly starving to death because she placed the laws of the nether world above those of the state. This Antigone is not a representation of the legendary figure of Greek literature depicted in emphatic relief. She is a gesture representing self-chosen death and nothing else. The cavernous walls about her sink too in a single gesture that fuses man and world in one. Or consider the figure of Penthiselea: the gesture of the rider in full flight, at once hunter and hunted, before the arrow strikes her and she falls. This primordial gesture of the hunt until the arrow strikes us hardly calls for explicit interpretation. Consider too the gesture of Orestes on the left of the tryptich: his head is bowed before imminent catastrophe. We need no special knowledge to understand that what we see is a sacrificial victim who holds his head ready for the final blow from a fate mightier than himself. Other images are even easier to recognize: the abandoned Ariadne, for example, standing upon the shore of Naxos, gazing into the blue distance in a gesture of sacrificial love. In Iphigenia, we see yet another sacrificial victim. The picture represents a massive gesture of submission to her sacrifice. This victim knows what self-sacrifice means and embodies it.

All these images present us with nothing but gestures, gestures that bear their meaning within themselves and far exceed any humanistic knowledge that we may possess. Even when they present human features, these symbolic gestures remain embedded in the textural surface of the painting itself: the myriad colors of the shimmering world play temptingly about Calypso as she offers herself to Odysseus, who appears in the moment of turning away as a universal representative for us all, as absent in spirit as some departed shade. It is characteristic of Scholz's work that the more he depicts human features, the countenance that expresses the inner life of human subjectivity, the more fragmented and even illegible his visual language becomes. With difficulty we can make out the individual gesture, the outline of a nose, the upturned gaze like that of Alcestis approaching the upper world. There is almost nothing psychological involved here and little interpretation of subjective interiority. Almost everything is merely the interiority of the mask that masks nothing, the interiority of rapt attention wholly absorbed in the enigma of our existence.

No one will claim that these images are conceived in a Greek way. On the contrary, I would claim that we cannot help seeing them in our own way and with our own eyes. By that I mean that we can only see them as people who have already experienced the whole history of Christian interiority. And yet it is precisely this that allows us to perceive the presence of Greece here. These paintings by a contemporary artist present anew the ancient enigma of man and the Greek response to it. Perhaps there is one picture in particular that shows in concentrated form something that is true of all of them. It is entitled "Iphigenia," and is painted predominantly in blue. Here we see no yearning figure pining for home, no grieving victim, forced to renounce both life and homeland. Nor do we find here the mythical story that recounts how she was torn from her home and carried off into strange lands. It shows a rapt Iphigenia facing the final boundary between this life and the invisible realm beyond. The picture presents the state of transport itself. Although the picture as a whole seems written in almost undecipherable characters, we can still divine in it a meaning that speaks to us directly.

The painting does not recount a story, nor interpret anew one with which we are already familiar. A certain heraldic quality informs the whole work. The images before us present human life in the language of heraldic emblems and devices. In them we can recognize ourselves, even though we are unable to understand or decipher them fully. They are symbols of the unfamiliarity in which we encounter ourselves and our increasingly unfamiliar world. Just as the language of Homer and the tragic poets lives again in the reflected light of translation, so the ancient legends can still live again in the art of today, concentrated in the simplicity of mighty gestures.

4. The speechless image

If one thing is certain in contemporary art, then it is the fact that the relation between nature and art has become problematic. Art no longer fulfills our naive pictorial expectations and we can no longer say what the content of a picture is. We all recognize the embarrassment of the artist who finally takes refuge in numbers, the most abstract signs of all, when he is expected to supply a verbal title for his work. The ancient classical relation between nature and art, that of mimesis, no longer holds.

Let us recall how Plato formulated the task of philosophy – "to see things together in respect of the one" or to elicit the universal *eidos* from the manifold appearances of things.[1] In this sense I would like to propose such an *eidos* or perspective from which we can describe and interpret contemporary art. I want to talk about the speechless language of the pictorial image. When we say that someone is "speechless" we do not mean that they have nothing to say. On the contrary, such speechlessness is really a kind of speech. In German the word *Stumm* (mute) is connected with the word *stammeln* (to stutter or stammer). Surely the distress of the stutterer does not lie in the fact that he has nothing to say. Rather, he wants to say too much at once and is unable to find the words to express the pressing wealth of things he has on his mind. Similarly, when we say that someone is struck dumb or speechless *(verstummt)*, we do not simply mean that he has ceased to speak. When we are at a loss for words in this way, what we want to say is actually brought especially close to us as something for which we have to seek new words. If we consider the rich, colorful, and resplendent eloquence that speaks to us so clearly and fluently from the classical periods of painting represented in our museums, and compare it with the creative art of our own time, we certainly have the impression of speechlessness. We must ask how we can account for this speechlessness which addresses us so forcibly with its unique mute eloquence.[2]

As far as European painting is concerned, this speechlessness began with the still-life and the landscape, which were originally hardly separate from one another. Previously there were many sacred or regal subjects thought worthy of pictorial representation, along with figures and stories familiar to everyone. The fact that the Greek word for picture *(zoon)* originally meant a living being shows how little mere things and nature without man were thought worthy of pictorial representation at all. Yet when we visit a traditional art gallery today, it is precisely the still-life paintings that strike us as particularly modern. When we encounter such subjects in a painting, they clearly do not require the same degree of interpretation as do the depictions of gods and men and their activities. It is not that these subjects were not also intelligible forms of self-presentation which were once immediately understood as such. Yet if a contemporary artist tried to use these forms of expression, his work would quickly strike us as too declamatory. And there is nothing our present age likes less than declamation. But what do we mean by declamation? The German word for such demonstrative pronouncements is *Aufsagen* and it is instructive here. Such demonstrative "saying" is not really a form of saying at all since, far from seeking just the right word for what is meant, it merely starts from the practiced and familiar word, from words selected at another time by someone else or even by ourselves when we actually meant something by them. If the creative artist of today were simply to employ classical pictorial subjects, that would be such a saying, a mere repetition of a previously forged language. But the still-life, typical of the period of early Dutch bourgeois society, is quite another matter. Here it seems as if the sensible world around us finds expression in a language that needs no words.

Of course, the still-life can only be regarded as a particular genre in its own right when it succeeds in supplanting the narrative painting. Whenever we merely encounter familiar motifs from still-life pictures in the context of purely decorative art, that is not a case of the true still-life, that is, of the speechless image. As a rule, therefore, the still-life is a moveable picture that can be hung in different places at will – although there is far more to it than this. Wherever it is placed, the picture invites us to assemble before it as if it had much to say to us.

And in fact, so it does. It is not an arbitrary selection from the physical world around us. On the contrary, there is an iconography of the still-life. In contrast to all other kinds of pictorial subjects, the very arrangement itself belongs to the essence of the still-life. Naturally, I do not mean to suggest that in all other cases the painter simply represents reality as he finds it. This is no more true of the landscape or portrait than it is of the religious or historical painting, for composition is always the contribution of the artist. But the still-life enjoys a unique freedom in the arrangement of its subject-matter precisely because the "objects" of composition in this case are things we can move around: fruit, flowers, everyday objects, sometimes even the spoils of the hunt – anything, in fact, that we choose to display. Compositional freedom thus begins with the subject-matter itself, and to that extent the still-life anticipates the compositional freedom of modern art, in which we find no trace of mimesis at all, and in which total speechlessness rules supreme.

The speechless silence of contemporary painting is a long way from the time when the still-life of nature and physical things first became a worthy subject of art. The Dutch still-life paintings which still make such an impression on us do not simply testify to the dis-covery of the physical beauty of the things about us. They imply a whole background that legitimates certain objects as worthy of pic-torial representation. It has been known for a long time and demonstrated through particular examples[3] that many symbols of vanity are to be found in Dutch still-life paintings. The mouse, the moth, the fly, and the burning candle are all symbols of the evanes-cence of earthly things. It may well be that in all their puritan seriousness, the people of that time always understood the language of these symbols when they enjoyed and admired the splendor of such earthly things. So that we should understand these pictures aright, they would even contain a skull or carry some edifying verse inscription expressing the vanity of all earthly things. In the Alte Pinakothek in Munich there is a painting by de Heem that bears the following inscription: "But one looks no more at the most beau-tiful flower."[4]

More important, however, and this is what first constitutes the picture as a speechless *language,* is the fact that even without all these symbols or any explicit understanding of them, the very subject of representation in all its sensuous richness expresses its own tran-sience. In my opinion it is the significant self-presentation residing in the very appearance of things as such that belongs to the true iconography of the still-life over and above the elements capable of explicit symbolic interpretation. Again and again in this iconography we encounter the motif of the half-peeled lemon, the peel dangling down to one side. No doubt many different things account for this common pictorial motif: the relative rarity of the fruit, the dialectic between the inedible peel and the aromatic fruit within (analogous to the effect of opened nut shells), the bitter acidic taste that attracts and repels at the same time. It is just these constantly repeated motifs that capture mortality, evanescence, and transience within the painting.

It is still an open question whether the genre of still-life is not Italian rather than Dutch in origin. If this is indeed the case, we can immediately perceive a relationship with the mosaics and decorative painting of antiquity, the remains of which were once more readily to be seen on the walls of decaying ancient buildings than they are today. For us, the newly excavated remains at Pompeii are the most well-known source of evidence.[5] There are two features in particular that serve to emphasize this iconographic relationship. In the first place, the decorative paintings of antiquity known to us that resemble the still-life genre tend in the direction of trompe l'oeil effect. They are depicted on the wall in such a way as to resemble views from small windows. There is nothing like this to be found in the still-life proper, since the very artificiality of its arrangemnt excludes such illusionistic effects. In the second place, whenever in these ancient paintings we come across, in addition to fruit and flowers, animals like snails and snakes, crabs and birds – precisely the things that may have exercised such an influence on the painters of early modern times – then there is always something purely decorative, festive, almost heraldic about these arrangements. But the lizard at the bottom of the flower arrangement painted by Jacobo da Udine for example, and many of the moths and flies, lizards and mice to be found in Dutch still-life paintings have a quite different function: the fleeting, fluttering, scurrying quality of these things lends to the still-life around which they play something of their own arrested and fleeting vitality.

We might add that the fruit characteristically depicted in Italian still-life painting is not the lemon but the pomegranate. Its symbolic meaning suggests a similar interplay of inviting richness and revulsion. It is true that in the succeeding period, the religious background of the still-life gradually recedes and gives way to the rich, decorative, and tempting depiction of attractively arranged fruit. But finally, at the end of a long and unusually persistent typological road (the lemon peel remained all but obligatory until the late nineteenth century), the still-life acquired new life in the revolutionary developments that established modern painting, albeit in a rather enigmatic fashion. We only have to think of Cézanne's still-life paintings where we no longer encounter tangible objects arranged in a space that we can actually reach into. Rather, it is as if the things are embedded in the very surface of the canvas that supplies their space.

Things, the unity of an individual thing, or the unity of arrangement, no longer provide a subject worthy of pictorial representation. Van Gogh's sunflowers are integrated into the surface articulation of the painting, just as in any modern portrait, and the objective significance of the things depicted hardly adds anything to the picture. Surely it is significant that, as with the half-peeled lemon of the Dutch still-life, we can similarly recognize in the modern still-life a favorite pictorial "subject" – for want of a better name for something that is no longer the subject, but is present nevertheless. I am thinking of the image of the guitar, which in the hands of Picasso, Braque, Juan Gris, and others, became a sort of privileged victim in the dislocation of form that we call Cubism. I do not wish to investigate the various theories that painters themselves have proposed or have been persuaded to accept in order to justify their new procedures. Is it not likely that the preference for this object in particular, with its distinctive form and vibrating contours, is connected with the fact that it is after all a musical instrument? As an object not created for contemplation, the instrument itself, suffused by waves of sound that arise from it to weave garlands of dancing notes on the picture's surface, seems to invoke, as the very ideal of the new painting, "absolute music," that art which has for centuries dared to abandon all linguistic content and renounce all extramusical reference. It may well be that other factors, like the rapid pace of modern life for example, have also suggested the disintegration of the regular forms of things. Malevich's early picture of the "Lady in the Big City" actually depicts the changes in our life-world that have caused the solid and permanent things of earlier times to disappear. In any case, it was truly a momentous event when at the beginning of the century the unity of our pictorial expectations began to dissolve and splinter into the inconceivable variety of possible forms. Only the relation of form and color, without reference to specific objects, remains as a kind of visual music which addresses us in the speechless language of modern art.

In this situation we must ask what it is that constitutes the compositional unity of modern pictures. It is certainly not the unity of a significant pictorial subject, nor the mute unity of corporeal things that we encounter here. Both these things seem to have lost their power. What then does constitute the unity of these pictures? It is not simply the unity of the object that is missing in modern pictures, so that what formerly made the picture into a mimetic image (whether it was myth, narrative, or simply recognizable objects) – the unity of what is represented – has disappeared. Nor is it the unity of a single view as it was understood in the age of linear perspective, when the picture gave a view onto an enclosed space. Even after the collapse of the long established iconographical tradition, a collapse that has affected all painting since the breakdown of tradition in the nineteenth century, the unifying focus of linear perspective continued to hold together the arbitrary selection of reality presented to our view. The picture frame belongs specifically to this kind of painting insofar as it holds together and encloses, thus inviting us to enter into the depth of what it has enclosed. It is one of the most remarkable features of historical existence that the new only gradually and with great effort succeeds in breaking through the ossified forms of the old. Even the inner surface power of Cézanne's paintings could not fully eliminate the obsolete gilt frame of the Baroque era. Now it is clear that a contemporary picture is not held together by its frame, if it still has one at all. On the contrary, the picture holds the frame together. What is the unity and force that allows it to do so?

This unity is no longer a unity of expression, either. It is true that expression did provide a new principle of unity that dominated artistic creation in the modern era once the imitation and repetition of established pre-given pictorial subjects became a matter of empty rhetoric. The unity of inner expression – the expression of the artist rather than what he represents – and the expressive power of his brush, this most sensuous of all forms of visual language, could appear the most appropriate form of self-representation to an age of inwardness, because in this way our initial response to the enigma of life found immediate realization as an image. Today, in the midst of the technological culture of our industrial age, this unity of subjective experience and spontaneous self-expression no longer provides an illuminating principle of unity for the creative arts.

It is indeed the case that the very concept of the picture that was characteristic of the traditional museum has now become too restrictive. The creative artist has eliminated the frame, and the articulation of surface constitutive of the picture points beyond itself into other contexts. It used to be said as a criticism of a picture that it was too decorative, but this is slowly losing its pejorative meaning. Just as in former times, when the layout of monuments, churches, squares, halls, and domestic interiors defined the pictorial demands that the artist had to fulfill, so today we are beginning once again to recognize such given pictorial demands. A look at contemporary art from this point of view confirms that commissioned art has been reestablished in all its ancient dignity. This is not only a matter of economics. In the first place, commissioned art does not mean that the creative artist must reluctantly bow to the whim of the one who has commissioned his work (even if this is unfortunately often the case). The real nature and true dignity of such art lies in the fact that it fulfills a task that is defined in advance and is not a matter of merely individual caprice. Thus there is no doubt that modern architecture enjoys a leading position among the arts today because it sets tasks in this way and draws the other visual and plastic arts into relationship with itself through its organization of space and proportion. Contemporary art can no longer reject the claim that the work should not refer solely to itself when it invites us to dwell upon it, but should simultaneously refer to a life-context to which it belongs and which it helps to shape.

So we ask once again: what constitutes the unity of the picture today? What can the picture tell us of the context of our lives? We are surrounded on every side by momentous transformations in our life-world. The rule of number is visible everywhere and manifests itself above all in the form of the series, aggregate, addition and sequence. These forms characterize the cellular and segmented structure of large modern buildings as well as the precision of modern work methods and the regulated functioning of transport and administration. It is the exchangeability of parts which typifies the sum and the series. The fact that an individual part can be exchanged and replaced is an essential component of the kind of life which we lead. "Let us now praise machine parts."[6] We live in a world of planning, design, assembly, technical completion, delivery, and sale, a world that is pervaded by advertising techniques that strive to render the finished product obsolete once it has become an article of consumption and to supplant it with something new. What can the uniqueness of the image mean in such a world where everything is replaceable?

Or is it perhaps the case that the unity of the picture acquires a new importance precisely in this world? We are no longer surrounded by constant and familiar things with a unity of their own. In view of the increasing facelessness that seems appropriate to human beings in our industrial world, the form and color of the picture fuse into a unity in tension that appears to be organized from within. But by virtue of what power does it do this? What gives the picture its stability?

The experimental element that has entered into the process of artistic creation is certainly something qualitatively different from the never-ending experimentation that once made a master out of an ordinary painter. The rational construction that dominates our lives also attempts to create a place for itself within the constructive labor of the artist. This is why his creative activity has something of the experiment about it: it resembles the series of experiments through which we acquire new data by means of an artificially posed question and look for an answer there. This aggregative and serial element thus penetrates contemporary artistic production – and not simply in the titles of works either. Yet here something that can be planned, constructed, and indefinitely repeated suddenly acquires the hallowed status of a unique achievement. The creative artist may often be quite uncertain which of his experiments really "counts." He may even sometimes wonder when the work is quite finished. There is always something arbitrary about calling a halt to the process of creation, particularly if it is final. Nevertheless, there does seem to be a criterion against which the finished work is measured: further work becomes impossible when the structure in question starts to lose in density instead of gain. The creation now stands independently set free in its own right, quite irrespective of the will (even the self-interpretation) of its creator.[7]

Ultimately then, the ancient relationship between nature and art that has dominated artistic creation for centuries through the idea of mimesis fulfills itself with new meaning. Certainly art no longer looks to nature in order to produce it anew. Nature no longer provides the exemplary model for art to follow. And yet even though it follows its own path, the work of art does come to resemble nature: there is something regular and binding about the self-contained picture that grows out from within. We might think of the crystal here. The pure regularity of its geometrical structure is entirely natural, and yet surrounded by a wealth of shapeless chaos, we encounter it as something rare, adamantine, brilliant. In this sense, the modern picture has something of nature about it, for it has no inwardness to express. It requires no empathy with the psychological state of the artist. Like the crystal, it has its own timeless necessity: folds of being itself, eroded lines, runes in which time come to a standstill. Abstract? Concrete? Objective? Nonobjective? It is a pledge of order. The modern artist finds himself in difficulty if he tries to answer the question what his work actually represents. But the self-interpretation of art is always a secondary phenomenon. We should follow Paul Klee here, who is in a position to know, when he rejects all "theory in itself" and emphasizes the works themselves, "and indeed those already produced and not those that will come shortly."[8] The modern artist is less a creator than a discoverer of the as yet unseen, the inventor of the previously unimagined that only emerges into reality through him. Yet, remarkably, the measure to which he must respond seems to be the same one to which the artist has always responded. Aristotle says – and when do we encounter a truth that is not already to be found in Aristotle? – that a proper work is one where there is neither too little nor too much, nothing in excess and nothing missing.[9] A simple but difficult measure.

5. Art and imitation

What is the significance of modern nonobjective art? Are the old aesthetic concepts with which we used to try and understand the nature of art still valid today? Many outstanding representatives of modern art emphatically reject the pictorial expectations with which we approach it. Such art generally tends to produce an explicit shock effect upon us. How can we explain the new stance taken by the painter who repudiates all our previous traditions and expectations? How are we to respond to the challenge of this new art?

There are many skeptics who believe abstract painting to be nothing more than a fashion and who like to regard the art business as ultimately responsible for its success. But we have only to take a look at the other related arts to realize that the root of the matter lies much deeper than this. For we are faced with a genuine revolution in modern art that began shortly before the First World War. We see the simultaneous emergence of so-called atonal music – an idea that sounds as paradoxical as that of nonobjective painting. At the same time we also see – in Proust and Joyce, for example – the disappearance of the naive, omniscient narrator who observes events hidden to others and lends them epic expression. In lyric poetry we hear a new voice that interrupts and inhibits the familiar flow of melodic language and eventually turns to experimentation with quite new formal principles. Finally, something rather similar makes itself felt in drama as well – less so here than elsewhere perhaps, but undeniably perceptible all the same – with the repudiation of realistic staging and its naturalistic psychology and the deliberate rejection of theatrical illusion in Brecht's new epic theater.

Of course, I do not think that a consideration of the other related arts is sufficient to explain the revolutionary process that has taken place in modern painting. This process still retains an aspect of arbitrariness and an obsessive love of experimentation, although it is quite different from the kind of experimental method that first arose in the natural sciences. For there, an experiment represents a question that we deliberately put to nature so that she reveals her secrets to us. As far as painting is concerned, there is no question of conducting experiments in order to obtain the desired results. Here, experimentation finds adequate fulfillment in itself, as it were, since the experiment itself is the sole outcome. How can we come to terms intellectually with an art like this, which rejects any chance of understanding it in the traditional way?

First, we should not take the self-interpretation of the artist too seriously. We are not speaking against artists when we say this, but rather for them, since the claim implies that they must create in their own artistic medium. If an artist could express what he has to say in words, he would not wish to create and would not need to give form to his ideas. At the same time, it is inevitable that language, the universal communicative element that supports and holds together our human community, constantly awakens in the artist a need to communicate and express himself in words, to interpret what he is doing, and to explain himself to others. And, as we might expect, the artist thereby comes to depend upon those who specialize in interpretation, such as aestheticians, philosophers, and all kinds of writers on art. If, like Arnold Gehlen, we take a work like Kahnweiler's important masterly book on Juan Gris to represent the relationship between philosophy and art (and Kahnweiler is an excellent contemporary example), then we fail to see that here too the owl of Minerva only begins its flight with the falling of dusk.[1] Kahnweiler's subtle investigations represent the inspiration of the interpreter rather than that of the creator. And as far as general literature about art and the constant self-interpretation of great contemporary artists in particular is concerned, then the situation here seems to me to be much the same. Instead of starting from these attempts at self-interpretation and other contemporary interpretations of art which are unaware of their dependence on dominant doctrines of the moment, I would like to turn as a matter of principle to the tradition of aesthetic thought accomplished by philosophy. We shall see how this tradition fares with respect to the new art and what it has to tell us about it.

I would like to develop these considerations in two parts. I shall begin first by identifying those dominant aesthetic concepts that are universally regarded as self-evident, although their origin and validity are not really considered. I shall secondly address certain philosophers whose aesthetic theories seem most suitable for revealing the secret of modern painting.

The first of the three concepts that will help me to approach the problem of modern painting is that of *imitation*. As we shall see, this concept can be understood in a sufficiently broad sense that, in the last analysis, it still possesses a certain truth. Imitation is a concept that originated in antiquity, but it attained its aesthetic and cultural peak in the French classicism of the seventeenth and eighteenth centuries before then exercising an influence on German classicism. This movement focused on the doctrine of art as the imitation of nature. Obviously, this fundamental doctrine of the classical tradition is connected with other normative claims, like the idea that we may legitimately expect art to represent "the probable."[2] The claim that art should never violate the laws of probability, the conviction that in a perfect work of art the very forms of nature should appear before us in all their purity, and the belief in the idealizing capacity of art to perfect nature – all these familiar ideas are implied in the phrase "imitation of nature." We are excluding here the trivial theory associated with extreme naturalism, according to which the meaning of art lies in straightforward faithfulness to nature. This idea has nothing to do with the traditional concept of imitation.

Nevertheless, the concept of imitation still seems inadequate for the modern age. If we look back at the historical development of aesthetic thought, we notice that the concept of imitation was successfully challenged and eventually defeated in the eighteenth century by a quite new concept, that of *expression*. It is no accident that this development can be traced particularly well in the realm of musical aesthetics. For music is obviously the art in which the concept of imitation proves least illuminating and its application most limited. So it was that the concept of expression grew out of the musical aesthetics of the eighteenth century, until it came finally to dominate aesthetic judgment as a matter of course during the nineteenth and twentieth centuries.[3] Thus it has become generally accepted that sincerity and intensity of expression secure the communicative content of a picture, even if we are then unable to answer the decisive question about the nature of kitsch. For kitsch certainly represents an intense form of expression, and its total lack of genuine artistic value does not disprove the subjective feeling and genuine sincerity on the part of either the consumer or producer. In view of the wholesale destruction of form in modern art, which no longer sanctions either the idealization of nature or the expressive display of inner feeling as possible subject-matter for art, it would appear that both imitation and expression prove to be inadequate.

A third concept therefore suggests itself: the concept of *sign* and *sign language*. This concept also has a respectable history. We recall that art in the early period of Christianity found its justification in the *Biblia Pauperum*, which represented for all those who could neither read nor write the celebration of sacred history and the good news of salvation. The familiar stories were read in turn from the pictures before them. Modern pictures seem to require a similar process of reading, although they present us with signs like those on the written page rather than with images as such. And yet for all the abstraction that they imply, these written signs are not the same as letters. Nevertheless, there is a sort of correspondence here. The truly momentous invention of alphabetic script enabled us to capture all human experience by means of the combination of abstract individual signs in an orthographic system. This must surely be one of the most revolutionary moments in the history of human culture. And in part it has already affected the way in which we perceive images. Thus we actually "read" every painting from the top left to bottom right. It is also a well-known fact that the reversal of left and right in the mirror-image (something easily done with modern methods of technical reproduction) results in the most peculiar distortion of compositional arrangement, as Heinrich Wölfflin demonstrated.[4] The influence of the ways we read and write seems to be even greater when we attempt to read the pictorial language of modern painting: we no longer see these paintings as copies of reality that present a unified view with an instantly recognizable meaning. Such pictures merely register or juxtapose in pictorial signs and characters a sequence of events that must be perceived consecutively before they are finally integrated with one another. I am thinking here of pictures like Malevich's "Lady in the City of London," which illustrates very well the principle of the distortion of form in one of its psychological versions. The picture registers and shapes into a pictorial whole the torrent of separate impressions of the woman, who is clearly disturbed by the really rather modest volume of traffic, given that it was 1907. The viewer who looks on is expected to synthesize the various different aspects and facets. We are acquainted with this general formal principle from the multi-faceted style of artists like Picasso or Juan Gris. There is recognition here, but this recognition is always drawn back instantly into the unity of the picture itself, which no longer appears as a perceptible totality with an expressible pictorial meaning. This kind of pictorial language, determining the compositional element of the whole like a kind of shorthand, implies a certain refusal of meaning. The concept of the sign thus loses its proper significance and the modern language of painting increasingly tends to reject the demand for legibility in art.[5]

Although there may well be a valid element of truth in the three aesthetic categories we have just described, they nonetheless fail to provide an adequate response to what is really new in the art of our century.

Consequently, we must look further back. Whenever we look back into the deep historical roots of the present, we deepen our awareness of the conceptual horizons already at work in our thought. To assist us in the interpretation of modern art, I shall draw upon three representatives of philosophical thought: Kant, Aristotle, and finally, Pythagoras.

If I begin with Kant first of all, it is not primarily because Kahnweiler and all the aestheticians and writers on art associated with the modern revolution in painting refer back to Kant in some way or other under the influence of the neo-Kantian thought of the recent past. Rather, it is because in philosophy as well the attempt is still being made to exploit Kant's aesthetic thought for a theory of nonobjective painting.[6] The starting point in Kant's aesthetics is the claim that taste, in judging something to be beautiful, not only represents a disinterested delight but also a nonconceptual one. That means that when we find a specific representation of an object beautiful, we are not passing judgment on an ideal of the object. Consequently, Kant asks what it is that allows us to describe the representation of an object as beautiful. His answer is that the representation animates the mind in a free play of imagination and understanding.[7] Kant claims that this free play of cognitive faculties, this animation of our feeling for life occasioned by the sight of the beautiful, implies no conceptual grasp of an objective content and intends no ideal of an object. Kant correctly saw this idea preeminently exemplified in the case of ornament.[8] Can we find a clearer example to show that we do not intend the conceptual content of a representation (even where it is possible to recognize such a content)? One has only to think of those unfortunate children whose bedrooms were decorated with wallpaper showing an endless repetition of the same particular object, an object that would then accompany their feverish dreams. There is no doubt that any good example of ornament expressly forbids this sort of thing. Things that are designed to decorate our surroundings and accompany our moods should not draw attention to themselves.

In fact it is quite wrong to try to read an aesthetic of ornament into Kant's *Critique of Judgment,* for that is certainly not the point of Kant's theory of art at all. In the first place, it is primarily natural beauty that Kant has in mind when he asks what it really means to find something beautiful. For him, the beautiful in art is not a pure example of the aesthetic problem, since art is produced in order to please. It is also true that a work of art always presents itself in an intellectual manner. By this I mean that the work always contains a potentially conceptual element. Of course, fine art is not supposed to represent concepts or ideals directly, as they are understood in the ethical sphere. Rather, art is legitimated for Kant because it is the product of genius. It arises from an unconscious ability, directly inspired by nature, to create exemplary things of beauty without the conscious application of rules, so that even the artist cannot say exactly how he has accomplished his work. It is the concept of genius, therefore, and not the "free beauty" of ornament, that actually forms the basis of Kant's theory of art.

Yet it is precisely the concept of genius that has become so suspect in our own time. No one today, least of all those most closely involved with modern art, would be prepared to credit the genius with such clairvoyant, somnambulant sureness of touch in all he does. Today we appreciate the degree of inner clarity, sober reflection, and even intellectual effort with which the painter experiments on canvas with his materials – something that surely must always have been the case. We shall have to be careful, therefore, if we wish to apply Kant's philosophy to modern art in any direct fashion.

In spite of all the classicist and anticlassicist prejudices in this field, I would like to call upon Aristotle as the principal representative of the classical theory of imitation to assist us in our attempt to understand modern art. For when it is correctly understood, Aristotle's fundamental concept of mimesis has an elementary validity.

To see this, we must first realize that Aristotle did not even develop a real theory of art in the broadest sense, least of all a theory of the plastic and visual arts – despite the fact that his ideas were formed in the fourth century, the great age of Greek painting. In fact, we only find his theory of art in the context of his theory of tragedy and the famous doctrine of catharsis, which states that the passions are purged by pity and fear, and which according to Aristotle provides the secret of tragic mimesis. It is with reference to tragedy, therefore, that Aristotle employs the concept of imitation or mimesis, a key concept already familiar to us from Plato's critique of the poets. In Aristotle, however, it assumes a fundamental and positive significance.

Clearly, the concept of imitation is supposed to apply to the essence of all poetic art, but in passing, Aristotle also considers in an analogous manner the other arts, especially painting. What does he mean, then, when he claims that art is mimesis or imitation? To support this claim, he initially draws attention to the natural human tendency toward imitation and the natural pleasure we all take in such imitation. It is in this context that he claims that the joy we take in imitation is really the joy of recognition. In more recent times, this claim has aroused considerable opposition and criticism, but Aristotle intends it in a purely descriptive sense and is clearly thinking of our everyday life. He points out that children enjoy doing this sort of thing.[9] We can understand what this joy in recognition means when we consider the joy that people in general, and children in particular, take in dressing up. Nothing annoys children more than someone failing to take their disguise seriously. In an imitation, therefore, we are not supposed to recognize the child who has dressed up as someone, but rather the one whom the child represents. This is the motivation behind all the mimetic forms of behavior and representation. Recognition confirms and bears witness to the fact that mimetic behavior makes something present. However, this does not imply that when we recognize what is represented, we should try to determine the degree of similarity between the original and its mimetic representation.

Of course, this is how Plato presents the situation in his critique of art. He condemns art because it stands at more than one remove from the truth. Art merely imitates things, which are themselves only contingent imitations of their eternal forms, essences, or ideas.

A gulf therefore separates everything that truly is from art as an imitation of an imitation at three removes from the truth.[10]

I believe that this Platonic doctrine is intended in a dialectical and extremely ironic sense, and that Aristotle deliberately intends to correct it by inverting Plato's dialectical thought. For there is no doubt that the essence of imitation consists precisely in the recognition of the represented in the representation. A representation intends to be so true and convincing that we do not advert to the fact that what is so represented is not "real." Recognition as cognition of the true occurs through an act of identification in which we do not differentiate between the representation and the represented. For what is recognition? It does not mean simply seeing something that we have already seen before. I cannot say that I recognize something if I see it once again without realizing that I have already seen it. Recognizing something means rather that I now cognize something *as* something that I have already seen. The enigma here lies entirely in the "as." I am not thinking of the miracle of memory, but of the miracle of knowledge that it implies. When I recognize someone or something, what I see is freed from the contingency of this or that moment of time. It is part of the process of recognition that we see things in terms of what is permanent and essential in them, unencumbered by the contingent circumstances in which they were seen before and are seen again. This is what constitutes recognition and contributes to the joy we take in imitation. For what imitation reveals is precisely the real essence of the thing. This is a far cry from the naturalistic theory of art and any kind of classicism. The imitation of nature does not imply, therefore, that it must inevitably fall short of nature simply by virtue of being an imitation. There is no doubt that we can best understand what Aristotle wants to say if we think about what we mean by miming. But where in the realm of art do we encounter mimicry? Where does it actually become art? Primarily in the theater, of course, although not exclusively there. We recognize the figures and effigies in any public carnival, for example, and take pleasure in doing so. Religious processions in which holy images and symbols are born aloft for all to see express clearly the same mimetic dimension. Whether the context is secular or sacred, the mimetic makes its presence felt in the very process of representation.

However, there is more to recognition than this. It does not simply reveal the universal, the permanent form, stripped of all our contingent encounters with it. For it is also part of the process that we recognize ourselves as well. All recognition represents the experience of growing familiarity, and all our experiences of the world are ultimately ways in which we develop familiarity with that world. As the Aristotelian doctrine rightly seems to suggest, all art of whatever kind is a form of recognition that serves to deepen our knowledge of ourselves and thus our familiarity with the world as well.

But then it is a disturbing question whether modern painting can possibly contribute to the task of such self-recognition. Recognition, as understood by Aristotle, presupposes the continuing existence of a binding tradition that is intelligible to all and in which we can encounter ourselves. Myth played this role in Greek thought, providing the common subject-matter for artistic representation. And it was the recognition of myth in pity and fear that deepened our familiarity both with the world and with ourselves. This recognition of who we are, which takes place through the terrifying stories presented in Greek theaters, was made possible and supported by the whole world of Greek religious tradition, its pantheon and the mythical tales that linked the Greek present with the mythical – heroic past. What is that to us? We cannot hide the fact that over 150 years ago, Christian art also lost its power to speak as myth. It was not the revolution of modern painting but the close of the Baroque, the last great European style, that really signaled an end – the end of the whole tradition of pictorial imagery within Western art, along with its humanistic heritage and its Christian message. Of course, it is true that the modern viewer also recognizes the subject-matter of such art insofar as he or she is still aware of that heritage. Even in most modern pictures, we can still recognize something we understand – if only fragmentary gestures rather than stories once rich in meaning. To that extent, the ancient concept of mimesis still seems to possess some truth. Even in those modern pictures built up out of meaningful elements that dissolve into something unrecognizable, we can still sense a last trace of familiarity and experience a fragmentary act of recognition.

But is that sufficient? Can we not on reflection see that we are quite unable to understand such a picture as long as we look at it as a purely objective pictorial representation of something? What is the language of modern painting? Surely a language in which gestures suddenly acquire momentary significance only to sink back again into obscurity is an unintelligible language. In the language of such pictures we seem to encounter the rejection of meaning rather than its expression. The concepts of imitation and recognition fail us and we find ourselves at a loss.

But perhaps it is possible to understand mimesis and the kind of knowledge that it brings in a more universal sense. In this attempt to find a key to modern art through a deeper understanding of the concept of imitation, I now wish to go even further back, before Aristotle, to Pythagoras. Not of course back to Pythagoras as a historical figure in order to reconstruct or discover his original doctrines, for we could hardly find a more controversial area of philosophic research. I simply wish to make a couple of quite uncontroversial points that will lead us in the right direction.

First, Aristotle tells us that Plato, in his doctrine that things participate in the ideas, merely introduced a different word for something that Pythagoras had already taught: namely the idea that things are really imitations or *mimesis.*[11] The context tells us what imitation means here. This talk of imitation obviously derives from the fact that the universe itself, the vault of the heavens, and the tonal harmonies that we hear, can all be represented in a miraculous way by numerical ratios, especially those between even numbers. On a musical instrument, the various lengths of string are all related in specific ways, and even the least musical person can appreciate how this very precision seems to possess almost magical power. It really seems as if the pure relationships among the intervals arranged themselves of their own accord, as if in tuning the instruments the tones were striving to attain the full and perfect reality produced when the pure interval is sounded. Aristotle, in contrast to Plato, taught that it is fulfillment, rather than striving, which constitutes mimesis. Mimesis reveals the miracle of order that we call the *kosmos.* This idea of mimesis, of imitation and recognition in imitation, seems broad enough to help us understand the phenomenon of modern art more effectively.

What is it that is imitated, according to Pythagorean teaching? The numbers and the ratios between them. But what are numbers? And what are these ratios? Clearly the essence of *number* is not something that we can perceive, but a relation that we can only conceive in our minds. The establishment of pure numbers through what we call mimesis does not only give rise in the sensible world to the musical order of tones. According to the Pythagorean doctrine, it also accounts for the miraculous order visible in the heavens above, where, apart from the irregular motion of the planets, which do not seem to describe a perfect circle around the earth, the same pattern constantly recurs. Alongside these two experiences of order, the music of the tones and the music of the spheres, there is also the order of the soul. This too may be an authentic early Pythagorean idea, for music played a part in cultic practice and helped purify the soul. The Pythagorean regulations concerning purity and the doctrine of the transmigration of souls clearly belong together. The earliest concept of imitation thus implies all three manifestations of order: the order of the cosmos, the order of music, and the order of the soul. What is the significance of the fact that all these different forms of order are based upon the imitation or mimesis of number? Clearly this is because the numbers and the pure relationships among them constitute the very nature of these manifestations of order. It is not that all these things are striving to attain the nature of numerical exactness, but simply the fact that there is a numerical order at work in all of them. For upon this depends every other kind of order. So it was that Plato made the correct observance and unadulterated preservation of musical order the basis for the order of human life in the polis.[12]

I wish to take up this idea and ask whether we do not in fact experience order in art of every kind, however extravagant its manifestations? Of course, the order that we experience in modern art no longer bears any resemblance to the exemplary order formerly revealed by nature and the structure of the cosmos. It reflects neither the mythical interpretation of human experience nor a world embodied in cherished and familiar things. All this is in the process of disappearing. The modern industrial world in which we live has not only banished the prominent forms of ritual and cult to the periphery of life, it has also succeeded in destroying "things" in the proper sense. In acknowledging this fact, I do not wish to adopt the judgmental tone of some *laudator temporis acti*. I am merely describing the reality in which we find ourselves and which, unless we are foolish, we must accept. However, in this situation, it is true that we no longer have anything to do with "things" at all. Everything is now an article that can be purchased at will precisely because it can be produced at will – that is, until the production of this particular model has come to an end. This is the nature of production and consumption today. It is fitting, therefore, that the only "things" we know are mass-produced in factories, marketed with intensive advertising, and finally thrown away when they are broken. They cannot help us to experience what things are. Through them we are unable to experience the presence of what is essentially irreplaceable. There is nothing historical about them and they have no life. This is what the modern world is like. Can any thinking person expect the visual arts of today to give us the opportunity of recognizing things that are no longer real, that we can no longer encounter around us, that mean nothing to us, as if that could deepen familiarity with our world? Nevertheless, as long as they do not simply represent an increasingly fragile sense of familiarity, modern painting and sculpture can create irreplaceable and substantial works – and we could say a great deal about architecture in this connection as well. Every work of art still resembles a thing as it once was insofar as its existence illuminates and testifies to order as a whole. Perhaps this order is not one that we can harmonize with our own conceptions of order, but that which once united the familiar things of a familiar world. Nevertheless, there is in every work of art an ever new and powerful testimony to a spiritual energy that generates order.

In the last analysis, therefore, it is irrelevant whether or not a painter or sculptor works to produce objective or nonobjective art. The only relevant thing is whether we encounter a spiritual and ordering energy in the work, or whether we are simply reminded of some cultural motif or the peculiarities of this or that particular artist. For that impugns the artistic value of the work. But art is present whenever a work succeeds in elevating what it is or represents to a new configuration, a new world of its own in miniature, a new order of unity in tension. This can occur whether the work presents us with specific cultural content and familiar features of the world around us, or whether we are confronted by the mute, yet profoundly familiar, Pythagorean harmonies of form and color. Consequently, if I had to propose a universal aesthetic category that would include those mentioned at the outset – namely expression, imitation, and sign – then I would adopt the concept of mimesis in its most original sense as the presentation of order. Testifying to order, mimesis seems as valid now as it was then, insofar as every work of art, even in our own increasingly standardized world of mass production, still testifies to that spiritual ordering energy that makes our life what it is. The work of art provides a perfect example of that universal characteristic of human existence – the never-ending process of building a world. In the midst of a world in which everything familiar is dissolving, the work of art stands as a pledge of order. Perhaps our capacity to preserve and maintain, the capacity that supports human culture, rests in turn upon the fact that we must always order anew what threatens to dissolve before us. This is what the productive activity of the artist and our own experience of art reveals in an exemplary fashion.

6. On the contribution of poetry to the search for truth

The classical title for the considerations that follow derives from Goethe, and certainly in his case the relationship between the two concepts of "Poetry and Truth" is not simply one of opposition, but one of mutual interference. When Goethe gave this title to his autobiography, he was clearly referring to the positive role that poetic recollection plays in truth itself, and not just to the poetic freedom he allowed himself in telling his life story.[1] It is absolutely true that in earlier cultural periods, particularly those of the epic, poetry's claim to truth went completely unchallenged. Herodotus tells us that Homer and Hesiod gave the Greeks their gods: even for a writer who stood on the threshold of the Greek enlightenment, it was still self-evident that the ancient poetry of the Greeks embodied the truth of religious knowledge.[2] Or does this remark of Herodotus already betray an incipient doubt? In any case, the task of poetry to instruct as well as to please has maintained its absolute validity in classical aesthetics and still remains valid for modern scientific thought – at least in a more reflected and indirect form, now that we no longer show the same naive readiness to learn that was characteristic of earlier times.

It seems incontrovertible to me that poetic language enjoys a particular and unique relationship to truth. First, this is shown by the fact that poetic language is not equally appropriate at all times to any content whatsoever, and second, by the fact that when such content is given poetic form in language, it thereby acquires a certain legitimation. It is the art of language that not only decides upon the success or failure of poetry, but also upon its claim to truth. Certainly the old Platonic and naive objection to the trustworthiness of poetry and poets – "Poets often lie" – opposes the belief in the truthfulness of art and seems to contradict art's claim to truth. Yet

this claim will not be silenced. In fact, the very objection confirms
the self-evident nature of the claim, for the liar wants to be believed.
The poet makes his claim on the basis of his art – the art of
language.

What is true of language in general and what constitutes the process of linguistic communication will certainly be true of that particular case of language which we call poetry. Yet I should like to put
it the other way round and maintain that poetry is language in a preeminent sense. If this is to carry any conviction, it is of course
necessary to emphasize a dimension of our everyday use of language
other than that of the mere exchange of information. The only way
in which we perceive the possibility of speaking with one another is
that we have something to say to each other. This is a privileged process compared with all those ways in which there is simply a
transmission of information – as can also take place with signs. If
someone is to say something to someone else, it is not enough that
there should be a so-called recipient who is there to receive the
information. For over and above that, there must be a readiness to
allow something to be said to us. It is only in this way that the word
becomes binding, as it were: it binds one human being with another.
This occurs whenever we speak to one another and really enter into
genuine dialogue with another.

What is really presupposed when we let something be said to us?
Obviously the primary condition for this is that we do not know
everything already and that what we think we know is capable of
becoming questionable. In fact the very possibility of dialogue rests
upon the interplay of question and answer. Now every single statement that we make acquires its ultimate meaning (that is, what it says
to someone) from the question to which it supplies an answer. This
is what I call the hermeneutic character of speech: when we speak to
one another we do not so much transmit well-defined facts, as place
our own aspirations and knowledge into a broader and richer
horizon through dialogue with the other. Every statement that is
understood or is intelligible finds itself drawn into the dynamic of
one's own questioning, so that it is understood as a motivated
answer. Speaking means speaking with one another: to be struck by
something said or to fail to hear what is said are both genuine
experiences of language.

But there is yet another experience of language which has its own
character, the experience of poetry. And here the hermeneutic situa-

tion is of a quite different kind. Someone who wishes to understand a poem intends only the poem itself. We have not even begun to approach the poem if we try to go beyond it by asking about the author and what he intends by it. We all know from our own experience the fundamental difference that exists between a genuine poem and, for example, those more or less well-intentioned forms of poetic communication that young people love to compose. When someone writes a love poem of this kind, there is certainly plenty of sincerity and impulsive emotional power in it, and such verses are best understood from the motivation behind them. On the other hand, any poem worthy of the name is quite different from all forms of motivated speech. When we read a poem, it never occurs to us to ask who it is that wants to say something to us or why. Here we are wholly directed toward the word as it stands. We are not recipients of some form of communication that might reach us from this or that person. The poem does not stand before us as a thing that someone employs to tell us something. It stands there equally independent of both reader and poet. Detached from all intending, the word is complete in itself.

Let us ask in what sense there can be truth in such a word. Clearly, it is in the nature of the poetic word to be unique and irreplaceable. Only then do we call something a poem. If this is not our impression and the words seem to have been arbitrarily chosen, then we judge the poem a failure. The truly remarkable thing, however, is that a work that carries conviction as a poetic achievement also convinces us by what it says. It is a matter of universal experience that not everything can be expressed in a poetic way in every age. Epic poetry, for example, has a great tradition that extends through Homer, Virgil, Dante, and Milton to find its final "bourgeois" fulfillment in Goethe's *Hermann and Dorothea.* But the epic is no longer a genuine possibility for poetic language. Similarly, one could ask whether drama can exist in every period, or whether it is not characteristic of certain epochs that particular kinds of poetry are dominant while others are simply excluded as impossible. For example, 1500 years of Christian history has produced no real drama.[3] The question forces itself upon us: what can we learn from the fact that certain forms of expression are possible while others are not? What kind of "truth" does this imply?

What does "truth" mean here? There is an old rule that says that if we cannot define our question exactly, we should restate it in a negative form. So I should ask: what does it mean to say that certain forms of poetic language are no longer "true"? What is the meaning of "truth" here? "Truth" already had a double sense in early Greek philosophy. As it was used in the living language of the Greeks, the expression *aletheia* is best translated as "openness." For it was always connected with words concerned with speech. To be open means to say what one means. Language is primarily not, in the familiar phrase, the means given us to conceal our thoughts. This primary meaning of truth, then, is that we tell the truth, we say what we mean. This is supplemented, particularly in philosophical usage, by a further sense in which *something* "says" what it "means": whatever shows itself to what it is, is true. So, when we say "real gold" for example, we mean that it not only glitters like gold, but that it is gold. We can say instead that it is "true" gold, just as the Greeks would say *alethes.* Our own use of language corresponds even more clearly to this when we say that someone is a "true friend." We mean by this that someone has proved himself or herself to be a friend and not simply given us the impression of friendly support and sympathy. It has emerged that this is a real friend. He is now "unconcealed," as Heidegger would say.[4] It is in this sense that I am asking about the truth of poetry.

What happens to language when it becomes the language of poetry? As with the case of the man who has proved himself a friend, we must ask what is revealed here. It can also be put in this way: when we say "a true friend," we mean that here the word accords with its concept. This man actually corresponds with the concept of a friend. And it is in just this sense that I now ask what the poetic word is. How does it correspond to the concept of a word?

When we ask this question, we are a long way from the kind of question posed by information and communication theory. Indeed, it is also true that the poetic word is capable of being a text, of being written – but as something written, it is a word in a particular sense: namely, a word *that stands written.* I use this Lutheran expression because it serves to clarify something.[5] What does it mean to say that something stands written? Clearly it does not simply signify that it is set down in such a way that its content can be realized again and again, since this is true of all possible ways in which we set something down in writing. This is the sense in which something is written down in the notes that I have before me when I lecture. But we would not say of them that "a word [. . .] stands written." Why not?

Obviously, what is written in the notes is simply there to refer to an idea that I wish to expound to my listeners. The notes' practical value lies exclusively in their subordination to the idea behind them. They do not belong to "literature." A poem, on the other hand, is not a reminder of an original performance of an idea, and is not simply in the service of further performances. It is the other way round – so much so that the text enjoys greater reality than any of its potential realizations can ever claim for itself. Whether the poet himself reads his works aloud or whether someone else reads them, we all know that the spoken word falls short of the poem as that which we actually intend and against which all realizations are measured. How is the word able to stand for itself in this way?

Now it is not only the poetic word that is "autonomous" in the sense that we subordinate ourselves to it and concentrate all our efforts upon it "as a text." I think there are two other such kinds of texts. Clearly, the religious text is one of these. What is the meaning of the Lutheran translation mentioned earlier: "It stands written"? In Luther's usage, this often applies to a particular kind of speech that I should like to call a "pledge" *(Zusage)*. We can always call upon something that has been pledged – as in the case of a promise that someone has made to us. When someone makes a promise, then he pledges something. I can call upon what is said and rely upon it. It is more than a communication: it is rather a binding word that pre-supposes mutual validity. It does not lie in my power alone to prom-ise something. It also depends upon the other who accepts my promise, and only then does it become a promise. For example, we can imagine a situation in which a man promises his wife that he will never again drink more than he really needs to satisfy his thirst. Perhaps his wife has known for a long time that he will never be able to keep his promise. For this reason, she does not accept it and says she cannot believe him. This reciprocal relationship between saying and answering belongs to the essence of a pledge. It is in this sense that the texts of revealed religion are a form of pledge since they only acquire the character of an address insofar as they are ac-knowledged on the part of the believer.

Another privileged form of text that may be found in the modern state seems to me to be the legal text. The law is in a sense binding by virtue of its being written down, and it has a specific character of its own. I should like to call this kind of saying a "proclamation" *(Ansage)*. As we know, the legal text only becomes valid by means of declaration, and the law must be promulgated. It is the nature of this proclamation, in which the word only acquires its legal existence through being stated and without which it cannot acquire it, that first constitutes its legal validity. So, for example, it was a terrible legal calamity when in Germany in 1933 a retroactive law was passed in the unhappy case of Lubbe. We all feel spontaneously that such a retroactively valid law contradicts the real meaning of a *statute* as something that stands written. In this sense, the promulgation of law belongs to the essence of the constitutional state.

These two forms of saying, the pledge and the proclamation, should serve as a backdrop for our discussion of the poetic text, which correspondingly I should like to call a "statement" (*Aussage*). The first syllable of the German word *Aussage* [literally, an "out-saying" – Ed.] expresses a claim to completeness. Such a statement expresses fully what the given state of affairs is. For example, the statement that we make before a court has just this character, since we are instructed as witnesses to tell the whole truth, that is, every-thing we know without addition or omission. In the legal context this is known as a statement. Here I shall ignore how the role of a witness before a court is problematic on other hermeneutical grounds. I only want to draw attention to the total or perfectionist character of such a statement. For it is here that the connection with poetic saying (*Sage*) may be found. It is a saying that says so com-pletely what it is that we do not need to add anything beyond what is said in order to accept it in its reality as language. The word of the poet is autonomous in the sense that it is self-fulfilling. The poetic word is thus a statement in that it bears witness to itself and does not admit anything that might verify it. In other cases, in a court of law for example, we might wish to check a statement to determine whether the witness, the accused, or whoever, is speaking the truth. Clearly, this is not the case with the poetic word. The question that ought to concern us here is: how can there be a saying in regard to which it would be quite meaningless and patently mistaken to seek further verification over and above the fact that it has been said?

I do not want to say anything about the religious use of the word or the analogies that there may be with the experience of prayer, for that exceeds my area of competence. But it is quite obvious that we find something analogous here, even if it does rest on a quite dif-ferent basis. To speak of truth in poetry is to ask how the poetic word finds fulfillment precisely by refusing external verification of any kind. Let us take a literary example at random – *The Brothers Karamazov* by Dostoevsky. The staircase that Smerdjakov falls down plays a major role in the story.[6] Everyone who has read the book will remember this scene and will "know" exactly what the staircase looks like. Not one of us has exactly the same image of it and yet we all believe that we see it quite vividly. It would be absurd to ask what the staircase "intended" by Dostoevsky really looked like. Through the way in which he tells his story and by his treatment of language, the writer succeeds in rousing the imagination of every reader to construct an image so that he thinks he sees exactly how the stairs turn to the right, descend for a couple of steps, and then disappear into the darkness below. If someone else says that it turns left, descends for six steps, and then is lost in the darkness, he is obviously just as much in the right. By not describing the scene in any more detail than he has, Dostoevsky stimulates us to construct an image of the stairs in our imagination. From this example we can see how the poet manages to conjure up the self-fulfillment of language. But how does the poet do this and what means does he employ?

I would just like to insert a small observation. Clearly in the language of poetry, the dimensions of sound and sense are inextricably interwoven. This fusion can exist to a lesser or greater degree, but in certain forms of linguistic art it reaches an extreme point where they become totally indissoluble. I am thinking here of lyric poetry, where we confront an unconditional case of untranslatability. No translation of a lyric poem ever conveys the original work. The best we can hope for is that one poet should come across another and put a new poetic work, as it were, in place of the original by creating an equivalent with the materials of a different language. There are of course levels of untranslatability. A novel is certainly translatable, and we must ask ourselves why this is, why we are able to see Dostoevsky's staircase in front of us so vividly that I could almost argue with someone about the direction in which it turns, although I know no Russian? How does language achieve this? Obviously, in this case the relation between sound and sense is weighted rather more toward the side of sense. Nevertheless, the language is poetic in the sense that it is not fulfilled by anything beyond itself, that is, by any confirmation we might seek through verification of the facts or through further experience. It fulfills itself. Self-fulfillment means that we are not referred to anything further. Thus poetic language stands out as the highest fulfillment of that revealing (*deloun*) which is the achievement of all speech.[7] For this reason it seems to me that an aesthetic theory that interprets the poetic word simply as a combination of emotional and signifying moments added onto everyday language is thoroughly misleading. That may well be the case, yet it is not because of this that a word becomes a poetic word, but because it acquires the power of "realization." So even Husserl's perceptive remark that in the realm of the aesthetic, the eidetic reduction is spontaneously fulfilled insofar as the "position" or positing of actuality is suspended, only represents half the story. Here Husserl speaks of "neutrality modification."[8] If I now point to the window and say, "Look at the house over there," then anyone who follows my directions will see the house over there as the fulfillment of what I said, simply by looking in the right direction. On the other hand, if a poet describes a house in his own words or evokes the idea of a house, we do not look in the direction of any particular house, but each of us constructs his own image of a house in such a way that it stands there for him as "the house." In all of this, an eidetic reduction is at work insofar as the house is a universal that is given through his words as a spontaneous "intentional fulfillment." The word is true in the sense that it discloses, producing this self-fulfillment. The poetic word suspends the positive and the posited as that which might serve to verify whether our statement corresponds with what lies outside it.

And yet it would be misleading to think that this represents an enfeebled consciousness of reality or a weakening of the positing power of consciousness. The reverse is true. The realization that occurs by means of the word eliminates any comparison with whatever else might be present and raises what is said above the particularity of what is usually called "reality." It is quite incontestable that we do not look beyond the word to the world for confirmation. On the contrary, we construct the world of the poem from within the poem itself. How can the poetic word provoke this immediate refusal to seek verification for what is said? This is quite clear in the case of Hölderlin, who announced the return of the gods. Anyone who seriously believes that he should await the return of the Greek gods because it has been promised as a future event has not grasped the nature of Hölderlin's poetry. "Their spirit breathes in song."[9] How does the poet achieve it? How does poetry enable the poet to frame his language so that it is suddenly "just so"? By that I mean that the poetic creation does not intend something, but rather is the existence of what it intends – so much so that even the poet who hears it cannot think of himself as the one who said it.

What does it mean to say that a poem is successful? What does it mean that a specific content intended in a particular way comes to stand in a poem by means of its emergence as a true word?

Let us recall the considerations with which we began. There we said that all speech says something, whether we let something be said to us or say something to someone else. And this presupposes that there is something clearly in question for us, so that what is said must be taken as an answer. How does this apply to the poetic work? What the poet intends or what motivates him to say this or that is not the issue. We are concerned with the question to which what has been successfully achieved in the poem is the answer, rather than anything standing "behind it." What sort of question is this? Why in our own time does poetry reject certain themes and prefer others? And how can we hear the poetry of today, where a new world of content stands before us, with the same alert and receptive poetic sense that we bring to Schiller, Shakespeare, or Goethe? How and in what respect does the poem succeed in overcoming the time-bound and occasional circumstances of its origin? I can put this in another way. What is the question to which a poetic creation always represents an answer? I do not think that it is sufficient to say that all poetic works address us because they supply an answer to the ultimate questions of human life. In certain areas that is quite true. It is reasonable to say that the "boundary situations" of death and birth, suffering and guilt, or whatever – all of which have been taken up into great tragedy as a particular form of art – are still open questions to which we seek an answer.[10] But must we not raise a more far-reaching issue? What is the question to which every poetic work is always an answer? Perhaps the answer to that question begins to suggest itself if I go back to what was introduced as the universal nature of all speech – namely, the fact that what the word evokes is there. It does not matter whether we are concerned with specific themes that are expressed in our own or any other time, for the decisive thing is that the word summons up what is "there" so that it is palpably near. The truth of poetry consists in creating a "hold upon nearness." What this hold upon nearness means becomes clear if we consider a counterexample. Whenever we feel something lacking in a poem, then it is because it is not a structure that hangs together. It jars because it contains something merely conventional or stale. A genuine poem, on the other hand, allows us to experience "nearness" in such a way that this nearness is held in and through the linguistic form of the poem. What is the nearness that is held there? Whenever we have to hold something, it is because it is transient and threatens to escape our grasp. In fact, our fundamental experience as beings subject to time is that all things escape us, that all the events of our lives fade more and more, so that at best they glow with an almost unreal shimmer in the most distant recollection. But the poem does not fade, for the poetic word brings the transience of time to a standstill. It too "stands written," not as a promise, nor as a pledge, but as a saying where its own presence is in play. Perhaps it is connected with the power of the poetic word that the poet feels a challenge to bring to language that which seems most closed to the realm of words. This self-fulfillment appears at its most mysterious in lyric poetry, where we cannot even determine the unified sense of poetic speech, as is especially the case with "pure poetry" since the time of Mallarmé.

Let us ask once again how and with what means the lyric poem fulfills itself? This "standing of the word" seems to point toward that fundamental human situation that Hegel described as feeling at home in the world.[11] As we know from our own experience of life, the basic task facing us is "to make ourselves at home" in the flood of impressions. This happens primarily as we learn our mother tongue and the totality of our linguistically interpreted experience is increasingly brought into order. We thereby acquire a growing familiarity with our mother tongue as the initial articulation of that world in which henceforth we make our way. Everyone knows what it means to have a feeling for language so that something sounds strange when it is not "right." We constantly find this with translations. Our expectation of familiarity is disappointed and our sense of nearness recedes. What is this familiarity that supports us as speakers? What is this nearness that surrounds us? Obviously, it is not only the words and phrases of our language that are constantly becoming more familiar to us, but what is said in those words as well. When we grow up in a language, the world is brought close to us and comes to acquire a certain stability. Language always furnishes the fundamental articulations that guide our understanding of the world. It belongs to the nature of familiarity with the world that whenever we exchange words with one another, we share the world.

The word of the poet does not simply continue this process of *Einhausung,* or "making ourselves at home." Instead it stands over against this process like a mirror held up to it. But what appears in the mirror is not the world, nor this or that thing in the world, but rather this nearness or familiarity itself in which we stand for a while. This standing and this nearness find permanence in the language of literature and, most perfectly, in the poem. This is not a romantic theory, but a straightforward description of the fact that language gives all of us our access to a world in which certain special forms of human experience arise: the religious tidings that proclaim salvation, the legal judgment that tells us what is right and what is wrong in our society, the poetic word that by being there bears witness to our own being.

7. Poetry and mimesis

The doctrine that art is the imitation of nature is one that can claim an ancient origin and a self-evident validity, but it only began to play its proper role in the politics of art with the classicist aesthetics of the modern age. French classicism, along with Winckelmann and Goethe, saw the faithful study of nature as the real school of the artist. In this way, the doctrine of imitation was put in a context in which the visual arts were accorded a decisive preeminence in aesthetics. In the eighteenth century, after Winckelmann, it was not so much Classical poetic literature that counted as Classical art, but rather what Hegel called the religion of art: that age of Greek sculpture in which the Greek world of the gods and the divine as such manifested themselves in human form. In Hegel's eyes, this was art as religion, and if after the decline of antiquity he feels the loss of this harmonious coincidence of the human and the divine and so claims that art as such is a thing of the past, then it is the visual arts, as a sensuous appearance of the absolute, that serves as his criterion.[1]

It is of course true that the ancient doctrine of imitation dominates poetic theory above all. Yet it seemed to justify itself most convincingly in the visual arts, for it is here that all talk of image and original most forcibly suggests itself – something that Plato made use of in his critique of the poets. There is something immediately convincing about the claim that a fundamental distinction remains between the original and the image in the visual arts insofar as the movement of life is contained and held in the image which does not move. So Plato employs the concept of mimesis in order to emphasize the ontological distance between the original and the image. When he plays this off against poetic and in particular dramatic language, it is in a violently polemical sense. Aristotle justified the concept of mimesis in another more positive sense. In his *Poetics,* which came to dominate subsequent aesthetics, Aristotle turned his attention to the "total work of art" represented by ancient tragedy.

The extent to which poetic theory (and rhetoric) determined the direction of aesthetic thought is well known. For example, modern art theory is dominated by the concept of style which, as the word indicates, derives from the art of writing and the stylus or slate pencil. But right into the eighteenth century it was still possible to cling to the doctrine of imitation as a representation of exemplary subjects of a sacred and profane nature. It was only during the eighteenth century that a change began which was to break down this restricted and confining concept of imitation as the concept of expression rose to a dominating position. This concept was originally employed in the aesthetics of music, but the immediate language of the heart as expressed through sound now became the ideal in terms of which the whole language of art in its rejection of all intellectualism was conceived.

Thus the old connection between poetic theory and rhetoric, both understood as the arts of fine speaking, was broken. The ancient alliance of rhetoric and poetics could no longer assume a proper place in modern aesthetic thought, especially after the aesthetics of genius, with the great poetic imagination of Shakespeare in view, had discredited the concept of poetic rules and finally even the idea of poetic artifice.

Instead, its place was taken by the new and intimate relationship between poetry and music, which attained its full classical development at that time. In German romanticism, poetry was held to be the universal language of mankind. The old aesthetic of imitation is no longer convincing when the essence of poetic language expresses itself less in the presentation of concrete images than in the intensity of mood created by the unending movement of poetic language–not to speak of the radical use of language in "pure poetry." The concept of mimesis seems to have become inapplicable.

However, the concept of mimesis can be grasped in a more original fashion than is suggested by classicism. I should like to show that in fact, the original concept of mimesis is capable of justifying the essential priority of poetry with respect to the other arts.

Nor should that surprise us, if we take the ancient concept of poetry as our point of departure. For the words *poiesis* and *poietes* themselves have a special significance in Greek. They not only signify productive activity or the producer himself as the case may be, but rather in a specific sense poetic creation and the poet as well. This is a significant double meaning that makes a semantic connection between a specific kind of making and producing and other forms of the same activity. From the social point of view, on the other hand, this corresponds to the fact that the poet occupied a position alongside the king and the orator, and was the only artist who was not considered a mere artisan. This understanding shared by both forms of *techne,* the manual and the poetic, is clearly determined by the kind of knowledge involved. For knowledge and facility direct the productive activity of both the craftsman and the poet. Now, as Plato in particular has stressed most strongly, it lies in the nature of all the productive arts that in general they do not carry within themselves the goal and measure of this knowledge and facility. Their activity is directed toward the work, or *ergon*, and this work in turn is destined for use. How the work is to be produced and what it should look like are determined therefore by the purposes and uses to which it will be put.

Now it is certainly true of everything that we call a work of art – the poetic work that is to be sung or performed, the image of the god to which sacrifice is made, or the decoration and embellishment of tools – that it is not really there to be used. The intention of the producer is realized not in the fact that the product serves a useful purpose, but clearly only in the fact that it is simply there. It is certainly true that although the work was independent of specific use-functions, it was still embedded in the functional context of life, where it occupied a position of its own: the sculpture as part of the process of religious or public life, or the poetic work in recitation or theatrical performance. But nobody would wish to apply the concept of functional art to such phenomena. For this modern concept implies that the superior concept of an art free from all use already exists beforehand. But that is a modernism: if a work of art serves different purposes, religious, political, or whatever, it is not on that account subordinated to another alien purpose, but rather manifests itself in its real nature. "Use" of this kind serves its existence as a work, and not the reverse. We are quite justified therefore in speaking of the fine arts when confronted by religiously committed art, for their characteristic feature is their freedom from utility and the independent significance of their existence and manifestation as something beautiful.

Now it is a peculiar feature of poetry that it is not actually there in the same sense as the works of the visual arts. Nothing stands there in its own right. There is no material, no dense intractability of matter, to be subdued by form. The poetic work possesses an ideal kind of being and depends on reproduction, whether dramatic play in the original sense, or recitation or reading. It is easy to understand how it is just here that the universal meaning of the poet as maker becomes eminently applicable. When it is language alone that lets something be there, the ideal of production is most clearly fulfilled. For the word enjoys unlimited power and ideal perfection. Poetry is something that is made in such a way that it has no other meaning beyond letting something be there. There is no respect in which a linguistic work of art has to be there *for* anything. It is thus properly speaking something "made."

But it also fulfills what we mean by mimesis in a specific way. No special historical investigations are required to recognize that the meaning of the word "mimesis" consists simply in letting something be there without trying to do anything more with it. The pleasure involved in mimetic behavior and its effects is a fundamental human pleasure that Aristotle had already illustrated with the behavior of children.[2] The pleasure of dressing up and representing someone other than oneself, and the pleasure of the person who recognizes what is represented, show what the real significance of imitative representation is: there is no question of comparing or judging the degree of accuracy with which the representation approaches what is intended by it. Of course, such critical judgment and evaluation do exist alongside any representation, but only as something secondary. Every representation finds its genuine fulfillment simply in the fact that what it represents is emphatically there. When Aristotle describes how the onlooker knows that "that is who it is," he does not mean that we see through the disguise and know the identity of the person dressed up. On the contrary, he means that we know who is represented.[3] Knowledge here means recognition. We recognize whom we know, whether it is the god, the hero, or even our own laughable contemporaries with whom we are acquainted. Mimesis is a representation in which we "know" and have in view the essential content of what is represented.

We can still see quite clearly in Aristotle that mimetic representation is part of a cultic event rather like the carnival processions with which we are still familiar. The act in which something is recognized here is not an act of distinction, but of identification. However ineliminable it may be, and however we may emphasize it, the distance between the image and the original has something inappropriate about it as far as the real ontological meaning of mimesis is concerned. When the work of art carries conviction, the *paradigma* (to which, according to Plato, every representation is related as an image, and which it necessarily falls short of) is not present as such (for *paradigma* means "what is shown alongside").[4] No one points to it as something that stands alongside the representation. The onlooker does not see anything in the representation beyond what is represented there, any more than the player distinguishes himself from the role in which he is totally absorbed.

When we know something *as* something, this certainly means that we recognize it, but when we recognize something, we do not simply know it for a second time after previous acquaintance with it. Recognition is something qualitatively different. Where something is recognized, it has liberated itself from the uniqueness and contingency of the circumstances in which it was encountered. It is a matter neither of there and then, nor of here and now, but it is encountered as the very self-same. Thereby it begins to rise to its permanent essence and is detached from anything like a chance encounter. It is not for nothing that Plato described the knowledge of the permanent essence of the idea as a remembrance, and explicated this knowledge in mythical form as a reminiscence of a previous existence. Aristotle is quite right to perceive the essence of mimetic representation, and thus of the work of art as well, in such knowledge. From there he arrived at his famous distinction between poetry and history, according to which poetry is the "more philosophical" of the two because history only recognizes things as they actually happened, while poetry on the other hand relates how they might have happened: that is, according to their universal and permanent essence.[5] Poetry thus participates in the truth of the universal.

On the other hand, when Plato in his critique of the poets relegates the imitative arts to the very lowest level because, unlike real things, they are not even simply imitations of the essential forms but rather imitations of imitations, then he is obviously inverting the

true nature of artistic representation. We should not infer from this
that he did not really understand the nature of artistic representation. In fact, this is an ironic distortion intended to emphasize the
claim of philosophy as dialectic to knowledge of true essences. In
other contexts Plato recognized perfectly well that, when we are
talking about art, it is precisely not the ontological distinction between the representation and the represented, but the total identification with what is represented that constitutes the nature of
representation. In the *Philebus,* for example, he refers to the delight
that the onlooker takes in the comic hero's blind ignorance concerning both himself and the world in which he moves.[6] Plato gives a
profound interpretation of the source of this comic delight expressed in gales of laughter at such a spectacle. Comic events on
stage count as the whole "comedy and tragedy of life."

Aristotle also observes the same connection. It is like this not only
in the sphere of artistic presentation, but in our social life as well:
whenever we meet with the absurd, we are already openly enjoying
a spectacle and taking innocuous pleasure in it. Yet behind such
"aesthetic freedom" there lies a profound sense of community that
dissolves all distance. In the liberating laughter with which we view
the comical, as in the traumatic experience of the tragic, an act of
identification, a deep and disturbing encounter with ourselves, over-
comes us. In this experience, any distinction between play and
actuality, appearance and reality, is eliminated. The distance between onlooker and player is as thoroughly overcome here as was
the distance between the representation and what it represented.

The concept of mimesis that expresses such "aesthetic" experience does not have to be artificially referred back to the original
Greek situation in which all the arts were still closely related to one
another, through the religious cult and its ritualistic representation
in word, sound, image, and gesture. The mimetic is and remains a
primordial phenomenon in which it is not so much an imitation that
occurs as a transformation. It is, to use a deliberately artificial
expression which I have employed in another context, "aesthetic
nondifferentiation"[7] that constitutes the experience of art. If we
renew the original meaning of mimesis, we can free ourselves from
the restrictions that the classicist aesthetic of imitation has imposed
upon our thought. Mimesis then does not imply a reference to an
original as something other than itself, but means that something
meaningful is there as itself. No given natural criterion decides

whether a representation is valuable or not. Certainly every representation that addresses us already represents an answer to the question of why it exists, whether it represents anything or just "nothing at all." In this sense, the nature of all productive activity in art and poetry still lies in the fundamental mimetic experience.

One may draw the conclusion, therefore, that anyone who thinks that art can no longer be adequately grasped using Greek concepts is not thinking in a sufficiently Greek way.

8. The play of art

Play is an elementary phenomenon that pervades the whole of the animal world and, as is obvious, it determines man as a natural being as well. Man shares a great deal with the other animals, whose enjoyment of play can astonish us – so much so that anyone who observes and studies animal behavior, in particular that of the higher mammals, is overcome by a feeling of delight coupled with horror. If animals and human beings resemble one another in so many respects, does not the borderline between them become blurred? The modern study of animal behavior has indeed made us more and more aware just how questionable such a distinction really is. Things are no longer as simple for us as they were made to seem in the seventeenth century. So overwhelming was the impact of Descartes' central insight at that time, that self-consciousness came to be seen as the mark of humanity, animals were simply considered to be automata, and man alone was distinguished among divinely created beings by his self-consciousness and free will.

This enthusiasm has utterly disappeared. For more than a century now, the suspicion has been growing that human behavior, on the part of both the individual and especially of the group, is determined by natural conditions to a much greater degree than is appropriate for a being who is aware of choosing and acting freely. For it is by no means the case that everything accompanied by the conscious feeling of freedom is actually the result of a free decision. Unconscious factors, compulsive drives, and interests not only determine our behavior, but our consciousness as well.

We may well ask whether a great deal of what we claim to be the exercise of free and conscious human choice cannot be much better understood in terms of animal behavior and its controlling instincts. Is it not the case that in the final analysis, human play is also determined by nature, and that artistic creation itself is an expression of a play-drive?

To be sure, we always think that we play "at something," and believe that our behavior is thereby quite different from the playful behavior of small children and animals. They play "with something," it is true, but they do not really "intend" this or that game so much as simply the act of playing itself – the expression of superabundant life and movement. On the other hand, the game that someone begins, invents, or learns how to play, has a specificity of its own that is "intended" as such. Here we are conscious of the rules and conditions of play, whether we are talking about the sort of games we play together or about competitive sports, which possess the character of play in an indirect sense. Our playful behavior is sharply distinguished from all our other forms of behavior by this specificity – much more sharply than is the case in the animal world, where forms of play slip easily into other kinds of behavior. The playfulness of human games is constituted by the imposition of rules and regulations that only count as such within the closed world of play. Any player can avoid them simply by withdrawing from the game. Of course, within the game itself, the rules and regulations are binding in their own way and can no more be violated than any of the rules that determine and bind our lives together. What is the nature of the validity that both binds and limits in this way? Doubtless, the kind of directedness to the matter at hand that is unique to man also finds expression in the characteristic of human play to include binding rules. Philosophers refer to this as the intentionality of consciousness.

Now this is indeed so universal a structure of human existence that we might well consider the directedness of play to be characteristically human. We are used to talking about the element of play proper to all human culture. We discover forms of play in the most serious kinds of human activity: in ritual, in the administration of justice, in social behavior in general, where we even speak of role-playing and so forth. A certain self-imposed limitation of our freedom seems to belong to the very structure of culture.

But does this mean that it is only in human culture that the act of play is objectified with the specificity of "intended" behavior? Play and seriousness seem to be interwoven in a still deeper sense. It is immediately apparent that any form of serious activity is shadowed by the possibility of playful behavior. "Acting as if" seems a particular possibility wherever the activity in question is not simply a case of instinctual behavior, but one that "intends" something. This "as if" modification is so universal that even the play of animals sometimes seems animated by a touch of freedom, especially when they playfully pretend to attack, to start back in fear, to bite, and so on. And what is the significance of those gestures of submission that can be considered the conclusive end of contests between animals? Here too, in all probability, it is a matter of observing the rules of the game. It is a remarkable fact that no victorious animal will actually continue the attack once the gesture of submission has been made. The execution of the action is here replaced by a symbolic one. How does this fit in with the claim that in the animal world, all behavior obeys instinctual imperatives, while in the case of man, everything follows from a freely made decision?

If we wish to avoid the interpretative framework of the dogmatic Cartesian philosophy of self-consciousness, it seems to me methodologically advisable to seek out just such transitional phenomena between human and animal life. Such borderline cases in the realm of play allow us to extend the comparison into a realm not immediately accessible to us, but which we can approach only through the works that it produces: namely, the realm of art. In this connection, however, I do not think we have found a really convincing borderline case in the universal constructive force manifest in the forms of nature, and in whose formative play we see an excess over and above what is strictly necessary and purposive. The astonishing thing here is precisely not the drive of the "constructive force," but rather the suggestion of freedom that accompanies the forms it produces. That is why symbolic actions like those described are particularly interesting. For in human fabrication as well, the decisive moment of technical skill does not consist in the fact that something of extraordinary utility or superfluous beauty has emerged. It consists rather in the fact that human production of this kind can set itself various tasks and proceed according to plans that are characterized by an element of free variability. Human production encounters an enormous variety of ways of trying things out, rejecting them, succeeding, or failing. "Art" begins precisely there, where we are able to do otherwise. Above all, where we are talking about art and artistic creation in the preeminent sense, the decisive thing is not the emergence of a product, but the fact that the product has a special nature of its own. It "intends" something, and yet it is not what it intends. It is not an item of equipment determined by its utility, as all such items or products of human work are. Certainly it is a product, that is, something produced by human activity that now stands there available for use. And yet the work of art refuses to be used in any way. That is not the way it is "intended." It has something of the "as if" character that we recognized as an essential feature of the nature of play. It is a "work" because it resembles something played. It is not encountered in its own right, but stands for something else. Just as a symbolic gesture is not just itself but expresses something else through itself, so too the work of art is not itself simply *as* a product. It is defined precisely by not being a piece of work that has just been turned out and could be turned out again and again. On the contrary, it is something that has emerged in an unrepeatable way and has manifested itself in a unique fashion. It seems to me, therefore, that it would be more accurate to call it a creation (*Gebilde*) than a work. For the word *Gebilde* implies that the manifestation in question has in a strange way transcended the process in which it originated, or has relegated that process to the periphery. It is set forth in its own appearance as a self-sufficient creation.

Rather than referring back to the process of its formation, such creation demands to be apprehended in itself as pure manifestation. What this means can be grasped particularly clearly in the transitory arts. Poetry, music, and dance have none of the tangibility of a material thing, yet the transient and insubstantial stuff of which they are made does compose itself into the compact unity of a creation – one that always remains the same. For this reason, creations, texts, compositions, and dance forms are certainly spoken of as works of art as such, but their essential identity depends upon the act of reproduction. In the reproductive arts, the work of art must constantly be reconstituted as a creation. The transitory arts teach us most vividly that representation is required not only for the reproductive arts, but for any creation that we call a work of art. It demands to be constructed by the viewer to whom it is presented. In a sense, it is not simply what it is, but rather something that it is not – not something we can simply use for a particular purpose, nor a material thing from which we might fabricate some other thing. On the contrary, it is something that only manifests and displays itself when it is constituted in the viewer.

The act of reading is a peculiar borderline case that can illustrate this vividly. Strictly speaking, as long as we do not read aloud or recite, nothing is produced as it is in the reproductive arts. Although we do not generate a new independent reality, we nevertheless always seem to be moving in that direction.

There has always been a tendency to link the experience of art with the concept of play. Kant characterized the disinterested, non-purposive, and nonconceptual quality of delight in the beautiful as an affective state of mind in which our faculties of understanding and imagination cooperate with one another in a kind of free play. Schiller then transposed this description onto the basis of Fichte's theory of drives, and ascribed aesthetic behavior to a play-drive that unfolds its own free potentialities in between the material drive on the one hand and the formal drive on the other. To this extent, modern aesthetic thought has fully recognized the "contribution of the subject" to the construction of aesthetic experience. Yet the experience of art also presents that other dimension in which the playlike character of the creation, the very fact of its being "played," comes to the fore. The proper basis for this is still to be found in the ancient Greek concept of mimesis.

The Greeks distinguished between two kinds of productive activity: manual production which fabricates utensils, and mimetic production which does not create anything "real" but simply offers a representation. Something of this second sense of production is preserved in our own language when we speak of mimicry. For it is not only when we want to describe someone's gestures or the play of expression on someone's face that we talk in this way, but particularly where the deliberate imitation of a person's whole manner of behavior is involved – be it the artistic assumption of a role by an actor or the impersonation of another outside the realm of art. The very idea of mimicry implies that one's own body is a vehicle for imitative expression and that, in the case of art, it represents itself as something that it is not. A role is "played," and this implies a unique ontological claim. The simulated astonishment or feigned sympathy that people play at in social intercourse is quite different from this. Imitative representation is not the kind of play that deceives, but a play that communicates as play when it is taken in the way it wants to be taken: as pure representation. That is the precise difference between them. For example, the hypocritical sympathy that is merely a play wants to be believed, and this claim persists even when we are able to perceive that it is feigned and artificial. Mimetic imitation,

on the other hand, does not intend to be "believed," but to be
understood as imitation. Such imitation is not feigned, is not false
show, but on the contrary is clearly a "true" showing, "true" as a
show. It is perceived just as it is intended, namely *as show, as
appearance.*

Even if we leave to one side the difficult problem concerning the
being of appearance, it is clear in any case that wherever such "being
played" is at issue, this manifest show belongs in the dimension of
communication. The play of art as appearance is played out between
us. The one takes the creation simply as a creation, just as the other
does. Communication takes place when the other person takes part
in what is imparted to him – and in such a way that he does not, as it
were, only receive in part what is communicated, but shares in this
knowledge of the whole matter that is fully possessed by both of
them. This is obviously what distinguishes genuine communication
from simulated participation. In the latter, the "appearance" is precisely not an appearance common to both partners, but a deception
that is intended to appear simply for the other. An artistic creation is
therefore a true show. So much is it common to all that even the artist enjoys no privileged status over those who experience his work.
Precisely because he has expressed what he has to say, he keeps back
nothing for himself, but communicates himself without reserve. His
work speaks for him.

We must not lose sight of the ontological significance of mimicry
and mimesis if we are to understand the essential sense in which art
possesses the character of play. Mimicry is imitation. But this has
nothing whatever to do with the relation between copy and original,
or indeed with any theory for which art is supposed to be an imitation of "nature", that is, of that which exists in its own right. A little
reflection on the essence of mimesis can save us from this crass
naturalistic misunderstanding. The original mimetic relation is not
an imitation in which we strive to approach an original by copying it
as nearly as possible. On the contrary, it is a kind of showing. Here
showing does not mean setting out something like a proof in which
we demonstrate something that is not accessible in any other way.
When we show something, we do not intend a relation between the
one who shows and the thing shown. Showing points away from
itself. We cannot show anything to the person who looks at the act
of showing itself, like the dog that looks at the pointing hand. On
the contrary, showing something means that the one to whom some-

thing is shown sees it correctly for himself. It is in this sense that imitation is a showing. For imitation enables us to see more than so-called reality. What is shown is, so to speak, elicited from the flux of manifold reality. Only what is shown is intended and nothing else. As intended, it is held in view, and thus elevated to a kind of ideality. It is no longer just this or that thing that we can see, but it is now shown and designated as something. An act of identification and, consequently, of recognition occurs whenever we see what it is that we are being shown.

Remarkably enough, even in the case of mechanical reproductions of art, this is often unmistakable. When we look at the frequently outstanding photographic reproductions in illustrated newspapers, it is remarkable how unerringly we are able to distinguish a photographic report of real events from the reproduction of a painting or even the most realistic of film scenes. That is not to say that the film is unnatural in any way, or that the realistic portrait is not painted realistically enough. Something else comes through here even when it is reproduced in a newspaper. Aristotle is quite right: poetry makes the universal more visible than that faithful narration of facts and actual events which we call history can ever do.[1] The "as if" modification of poetic invention and the formative activity of sculpture or painting clearly make possible a form of participation that is beyond the reach of contingent reality with all its limitations and conditions. The photographic documentation of such contingent reality – the picture of a statesman, for example – only acquires its significance within a familiar context. The reproduction of a portrait painting has significance in its own right even when we do not know the identity of the person it represents. It not only allows us to recognize the universal, but thereby unites us by virtue of that which is common to us all. It is because what has been reproduced is not a "real" photograph, but only a painting that has the character of play, that it embraces us as participants. We know how it is intended and we take it as such.

From this perspective we can judge just how inappropriate the understanding and practice of art in the age of the culture industry have become. It is an industry that reduces participants to the level of exploited consumers. But a false self-understanding is thereby demanded of us. The mere onlooker who indulges in aesthetic or cultural enjoyment from a safe distance, whether in the theater, the concert hall, or the seclusion of solitary reading simply does not exist. Such a person misunderstands himself. For aesthetic self-understanding is indulging in escapism if it regards the encounter with the work of art as nothing but enchantment in the sense of liberation from the pressures of reality through the enjoyment of a spurious freedom.

The comparison between the forms of play discovered and created by men, and the uninhibited movement of play exhibited by superabundant life, can teach us that precisely what is at issue in the play of art is not some substitute dream-world in which we can forget ourselves. On the contrary, the play of art is a mirror that through the centuries constantly arises anew, and in which we catch sight of ourselves in a way that is often unexpected or unfamiliar: what we are, what we might be, and what we are about. In the last analysis, is it not an illusion to think that we can separate play from seriousness and only admit it to segregated areas peripheral to real life, like our leisure time which comes to resemble a relic of lost freedom? Play and seriousness, the exuberance and superabundance of life, on the one hand, and the tense power of vital energy on the other, are profoundly interwoven. They interact with one another, and those who have looked deeply into human nature have recognized that our capacity for play is an expression of the highest seriousness. For we read in Nietzsche, "Mature manhood: that means to have found again the seriousness one had as a child – in play."[2] Nietzsche also knew the reverse of this as well, and celebrated the creative power of life – and of art – in the divine ease of play.

Insistence on the opposition between life and art is tied to the experience of an alienated world. And failure to recognize the universal scope and ontological dignity of play produces an abstraction that blinds us to the interdependence of both. Play is less the opposite of seriousness than the vital ground of spirit as nature, a form of restraint and freedom at one and the same time. It is precisely because what we encounter in the creative forms of art is not merely the freedom of caprice or of the blind superabundance of nature, that their play is capable of penetrating all the dimensions of our social life, through all classes, races, and levels of cultural attainment. For these our forms of play are forms of our freedom.

[democracy]

9. Philosophy and poetry

The curious proximity between philosophy and poetry which after Herder and German Romanticism found its way into the common consciousness has not always been welcomed. This could well be regarded as evidence of the poverty of the post-Hegelian age. The philosophy to be found in the universities of the nineteenth and twentieth centuries forfeited its status – and not only as a consequence of Schopenhauer's insulting tirades. This occurred when it was confronted by great writers who were also outsiders, like Kierkegaard and Nietzsche, but even more when it was overshadowed by those great luminaries of the novel, particularly by the French (Stendhal, Balzac, Zola) and by the Russians (Gogol, Dostoevsky, Tolstoy). Philosophy either lost itself in the realms of historical research or defended its scientific character in the context of sterile epistemological problems. When in our own time the philosophy of the universities regained a certain validity – to mention here only the so-called philosophers of existence, Jaspers, Sartre, Merleau-Ponty, Gabriel Marcel, and above all, Martin Heidegger – it was not without a daring approach to the borders of poetic language. This frequently encountered bitter criticism: the prophet's garb ill becomes a philosopher who wishes to be taken seriously in the age of science. Why would any philosopher ignore the great achievements of modern logic over the last hundred years, with its astonishing advances over Aristotle, and increasingly hide himself among the shadows cast by poetry?

Yet this proximity and distance, this fruitful tension between poetry and philosophy, is hardly a problem of our immediate or recent history alone, for it has all along accompanied the path of Western thought, which is distinguished from all oriental wisdom precisely by virtue of having to sustain this tension. Plato spoke of "the ancient quarrel"[1] between poetry and philosophy, and rejected poetry from the realm of Ideas and the Good. And yet at the same time, he adopted poetry himself as a teller of mythical tales who knew how to combine in an inimitable fashion the festive with the ironical, the remoteness of legend with the clarity of thought. One may well ask who would want to separate poetry and philosophy, image and concept, united as they are in the Old and New Testaments and a thousand years of Christian thought and literature.

There has always been a question as to why and how language, as the only medium of poetry and thought, is able to encompass what is common to them and what is not. Certainly in our everyday use of language, this affinity does not emerge, and poetry and thought do not even come to interfere with one another. Naturally, speech of every kind is always capable of evoking image and thought. But in general, our speech acquires meaningful determinacy and clarity from a living context that is concretely realized in a situation in which we are addressed. The word spoken in such a concrete and pragmatic context does not simply stand for itself: in fact, it does not "stand" at all, but on the contrary passes over into what is said. Even when such speech is set down in writing, nothing changes – although the task of understanding the text that has been detached in this way has its own hermeneutical difficulties. The language of poetry and philosophy on the other hand can stand by itself, bearing its own authority in the detached text that articulates it. How can language accomplish this?

It is incontrovertible that language as we encounter it in its everyday use is unable to do this, and that it does not need to do so: whether it approaches the ideal of the unambiguous characterization of what is meant, or whether it remains a long way from this ideal (as in political speeches, for example), language never stands for itself. It stands for something we encounter in the practical activities of life or in scientific experience, and it is in this context that the views we express prove themselves or fail to do so. Words do not "stand" on their own account. Whether they are spoken or written, their meaning is only fully realized within the context of life. Valéry contrasted the poetic word with the everyday use of language in a striking comparison that alludes to the old days of the gold standard: everyday language resembles small change which, like our own paper money, does not actually possess the value that it symbolizes.[2] The famous gold coins still in use before the First World War, on the other hand, actually possessed as metal the value that was imprinted upon them. In a similar way, the language of poetry is not a mere pointer that refers to something else, but, like the gold coin, is what it represents.

I know of no similar remark concerning the language of philosophy – unless it lies hidden in Plato's famous attack upon the written word and its inability to defend itself against misuse by others.[3] For his criticism does indeed point to the ontological status of philosophical thought. The Platonic dialogue stands by itself, so much so that through its poetic mimesis, it could establish the dialectical character of dialogue. It is indeed a special kind of text, one that repeatedly involves the reader in the dialogue that it portrays. For philosophy as the infinite "toil of the concept"[4] is only constituted in the dialogue or in its silent internalization which we call thinking. Everyday speech with its ubiquitous opinions *(doxai)* is left far behind. But does not that mean that philosophy leaves the mere word behind as well?

Poetry and philosophy are both set off from the exchange of language as it takes place in practical activity and in science, but their proximity seems in the end to collapse into the extremes of the word that stands, and the word that fades into the unsayable. The following discussion pursues this proximity, which exists and can be justified.

As a first indication in this direction, I should like to point out that Edmund Husserl, the founder of phenomenology, developed for philosophy a method of self-understanding by rejecting all the naturalistic and psychologistic misunderstandings that had become widespread during the late nineteenth century. He called this the "eidetic reduction," by which all experience of contingent reality is bracketed as a point of method. This is something that occurs de facto in all true philosophizing. For it is only the a priori essential structures of all reality that have always and without exception formed the realm of the concept, or the realm of Ideas, as Plato called it. Whoever seeks to describe the mysterious character of art, and above all of poetry, will not be able to avoid expressing himself in a similar way, and will talk of the idealizing tendency of art. Whether the artist travels the road of realism or of total abstraction, he will not deny the ideality of what he has created and its elevation to an ideal spiritual reality. Husserl, who taught the eidetic reduction, which implies the suspension of the positing of reality as the very method of philosophy, could say that the eidetic reduction is "spontaneously fulfilled" in the realm of art.[5] Wherever art is experienced, this bracketing, the so-called *epoche,* has always already occurred: in fact, no one takes a painting or a statue for the real thing, not even in the extreme case of illusionistic painting, which raises the illusion of reality into the sphere of ideality to exploit its aesthetic delight. We have only to think of the vaulted ceiling of St. Ignatius in Rome.[6]

In the case where language is the medium, we must ask a question that particularly concerns the relation between philosophy and literature: how do these two preeminent and yet at the same time contrary forms of language – the poetic text which stands on its own account, and the language of the concept which suspends itself and leaves everyday reality behind it – relate to one another?

Following a tried phenomenological principle, I should like to approach this question from an extreme case. For this reason, I shall take as my starting point the lyric poem and the dialectical concept. The lyric poem is an extreme case because it implies in the clearest possible way the inseparability of the linguistic work of art and its original manifestation as a language, as the untranslatability of such poetry shows. And within the realm of lyric poetry, we will turn to its most radical form: "pure poetry" as programmatically developed by Mallarmé. The very question of translatability – however negative our answer may be – demonstrates that even in this extreme case, where the musicality of the poetic word is intensified to the very highest degree, it is still a question of the musicality of *language.* The form of the poem is constructed by the constantly shifting balance between sound and sense. If we pursue the analogy suggested by Heidegger when he says, for example, that color is never more color than when it appears in the painting of a great master, stone is never more stone than when it belongs to a column bearing the pediment of a Greek temple – and we all know that it is only in music that the tone first becomes *tone* – then we may ask what it means for the word and language of the poem to be word and language in a preeminent sense.[7] What does that tell us about the ontological constitution of poetic language? The structuring of sound, rhyme, rhythm, intonation, assonance, and so on, furnishes the stabilizing factors that haul back and bring to a standstill the fleeting word that points beyond itself. The unity of the creation is constituted in this way. But it is a creation that at the same time possesses the unity of everyday speech. This means that the other logico-grammatical forms of intelligible speech are also at work in the poem, even though they may recede into the background in favor of the structural moments of the creation that we have just listed. The syntactic means at the disposal of language may be used extremely sparely. By standing for themselves, individual words gain in presence and illuminating power. Syntactic indeterminacy is responsible for the free play of both the connotations to which the word owes its rich content and, even more, for the semantic weight that inhabits every word and suggests a variety of possible meanings. The consequent ambiguity and obscurity of the text may be the despair of the interpreter, but it is a structural element of this kind of poetry.

With this we restore the word of everyday speech to its original possibility – naming. To name something is always to call it into presence. Of course, without some contextual determinacy, an individual word as such can never evoke the unity of meaning, which arises only through the totality of what is said. And when, for example, modern poetry shatters the unity of the imaginative picture and altogether abandons the descriptive attitude for the sake of the surprising richness produced by relating quite disparate and unconnected things, then we may ask ourselves what these words that name actually mean? What is named in this case? It is true that lyric poetry of this kind is the successor to Baroque poetry, but we miss the unified background of a cultural tradition of shared imagery such as the Baroque age possessed. How can a whole be formed out of configurations of sound and fragments of meaning? This question leads to the hermetic character of "pure poetry."

In the end, it is easy to appreciate why in the age of mass communication such lyric poetry necessarily has a hermetic character. How can the word still stand out amid the flood of information? How can it draw us to itself except by alienating us from those all too familiar turns of speech that we all expect? The successive verbal constructions are gradually superimposed in order to constitute the poem as a whole, although the contours of each such segment are emphasized in their own right. In certain very modern poems, this process can go so far that the intelligible unity of speech is altogether rejected as an inappropriate demand. I think this is a mistake, for the unity of sense is retained wherever speech exists. But this unity is concentrated in a complex fashion. It almost seems as if we cannot

really perceive the "things" named, since the order of the words can
neither be accommodated to the unity of a train of thought nor let
themselves be dissolved into a unified image. And yet it is precisely
the force of the semantic field, the tension between the tonal and the
significative forces of language as they encounter and change place
with one another, that constitutes the whole. Words evoke images,
which may well accumulate, intersect with one another, and cancel
one another out, but which remain images nevertheless. There is not
a single word in a poem that does not intend what it means. Yet at
the same time, it sets itself back upon itself to prevent it slipping into
prose and the rhetoric that accompanies it. This is the claim and
legitimation of "pure poetry."

Naturally, "pure poetry" is an extreme case that enables us to
describe the other forms of poetic speech as well. The complete
scale of translatability ascends from lyric poetry through epic and
tragedy – a special case of the transition into visibility[8] – leading up
to the novel and any demanding prose. In all these cases, it is not
simply the various linguistic means described above that insure the
stability of the work. Here we are concerned respectively with a
reciting or a staging of the work, a novelist or an author who, like an
orator, speaks in a literary way. Consequently, it is correspondingly
easier to translate such forms. Yet even within the genre of lyric
poetry, there are forms like the *Lied,* which share with musical song
the stylistic means of the strophe and the refrain, or like the
politically engaged ballad, which employs these same rhetorical
forms and others as well. Nevertheless, even among these cases,
when we look at them in terms of their use of language, the case of
"pure poetry" remains definitive: so much so that the lyrical form of
the *Lied* can rarely be transferred into the medium of music without
loss, least of all where it is song in its own right. For then it has its
own "tone," as Hölderlin says,[9] to such an extent that it cannot be
transposed into any other melodic form. The same criterion is to be
applied to "engaged" poetry, and indeed, primarily to it. For all
direction to a goal as we find it in military or revolutionary poetry is
clearly distinguished from what is to be called "art," and for no
other reason than that insofar as it is purely directed to a goal, it
manifestly lacks the concentrated form of poetry. This also provides
the basis for the simultaneity of poetry through the ages, filtering
down across historical distance, continually returning and renewing
itself in the course of time. Although its contemporary relevance is

dead – and in the case of Greek tragedy, its musical and choreographical accompaniment has passed away – the pure text lives on
because it stands on its own account as a form of language.

What has all this to do with philosophy and the proximity between poetry and thought? What is language in the context of
philosophy? The only sensible course, in accordance with the same
phenomenological principle of the extreme case, is to take as our
object dialectic, especially in its Hegelian form. In this case, we distance ourselves from everyday speech in a quite different way. The
problem is not that everyday prose threatens to infiltrate the
language of the concept, but that the logic of the proposition takes
us in the wrong direction. As Hegel expressed the matter, "The
proposition in the form of a judgment is not suited to express
speculative truths."[10] What Hegel means by this remark is by no
means limited to the peculiar nature of his own dialectical method.
On the contrary, Hegel here exposes the common characteristic of
all philosophizing, at least since Plato's "turn" toward the *logoi*.[11] His
own dialectical method only represents a particular kind of philosophizing. It is the common presupposition of all philosophizing that
philosophy as such does not possess a language that is adequate to the
task assigned to it. Of course, in philosophy as in all speech, we cannot avoid the form of the proposition, the logical structure of pred-
ication in which a predicate is referred to a given subject. Yet this
form constitutes a misleading presupposition and suggests that the
object of philosophy is given and known in advance, like the processes and things that we observe in the world. But philosophy
moves exclusively in the medium of the concept: "in Ideas, through
Ideas, toward Ideas."[12] The relation that these concepts have to one
another is not explicated through "external" reflection, which
envisages the concept of the subject from without, that is, from this
or that "point of view." Because of the arbitrariness of this way of
looking at the matter, where one attribute or another is predicated
of a subject, Hegel describes such "external reflection" as precisely
the "sophistry of perception."[13] On the contrary, the medium of
philosophy is speculation as the mirror-play of the categories
through which the matter of thought is immanently and dynamically
articulated. It is immanent because as being and as spirit it tends
toward the concept intended by thought as a concrete totality. Hegel
considered Plato's *Parmenides* to be the greatest masterpiece of
ancient dialectic, precisely because in this work Plato proved the

impossibility of determining any single Idea by itself, independently of the totality of Ideas. Hegel also correctly understood that the Aristotelian logic of definition as the instrument for all conceptual clarification of experience also reaches its limits in the realm of philosophical principles. These first principles cannot be classified, but can only be approached by a quite different kind of reflection which Aristotle, following Plato, called *Nous*.[14] For all their variety, these "first" most comprehensive categories, which are transcendental in the sense that they go beyond every particular realm as delimited by the genus, constitute a unity. Hegel describes them all with the striking singular term, "the category."[15] They are all "definitions of the Absolute," rather than definitions of things or kinds of thing in the manner of Aristotle's classificatory logic, according to which the essence of a thing is determined by the concept of the genus and the specific difference.[16] These categories represent boundaries that bind and delimit in the literal sense of the word *Horos*.[17] They are boundaries that are only defined reciprocally within the totality of the concept, and they only represent the whole truth of the concept when they are all taken together. Such speculative propositions mirror the *Aufhebung* or sublation of their own immanent positing. They are like the sayings of Heraclitus which express the One, the sole wisdom, in a contradictory form. They preserve the thought within themselves by recovering it from all externalization in such a way that it is reflected "into itself." The language of philosophy is a language that sublates itself, saying nothing and turning towards the whole at one and the same time.

Just as the language of "pure poetry" is a standard and a limiting case that leaves behind all prose, or rather all customary rhetorical figures, so the Hegelian dialectic is both a standard and a limiting case. Hegel's own attempt by means of the dialectically mediated progression of thought to contain this limit within the parameters of a Cartesian methodology still remains only an approach. Perhaps this attempt is limited in the same way that the interpretation of any poem is limited. In any case, Hegel was well aware that the rich totality of thought remains a task that can never be completed. He himself talked about the possibility of improving his logic, and frequently replaced earlier dialectical derivations with different ones. Like every continuum, the continuum of thought is infinitely divisible. And poetry? It is not simply that no poem can ever be given an exhaustive interpretation; the idea of "pure poetry" itself remains a never-to-be-completed task for poetic composition. In the final analysis, this is true of every poem. Mallarmé, the originator of "pure poetry," seems to have been aware of this correspondence between poetry and philosophy. At least we know that he spent some years in an intensive study of Hegel, and through his irreplaceable works, he was able to capture in language the encounter with nothingness as well as the invocation of the Absolute. Self-bestowal and self-withdrawal – such a dialectic of uncovering and withdrawal seems to hold sway in the mystery of language, both for poets and for philosophers, from Plato to Heidegger.

Thus both the poetical and philosophical types of speech share a common feature: they cannot be "false." For there is no external standard against which they can be measured and to which they might correspond. Yet they are far from arbitrary. They represent a unique kind of risk, for they can fail to live up to themselves. In both cases, this happens not because they fail to correspond to the facts, but because their word proves to be "empty." In the case of poetry, this occurs when, instead of sounding right, it merely sounds like other poetry or like the rhetoric of everday life. In the case of philosophy, this occurs when philosophical language gets caught up in purely formal argumentation or degenerates into empty sophistry.

In both these inferior forms of language – the poem that is not a poem because it does not have its "own" tone, and the empty formulae of a thinking that does not touch on the matter of thought – the word breaks. Where the word fulfills itself and becomes language, we must take it at its word.

10. Aesthetic and religious experience

Like all other kinds of experience, aesthetic and religious experience seek expression in language. If we bear in mind their original Greek meaning, the words *poetry*, literally a making through the word, and *theology*, literally speech about the divine, make the point. However, we must not simply assume that poetic and religious speech are completely different from one another. Anyone who is familiar with Greek theology and poetry knows very well that it is quite impossible to distinguish between the language of poetry and that of the mythological tradition. For it was precisely the poets themselves who mediated that tradition. A question posed in the form "poetic *or* religious language?" is even less appropriate when we confront the Indian or Chinese traditions of thought, for there we cannot even ask whether we are dealing with poetry, religion, or philosophy. The fraught dispute between the religious and poetic tradition on the one hand and the newly emergent claims of science and philosophy on the other is clearly a characteristic feature of intellectual and spiritual development in the West. It was precisely this tension that ultimately led to the distinction between poetic and religious speech. We cannot therefore thematize the problem involved here in an abstract and ahistorical sense. Rather, we must pose the question concerning the relationship between these kinds of speech and the experience that underlies them from within the Christian tradition of the West.

Furthermore, this question arises for us because it is in the Judaeo-Christian tradition that we first encounter a religion based upon a holy book, a set of writings with canonical validity. In English, for example, the word "scripture" is immediately understood to mean the Bible.

It is only in this context that our theme becomes a pressing question at all. It would be quite meaningless to ask whether Lao-Tze should be regarded principally as a poet, a religious teacher, or a philosopher.

Our theme thus concerns a question that is by no means a self-evident one. Rather it implies a definite pre-understanding that is to be clarified. And insofar as it is a question concerning speech and written language, it is a hermeneutic theme. "Hermeneutics" is a word that had become quite common in the eighteenth century, but which then virtually disappeared for a hundred years. Originally it was almost a word of everyday language, so that it could be applied to someone whom we would describe as an understanding sort of person, someone who knows how to relate to another human being and perceive what is only tacit and not explicitly expressed by the other. Even Schleiermacher, the famous founder of universal hermeneutics, repeatedly claims that the art of hermeneutics is also indispensable in our social life. As he says, "Who could move in the company of exceptionally gifted persons without endeavoring to hear between their words, as it were, just as we read between the lines of original and tightly written books? Who does not try in a meaningful conversation, which may in certain respects be an important act worthy of an equally close examination, to lift out its main points . . . ?"[1]

Thus the hermeneutic art is in fact the art of understanding something that appears alien and unintelligible to us.

In our experience of life generally, we face this task at its most extreme whenever we have to let something be said to us. We might well say that learning how to do this properly is a never-ending task laid upon each of us in our own lives. But even if we ignore this moral inhibition caused by our self regard, we can certainly claim that we encounter different levels of difficulty in the task of understanding, and that it is especially difficult where we must reawaken the petrified language of writing so that it speaks anew. To that extent, it is clear that understanding represents a particular task whenever we are confronted by texts or anything that has been committed to writing – the task is to let the text speak to us once again.

Of course, it is not the mere fact that something is written down that is decisive here. It is certainly true that all forms of writing have to be brought to speak. Yet the usual function of writing lies in its referring back to some original act of saying, so that in this sense the text does not claim to speak by virtue of its own power. When I read the notes that someone has made, it is the speaker rather than the text that is, as it were, to be brought to speak again. However, in the case of "literary" texts (in the broadest sense), it is clearly not the speaker who is to speak again, but precisely the text, the message, the communication itself. How this comes about is a problem in its own right. In fact, we call writing an *art* when poetry or literature succeeds in "speaking" to us. We might ask how the artist of the written word brings it about that his text speaks in its own right, so that we feel no need to refer back to the original act of speech, the living word. Of course, the situation is essentially different as far as the texts of the Judaeo-Christian tradition are concerned. What speaks to us in Holy Scripture certainly does not rest primarily upon the art of writing, but upon the authority of the one who speaks to us in the Church.

If we wish to analyze the problem of "poetic and religious speech," we find ourselves confronted by two kinds of special texts. We must clearly appreciate the particular implications of what these different kinds of texts represent. First of all, there is the text that we call "literature" in the narrow sense. It is what I call an "eminent" text, for it does not resemble the written notes we make when we wish to preserve a written record of the lecture, for example, or write a letter instead of making an oral communication. In all these cases, the written form refers back to the original speech as a reminder of our own thought. An eminent text, on the other hand, is one that we intend as a text, so that we point to it as something that "stands written."[2]

Of course, we have to admit that linguistic usage allows us to apply the word "text" outside such eminent cases as the Biblical, the legal, or the "literary" text. But that merely reflects the "technical" task of understanding insofar as the work of the interpreter defines the object to be understood as a text, and this simply represents the "technical" givenness of the text rather than the autonomy of "literature." A genuine text, on the other hand, is exactly what the word literally says: a woven texture that holds together. Such language, if it really is a proper text, holds together in such a way that it "stands" in its own right and no longer refers back to an original, more authentic saying, nor points beyond itself to a more authentic experience of reality. Wherever that happens without the

support of legal or ecclesiastical practices, we have an autonomous "text."

We took as our point of departure the fact that in the Greek tradition, it is impossible to separate specifically poetic and religious
language. Of course, there was cultic ritual along with its appropriate linguistic forms of expression, but it was through poetry that
the real religious tradition of the Greeks was transmitted. We call
this a mythical tradition, because it demands no other validation
beyond the fact that it is told. The original stories are concerned
with the deeds of gods and heroes. But the form in which these
stories are originally told, retold, and told yet again, always represents a fresh interpretation. This includes even the critique of the
gods that we constantly find in the great Greek poets who followed
the age of epic composition - we remember the criticism of the
behavior of the Homeric gods, for example. The indissoluble unity
of religious and poetic speech is clearly seen in the fact that even the
philosophical critique of the religious tradition remains in the last
analysis a form of theology too. If Plato can forge his myths with
unique mastery from an elaborate combination of traditional
religious themes with philosophical concepts, he thereby preserves
the characteristic feature of the Greek tradition as a whole: its ability
to combine the true and the false, to announce higher things while
enjoying the freedom of play.

The self-understanding of Greek poetry begins with Hesiod's
proem in which the muses appear before the poet and make their
promises to him: they are capable of telling both much that is false
and much that is true.[3] These lines are peculiarly ambiguous, so that
anyone with an ear for poetry cannot fail to see what this means: the
muses always tell us both the true and the false (even if the poet
invokes them to vouch for the truth of his theogony). The problem
is already clearly revealed here. What sort of claim to truth is
coupled with the poet's freedom of invention? This is a question
with which we are quite familiar. We must not let ourselves be
misled by an all too modernistic concept of the aesthetic or purely
poetical, as if the situation had ever been any different, as if poetry
had ever merely consisted in the formal mastery of linguistic means
rather than in presenting something true *through* the formal mastery
of language. In my previous investigations, this is what I have somewhat inelegantly called "aesthetic nondifferentiation": it belongs to

the essence of poetic understanding that we do not specifically
attend to the process of composition as such, the *exergasia* (to employ
a term from Greek painting). On the contrary, the inevitable
formal – linguistic articulation communicates a content and elevates
that content into a vivid and tangible presence so that it entirely
fulfills us.

We must ask again how this relates to the beginnings of Greek
thought. Where does myth stand in relation to poetry and truth? I
would say that the primary thing about myth is the act of telling
itself. This is a bold claim for someone who was in Marburg in the
1920s (and so shared the friendship of Rudolf Bultmann), but I must
express it in this way. We should always be clear about what is
involved in such telling: it is an intrinsically inexhaustible process
that can go on indefinitely. A storyteller who does not manage to
give the impression that he could in principle continue his story is
not a real storyteller at all. This means that when stories are told
concerning the gods, the very form of transmission implies the
moment of continuation – "and so forth" – which goes beyond what
has already been said to something that still lies beyond it. The
dimension of the divine that is recounted in stories – the behavior of
the gods and their dealings with men and heroes – yields an infinite
range of possibilities for storytelling, and the epic form of literature
is an expression of this range.

A further use of speech that is closely connected with this seems
to be the invocation, or perhaps we might simply say, the naming
itself. Naming – in the sense in which I am using the word in connection with the act of invocation – is clearly not to be confused
with that process of naming all things through which Adam took
possession of the created world. The experience with which we are
here concerned is that of the invocation. Homer constantly recounts
how mortals call upon the gods by name although they are fully
aware that they do not know whether they are really calling upon
them with the right name. "Zeus, or however you wish to be called"
is a familiar catch-phrase of epic invocation. Such invocation clearly
points beyond what we know and reveals something that remains
hidden from our grasp, something at least that exceeds what we
know about it. The pleasure the poet takes in naming, in explicitly
recounting names as such, is an essential moment of the epic attitude
of the teller, as both Homer and Hesiod clearly demonstrate.

Now the step from this kind of mythical and poetical tradition to "literature" is – if I may condense it into a formula – the step from the recounting of stories to the work. Of course, the concept of the work and of the work of art is not without problems. As is well known, the attempt has been made in contemporary progressive aesthetics to eliminate the concept of the work entirely. It has been claimed that the essential thing is not the work which allows the "consumer" a certain distance from which to contemplate and enjoy art, but the act of shock itself. Nevertheless, I believe there are good hermeneutic reasons for saying that the work still remains the work. Any identifiable configuration to which we can apply such expressions as "beautiful," "well-wrought," "eloquent," and so on, has already been identified in its own right as soon as we characterize it in this way. I do not claim that this transition to the work belongs to the religious cult: the ritual and ceremony, all forms and expressions of religious observance that are already established, can be repeated again and again according to hallowed custom without anybody feeling it necessary to pass judgment upon them. On the other hand, it is true that even a mobile enjoys an identity of its own, just as a unique dance, a bravura performance, or an organ improvisation does. It is perfectly possible to describe such a thing as "beautiful" or as "vacuous," as the case may be. Something presents itself here as something upon which we pass judgment. Even if it has only been seen or heard once, it still represents something that has taken shape as a work. I would say that we can observe such a gradual transition from ritual to the "work" in the development of Greek literature, a transition that eventually culminates in a work written to be read. We can trace the process in which all forms of poetic and religious speech, indissolubly connected with one another, begin to take shape as works: in the development of rhapsodic performance that went beyond ritual; in the choreographical staging of the choral lyric, which had certainly emerged from the observance of everyday religious practice; in the spectacle of tragedy, which was a special occasion in its own right for which prizes were awarded even though it was embedded in the context of religious life. In short, we can see that all these things already find themselves on the road to the autonomy of the text, so that their transition to written works, and works principally intended for reading, is neither surprising nor difficult to see.

What, though, is actually implied by the fact that something has finally become "literature," that it has taken shape as a text or a work in such a way that it can be brought to speak as "literature"? That we are here really dealing with a work that has become autonomous – and not with the words of an individual author – when we let it speak to us is shown by the fact that any reproduction – even on the part of the author or reader – contains an inappropriate contingent moment. A genuine text in this eminent sense is never measured against the original way in which it was originally said. There is always something disturbing about hearing a poet reading his own works: we ask why the poet sounds just like *this* and why he performs it in just this kind of way. Every speaker of a "text" knows that no possible vocal realization – not even his own – can ever completely satisfy our inner ear. The text has acquired an ideality that cannot be obviated by any possible realization.

The problem of theatrical "reproduction" in the sense of a scenic realization is something else that equally confirms the ideality of "literature." By virtue of a kind of second creation, an autonomous level of reality here comes into play. But even a dramatic text still remains, on account of the ideality of its literary form, the criterion for such "secondary" creations. We might think here of the conception of a role and the amount of leeway that the poetic text permits us. But there is a complex problem of overlay here between one ideality and another which I cannot pursue at the moment. Yet I would like to draw one general conclusion from the ideality involved in the "speaking character" of texts to which no speaker can ever correspond. The ideal of texts speaking as texts ultimately implies their untranslatability.

It is obvious that "literature," compared with anything else handed down in written form, is characterized by the fact that its actual linguistic manifestation, and not merely its "meaning," is what matters. This is why the translation of literary texts itself represents a literary – poetic task that can only ever achieve an approximation to the original. Obviously, we meet the extreme case of a "literature" that almost completely defies translation in "pure poetry," the very ideal of symbolist lyric poetry. Poetry of this kind is a radical consequence of a form of language that abandons the rhetorical element along with the usual linguistic means by which content is communicated. When sound and sense are in perfect equilibrium as centers of gravity, so that the unity of speech is achieved without any other syntactic means whatsoever – and in a certain sense this was Mallarmé's ideal – that does not mean that the unified sense of speech has been endangered or eliminated. That seems to me to be a misunderstanding. But this ideal does reject any kind of speech in which language does not speak to us in its unimpaired sensuous ideality, and ideality that cannot, as we saw, be fully attained by any realization. Here the work seems to have grown out of the preliterary forms in which myth and legend were once communicated to the point where "everything is a symbol."[4]

In a second step, I should like to juxtapose the written text and the holy book according to the formula: the original historical story becomes the original proclamation. The word *proclamation* is here meant to carry its full meaning of a "binding document." This clearly represents something quite new. Why is this testament in the form of a binding document necessary? In our own Western tradition, we know of no ancient religion that recognized the idea of false gods. In these religions, the gods represented a realm of being "beyond" the everyday, the sphere of the divine that could be approached by ever-new interpretations and illustrations of a poetic and "philosophical" kind. The incontestable reality of religious experience was the presupposition of all this: other peoples could not but believe in this overpowering reality of the divine. Consequently the well-known adoption of the gods of vanquished peoples or conquered cities into the pantheon of the Roman gods was nothing strange. It was not simply a manifestation of political prudence, but an expression of a quite general attitude to the universal presence of the divine. As far as the revealed religions are concerned, the situation is quite different. If I can ignore Islam, whose religious proclamation represents a special problem that I cannot go into now since I have no knowledge of Arabic whatsoever, the term "revealed religion" can really only be applied to the Jewish and Christian religions. Both religions possess an original canonic document that does not simply tell a history but rather testifies to it. The original history of the chosen people is not a story of a transcendent divine world like those we find in the mythical traditions of other religions. The Old Testament claims to be the word of God, an obligation, a law, a pledge based upon the observance of the law: the wrath of God and the faithfulness that strengthens the promise belong together. The scriptures testify to the faithfulness of the covenant in the relation of law and obedience to the law. And in the second century, it was precisely those writings that, as their founding document, held the religious community of the Jews together.

Let us now compare the original Christian story with the original history of the Jewish people. The "new covenant" is no longer like the old: instead of "obedience" and "law," we must now speak of *kerygma* – message – and "faith." If I wanted to give a secular illustration of the structural relationship between the message and the faith in order to distinguish it from the relation of law and obedience found in the Old Testament, I would draw attention to the nature of promising. Of course, a promise is something binding, but it is not like the law, which is binding in the sense that everyone has to obey it. The new covenant is not simply the contractual faithfulness between two parties, either. It is not simply that the one who promises freely enters into a relationship. It is not simply the one who promises who is free in this sense, for all promising is essentially oriented toward freedom. Not only is it impossible to enforce its fulfillment by legal means, as we could in the case of a contract, it only really becomes a promise at all if and when it is accepted. Thus we are all familiar with the situation in which someone promises too much and we benevolently advise them not to promise it at all. It is the acceptance alone that gives binding validity to the promise, and not anything that we might perform in addition. This seems to me to provide a good secular, structural analogy for the concept of faith. The gospel message is freely proferred and only becomes the good news for one who accepts it.

If I may describe the matter this way – without any theological expertise – it is possible to draw a hermeneutic conclusion. If the Christian message does represent such a freely made offer, a free promise, which is directed at each of us although we have no claim on it, then the task of proclaiming it is implied by our acceptance of it. Proclaiming the message does not mean merely repeating it. Anyone who proclaims the message in a senseless way, that is, in a literal way that is unrelated to a concrete context so that it receives a false interpretation in a given situation, is not really proclaiming it at all. Proclaiming the message requires that we understand what it means and whom it is addressed to. That is why it must be proclaimed in such a way that it actually reaches the person to whom it is directed. Thus, understanding belongs essentially to the communication of the message and gives rise to intelligent transmission. In the last analysis that means that it requires translation. Thus, universal translatability belongs to the essence of the Christian message. The missionary task of the Christian Church necessarily follows from the nature of the gospel message itself. And if following the message means transmitting it to another in such a way that it is understood, then it is a fundamental and rational necessity to translate the Bible into the vernacular and ultimately to proclaim the gospel in every language. Thus we have the original Greek version of the Gospel story, the introduction of Latin translations, the translation into Gothic, and so on. Eventually, the Reformation carried this missionary task to its ultimate conclusion.

The proclamation of the gospel message seems to me to be the foundation upon which all the different forms of religious speech and usage in the Christian tradition are defined. The public proclamation takes the form of the sermon. All forms of cultic speech in the Christian order of service, Catholic or in particular Protestant, ultimately serve the task of proclaiming the paradoxical message of faith. Here we meet in its most acute form the difficulty that we mentioned above, of letting something be said to us. For the message we hear is an incredible one that does not build upon our natural understanding of death and immortality, nor upon salvation and redemption as the usual consolations of religion do. On the contrary, the Christian message represents a challenge that shatters all our natural expectations, for it does not correspond to our guiding ideas of reward and punishment or merit and blame. Flacius, the founder of Protestant hermeneutics in Wittenberg, rightly showed, it seems to me, that the genuine task of hermeneutics arises from the peculiar nature of the Christian proclamation. All the strange features that we encounter in the Bible, the remoteness of the language, the grammar, the customs, and so on, certainly require specialist knowledge in order to facilitate a better understanding of this alien text. But the real task of hermeneutics here is to overcome the fundamental strangeness and alien quality that lies in the Christian message itself, culminating in the idea that even faith is exclusively a gift of divine grace so that all our criteria of merit and worth lose their significance. This is directed against *any* natural understanding of human nature. For this reason, because we are here solely concerned with this challenge of faith, it seems to me that all forms of religious speech that we encounter in Christianity represent aids to faith.

In the Protestant order of service, this is expressed by the central role of the sermon. And yet all the other forms of Christian worship, the whole life of the Church, in the last analysis represent aids to

faith: hymns, prayers, blessings, the eucharist, and all the other
aspects of the liturgy. The life of the community means solidarity in
the faith, and this has found dogmatic expression in the doctrine of
the Holy Spirit. Yet in relation to all these other forms of religious
life, the sermon is unique in being the word of an individual who
certainly subscribes to the belief of the Church, but who bears witness as an individual and speaks publicly as a helper of the word.
That is why the sermon is the real acme of ecclesiastic rhetoric in
which one individual speaks to many and seeks to communicate to
them the message of salvation.

   The conclusion I wish to draw from this juxtaposition is that even
if it is true that in the Christian tradition poetic and religious speech
have diverged from one another to become two different kinds of
speech, this does not mean that religious content ceases to be communicated through poetry. Nor, conversely, does it mean that
religious texts cannot also have a poetic – literary aspect that marks
them off from other religious texts. This leads to our final task, that
of rendering intelligible the mutual interference of these two
aspects. For this purpose, I would like to supplement the concept of
the symbolic, which already plays a central role in the theory of art
as well as in the phenomenology of religion, with the counterconcept of the sign, which I would like to endow with a new dignity.

   We can define the symbol as that through which someone or
something is known and recognized. This reflects the original meaning of the Greek word, where the "symbol" played the familiar role
of a kind of passport for the ancient world. It is obviously in a similar
sense that we talk about religious symbols. A congregation understands its symbols and finds confirmation of itself in that recognition. When classical German aesthetics gave a universally expanded
significance to the concept of the symbol which originally derived
from Christian Platonism, but later became quite common in the
confessional religious disputes of the sixteenth century, it was
following the original meaning of the word "symbol" as something
that facilitates recognition. In the ecclesiastical context, that meant
shared articles of belief, whereas today the symbolic power of the
work of art is defined the other way round: it does not perform the
representative function of pointing to something already universally
shared, but precisely in awakening a shared consciousness of something through its own expressive power. The experience that "this is
you" can range from the most terrifying intensity of tragic catas-

trophe to the lightest touch of meaning, from the encounter with King Oedipus to a confrontation with one of the silently brooding paintings of Mondrian: in all these cases, we become conscious of something shared. The recognition that the work of art procures for us is always an expansion of that infinite process of making ourselves at home in the world which is the human lot.

The situation is quite different in relation to the proclamation of the good news and the messianic promise. What is the meaning of the "this is you" in the context of the incarnation and Easter message? It is certainly not a further step in the process of making ourselves at home in the world, even in tragic experience of catharsis through pity and fear. It is not the infinite wealth of life possibilities that is encountered in such a "this is you," but rather the extreme poverty of the *Ecce homo*. The expression must be given a quite different emphasis here: "this is you" – a man helplessly exposed to suffering and death. It is precisely in the face of this infinite withholding of happiness that the Easter message is to become the Good News.

The symbolic structure of these two experiences of recognition appears to be the same, yet the kind of familiarity upon which the act of recognition rests is in each case fundamentally different. The claim of the Christian message – and this is what gives it its exclusivity – is that it alone has really overcome death through the proclamation of the representative suffering and death of Jesus as a redemptive act. In the face of this exclusive claim, all the sublime solemnity and festive transfiguration involved in the veneration of the dead that was cultivated by the older religious cultures seems like one great flight from death. We remember how Novalis made this the point of departure for his philosophical vision of history in his "Hymns to the Night."

Now I think it is reasonable to try to articulate this ambiguity and difference involved in the recognition "this is you" by means of the concept of the sign. Of course, in this connection it is necessary to abstract entirely from the whole art and science of signs that we call semantics and semiotics. I am here talking about signs in the religious sense. It is not simply a question of the pietistic tradition of reading the Bible, where we ponder the religious language of holy scripture in the expectation of receiving a sign. Rather, it seems to me a universal challenge implied by the acceptance of the Christian message, something that Luther expressed in the formula *pro me*.

There is more involved here than merely assembling before shared symbols. This may well be one of the results and it is certainly an element of all cult in any religion, but a sign is something only given to one who is ready to accept it as such.

A friend once told me a story that is not a particulary flattering one for churchmen, but is rather comforting all the same: one day a man who was simple and devout in his own way, an internationally famous type designer, was taking part in a Protestant service with a friend of mine. As they left the church, my friend said to him, "Didn't the pastor prattle on?" To which the other replied in surprise, "That may well be, but I didn't notice it." Clearly, the man had really listened to the sermon, to what it was trying to communicate of the gospel message. Hence only the message as such existed for him. This is an illustration of what I mean by a sign. It is not something that everyone has been able to see, not something to which one can refer, and yet, if it is taken as a sign, there is something incontestably certain about it. There is a saying of Heraclitus that illuminates this matter very well: "The Delphic god neither reveals nor conceals, but gives a sign."[5] One needs only to understand what "giving a sign" means here. It is not something that takes the place of seeing, for what distinguishes it precisely from all reports or from its opposite, silence, is the fact that what is shown is only accessible to the one who looks for himself and actually sees something there.

Without introducing the concept of a sign, we cannot properly describe the real difference between poetic and religious speech as it has taken shape in the course of Christian history and led to the extension of the concept of symbol beyond the religious context. It is well known that whereas in antiquity, art represented a self-evident medium for the transmission of religious truth, the recognition of art posed a very serious problem in the context of the Christian world. The visual and plastic arts became particularly problematic on account of the Jewish heritage which lived on in the history of the Christian church. Eventually, Christianity did in fact decide in favor of the image, and thus the visual and plastic arts. The decision was justified by the priority given to the written proclamation of the word, and thus the principle that art serve as an aid to faith came to the fore. The visual arts functioned as a *Biblia Pauperum*, as a kind of script for the illiterate. Similarly, the art of music played a significant role in Christian ritual – as a part of the liturgy itself, as an expression and affirmation of the congregation, whether in the sung mass and its increasingly elaborate development, or in the more heartfelt form of the rather ponderous congregational chorales of the Protestant service. But poetry and poetic qualities can also be encountered in the context of religious speech. Thus we admire the high quality of Hebrew poetry, which was wedded so powerfully and intimately to the language of religious tradition that no conflict was felt here. In the end we should also recognize that the peculiar way in which the original sources of the New Testament tell their story illustrates the art of narration. Perhaps it cannot compare with the very high level of many Old Testament texts, but there are passages in the New Testament with a densely wrought narrative quality, like many of the parables in the gospel of Mark. Of course, that does not alter the fact that, considered in the Biblical context, this is not really an autonomous text of literature. The message that is told here intends to be heard as the good news. But that means that it speaks to me as a sign rather than as a symbolic form of recognition.

In all cases, it would be quite meaningless to construct an opposition between art and religion, or even between poetic and religious speech, or to attempt to deny any claim to truth in what art says to us. In every expression of art, something is revealed, is known, is recognized. There is always a disturbing quality to this recognition, an amazement amounting almost to horror, that such things can befall human beings and that human beings can achieve such things. At the same time, the claim of the Christian message transcends this and points in the opposite direction: it shows what we cannot achieve. This is what gives rise to its specific claim and accounts for the radicality of its message. If the uniqueness of the gospel message lies in the fact that it must be accepted against all expectation and hope, then we can also understand the radicality of the Enlightenment which grew out of Christianity. For the first time in the history of mankind, religion itself is declared to be redundant and denounced as an act of betrayal or self-betrayal.

Appendix

Intuition and vividness

Translated by Dan Tate

Even a glance at the history of aesthetics teaches that art and literature are bound up with the concept of intuition and, at least in the latter case, with the conceptual value of vividness.[1] Certainly aesthetics is one of the youngest philosophical disciplines, yet we cannot fail to see that the grounding of aesthetics went hand in hand with its delimitation from concepts and conceptual knowledge – and with that, the concept of intuition underwent a decisive reevaluation. Even Baumgarten's formulation of a *cognitio sensitiva,* which characterizes the *pulchre cogitare,* points in this direction.[2] Moreover, Kant's *Critique of Judgment* not only conceives aesthetic pleasure as entirely "without concept," but also underscores the concept of imagination in the play of the cognitive faculties that constitutes aesthetic delight. "Intuition" here means nothing but a "representation of imagination."[3]

To be sure, the Kantian concept of intuition receives its real terminological stamp not in the context of aesthetics, but in the center of the *Critique of Pure Reason.* There it forms the critical counterpart to the concept of "concept" as a corrective to rationalist metaphysics. According to Kant's doctrine, something can be "given" to finite human beings only through space and time, the forms of intuition. Ultimately, this doctrine legitimates "intellectual intuition" (which Kant's idealist successors made so essential) as the distinctive feature of the "infinite intellect" that is not granted to human beings. In Kant's conception, the infinite intellect "sees into being" *(ins Sein schaut)* the thoughts that it thinks, just as later, Fichte's transcendental reflection understands intuition as an active seeing into *(Hinshauen).* Yet all of that is a part of Kant's critique of metaphysical knowledge. The *Critique of Pure Reason* demonstrates that concepts without intuition are empty and incapable of yielding knowledge.

Even though Kant's critical delimitation of intuition ties finite intuition to the sensible given in perception, it should not be forgotten that "imagination" is not restricted to its function in theoretical knowledge. Imagination is the general capacity to have an "intuition (representation) even with our the presence of the object."[4] Thus it is only from the perspective of imagination that intuition becomes a problem in the realm of art and aesthetics.

The site of the problematic would thus be missed right from the outset if the concept of perception or even that of perceptual judgment were taken as the point of departure. Even with theoretical knowledge, we must not overlook the fact that for Kant, "intuition" is just as much an analytic element of cognitive judgment as the "concept" is, and that knowledge is only accomplished through their cooperation. Within the framework of the *Critique of Pure Reason,* of course, cooperation stands in service to theoretical knowledge. In the case of aesthetic delight, by contrast, it is a matter of the "free" play of the cognitive faculties. But cooperation with the understanding and its concepts nonetheless belongs to the self-evident conditions of both aesthetic delight and the art of genius. Here, however, intuition is not related to a given object.

It is not accidental, therefore, that I have combined the concept of "intuition" with that of "vividness" in the title of my essay. The point is that intuition, as an aesthetic problem, must not be viewed from the standpoint of epistemological inquiry, but is rather related to the broader realm of imagination in its "free" play and productivity. It thus seems to me important from the start not to limit our viewpoint to visual objects or visual works of art, but to keep the linguistic arts – above all poetry – in mind. For it is here, in the use of language, in rhetoric and literature, that the concept "vivid" is truly at home: namely, as a special quality of description and narration such that we see "before us," so to speak, what is not as such seen, but is only told.

That is clearly an aesthetic quality. The words *anschauen* (to intuit) and *schauen* (to look upon), both related to the English word *show*, are connected in some way with the German word for the beautiful – *das Schöne. Anschauen* thus refers, as so many German words do, to the spere of the visible, but with a peculiarly indeterminate direction toward what is there to be seen. Thus the word was first used for the mystic's vision of God *(Gottesschau)*. We also encounter it in this meaning in contemporary usage like *Schauplatz* (theater) and *Schaubühne* (stage), as well as in phrases like *etwas anschauen* (to look upon something), *etwas beschauen* (to contemplate something), or even *zuschauen* (to watch). In all of these usages of the word, we cannot miss the temporal component of tarrying and dwelling, which our absorption in the act of intuition implies. I am reminded here of Hegel's poetic effort, *Eleusis,* which has the line "Sense loses itself in intuition."[5]

In the context of philosophical reflection and the course of its tradition, German words are more or less artificially assigned to Greco-Roman words and concepts. Thus the mystic's vision of God is traced back to the *videre deum per essentiam* which charaterizes the *status beatitudinus* and, from there, back to the Latin equivalents for the Greek *nous: intellectus* and *intelligentia.* The corresponding Latin terms take us back to the Classical conceptual world of *logos, nous, dianoia, theoria,* and *phronesis.* It will be helpful to keep these semantic fields in mind in order to secure for the concept of intuition its proper breadth.

It might at first appear that such a return to Greek thought threatens instead to narrow that concept. The opposition of sensible and intelligible intuition, of *aisthesis* and *noesis,* which goes back to Plato, reminds us of the influence that the Platonic heritage – more or less unconsciously – exerts upon modern thought. On the one hand, Plato's distinction between the sensible and the intelligible was a great achievement that enabled mathematics to understand itself for the first time. On the other hand, the distinction meant the introduction of a concept of intuition formed according to the model of sense perception, and it seemed to imply thereby its exclusive opposition to conceptual thought. Actually, Kant's critical turn against the rationalism of the eighteenth century represents (as the title of his dissertation already reveals[6]) the conscious adoption of such Platonism. However, the application of the concepts of the sensible and the intelligible to the experience of art does not seem to be really appropriate. In fact, Kant avoids this insofar as he emphasizes the play of the cognitive faculties and does not determine the object of aesthetic delight in terms of the opposition of sense and reason. So much is obvious from Sections Three and Four of the *Critique of Judgment.* Of course, the Platonic heritage continues to make itself felt wherever the concept of intuition, oriented as it is toward sense perception, is extended to conceptual knowledge and is treated critically as intellectual intuition. It seems to me that the adoption of this concept leads to misunderstandings that plague the concept of intuition in the realm of aesthetics and art theory.

In fact, as the immediacy of sensible or intellectual givenness (which Husserl calls "bodily givenness" or the intuitive fulfillment of an intention[7]), intuition is a pure limiting concept, an abstraction from the mediations through which human orientation in the world is achieved. That can already be verified in Aristotle. Even though he understands *aisthesis* as a sense perception, Aristotle can still say that it tends toward the universal: we see a man and not "something white."[8] Conversely, he cannot properly speak of *nous* as having a distinct ontological status – the way he can speak of knowledge, of *techne,* of the rationality of *phronesis,* or even of wisdom. For the ultimate "noetic grasp" of the principles does not occur in its own right, but only in the process of mediating thought.[9] We live in the *logos,* and the *logos,* the linguistic dimension of human being-in-the-world, fulfills itself by making something visible so that the other sees it. The Aristotelian word for this is *deloun,* which contains the "de" root of deictic comportment or showing.[10]

In this way, the abstract opposition of sensible and intellectual intuition – in relation to the opposition of intuition and concept – is in fact transcended. That, in turn, can help us remove from intuition and its associated cognates their exclusive reference to theoretical knowledge and scientific experience, and thus recognize its function in the realm of aesthetics and art theory. When seen against the background of ancient thought, it is obvious that the concept of intuition is not really defined by its relation to the sensible. By taking sensible givenness as its point of departure, modern thought has gone astray. An epistemology that refuses to recognize the formative power of distinction operative in all perception succumbs to a dogmatic concept of objective givenness, and art theory is easily confused by the rationalist concept and counterconcept of a *cognitio sensitiva.* The experience of art cannot be understood in terms of an abstract opposition to conceptual knowledge. This is shown by the fact that poetry is able to take the form of a literature no longer restricted to the spoken word without thereby losing its specific essence. It is not the immediacy of sensible givenness that provides the basis of all the arts, but rather what Kant calls the "representation of the imagination (*CJ,* § 49)," the formative process of intuition together with the resulting formed intuition. The object of ⟨ aesthetics as the theory of art would then be appropriately called *cognitio imaginativa*. For even in aesthetics, it is a question of a kind of cognition. Nevertheless, it is difficult to recognize the cognitive dimension of art on the basis of Kantian presuppositions. One can hardly appeal to the classical distinctions with which Kant's "Analytic of the Beautiful" begins. For the starting point is simply the "standpoint of taste," and that means the ideal of "free" beauty for which decorative art and natural beauty provide the model. From this it would follow that art is seen not as art but as decoration. It seems to me that because neither Adorno nor Bubner see that, they fail to appreciate why Kant's "Analytic of the Beautiful" cannot satisfy the needs of art theory. Consequently, they do not understand why Hegel's *Aesthetics* remains closer to us in spite of the systematizing tendency to which he succumbs.

The situation is much the same when we consider the tendency to abandon the concept of the work, a tendency very much in vogue in contemporary art theory. Both of these positions seem to me to represent an unacceptable foreshortening of aesthetic inquiry. The questions that art theory asks must address the whole, must address art both before it understands itself as "art" and equally after it ceases to understand itself as such. What is it that allows pictures, ⟨ statues, buildings, songs, texts, or dances to appear beautiful, and, if "no longer beautiful," as art nonetheless? "Beauty" does not mean the fulfillment of a specific ideal of the beautiful, whether classical or baroque. Rather, beauty defines art as art: namely, as something that stands out from everything that is purposively established and utilized. Indeed, beauty is nothing but an invitation to intuition. And that is what we call a "work."

Intuiting, however – and this is the point of our inquiry – is in fact not that ideal of theoretical knowledge, the *unus intuitus,* in which something otherwise accessible only in steps is "present" all at once. Nor does intuition correspond to – in Epicurus's phrase – the *athroa epibole,* to which the concept of intuition may be traced.[11] Rather, intuition itself is something that first has to be formed through the process of intuition, a process that implies a certain progression from one thing to another. Kant himself explicitly says that temporal succession cannot be separated from the concept of intuition (*CJ*, §27, p. 98). The act of intuition builds up something so that it "stands" for a while. We must not think, though, that the so-

called visual arts possess the character of intuition in a privileged
sense just because they are realized in visual objects and not in the
fleeting passage of sound or word, while the transitory arts can only
approach the visual arts insofar as they are themselves "vivid." It is
certainly true that one ordinarily praises linguistic presentations, and
particularly narratives, for being vivid. However, one does not
similarly praise pictorial works. It is almost as if the latter were ipso
facto vivid and that therefore only vivid narratives can be praised for
being such.

In fact, what is decisive here is not the distinction between the
"static" and the "transitory" arts, but rather the relation of word
and concept to intuition, which only becomes problematic in the
realm of language. The fact that we would rarely describe music as
vivid is surely instructive. By contrast, a drawing, for example, a
preliminary sketch, is called vivid if we can "vividly imagine" what
is so presented. Clearly, it is the descriptive character of the sketch
or design that allows us to say this, because it vividly captures a certain pictorial character, just as a verbal description does. The
"aesthetic" quality of such a description can serve a practical function, just as the vivid narrative of an historian, however deserving of
aesthetic appreciation, serves to communicate historical knowledge.
Similarly, we would not describe a dramatic dialogue written for the
stage as vivid, for it would actually be presented in front of us. And
it is only with some reservation that we praise the vividness of lyric
poetry, for its affective and tonal values are much more important
than objective description. "*Füllest wieder Busch und Tal still mit
Nebelglanz,*"[12] is indeed "vivid." It is, however, at the same time
much more an affective whole in which everything vividly described, the landscape and the dreaming I, is immersed and en-
veloped. This verse is not a description that allows us to see
something vividly. Such a poetic statement is rather an incantation,
indeed a ritual of the soul, which dissolves all distance.

"Vividness" is thus primarily predicated of descriptions that may
also be given in an abstract form, by signs, schemata, or conceptual
expressions, in which case we demand only that they be clear and
intelligible – not that they be vivid. The additional characteristic –
that descriptions can be vivid – clearly belongs to the "art" of discourse, primarily to narrative and particularly to literature. Vividness is here an authentic presence of that which is narrated: "we
literally see it before us." And yet we also know that here it is the

imaginations of the reader and listener that bring such presence ⟵
about – a singular form of presence, which is surely not that of an
unequivocal and fixed pictorial representation.

The problems concerning the graphic accompaniment of narrative texts of all sorts (including other cases like stage painting as
well) are well known to the aesthetics of book illustration. Illustration must gather the "fertile moment" into an image, and should
thereby stand midway between the autonomy of the image on the
one hand and its reproductive function on the other, which are both
necessary for illustration. The vividness that we praise in a narrative
text, by contrast, is not that of an image that could be reproduced in
words. It is much closer to a restless flux of images that accompanies
our understanding of the text, but that does not finally become a stable intuition, as some kind of result. It is this capacity of the "art" of
language to arouse intuitions in the imagination that establishes the
linguistic work of art in its own right and makes of it a "work" –
like a kind of self-giving intuition – so that such discourse is capable
of cancelling or forgetting any reference to reality that discourse
normally has. There are many different transitional forms here.
Language can also stand out and be described as vivid even when it
does not attempt to be art, but merely a simple report of some real
event. Indeed, the art of anecdote (about which we are tempted to
say that it is too beautiful to be true) can illustrate very well the ⟵
essential issue about these traditional forms. Anecdotes have an
essential relation to history and its participants, even though there is
no guarantee of truthfulness to the historical facts. This is also the
case for the historical novel – indeed, even for historical paintings
and, to a certain extent, for portraits. The vividness of a narrative is
not to be measured by its reproductive fidelity.

We certainly do not want to restrict the role that intuition plays in
the realm of art to the value accorded to vividness. Indeed, we saw
that we only praise vividness – which sets our intuitive capacities in
motion – when it particularly enlivens our "symbolic" or "conceptual" understanding. But that is not all. Above all, intuition plays a
constitutive role whenever a work of art addresses us. Here we must
exclude every merely ancillary function of intuition, particularly
anything with a merely illustrative character. Kant's own treatment
of the relation among concept, idea, and intuition in the *Critique of
Judgment* sometimes too readily suggests illustration (*Veranschau-
lichung*), insofar as the free play of imagination should be purposive

in the presentation of the "given concept" (*CJ*, § 49, p. 161). In fact, Kant tries to liberate himself from this primacy of the "given concept" by means of the concept of genius, but with only limited success. In any case, "illustration" actually has to do with cognitive processes. Here illustration may overstep the limits of intuition (for example, through intuitive comparisons), because certain things can only be presented symbolically – for example, large numbers, or four (or more) dimensional spaces. Such "illustration" clearly has nothing to do with the role of intuition in art.

In art, intuition is not a secondary moment. Art is rather to be characterized as intuition, indeed, as a world-view, *Welt-Anschauung* – literally, an intuition of the world.[13] This does not simply mean that art justifies its own claim to truth over and against scientific knowledge, insofar as the free play of imagination tends toward "knowledge in general." It also means that the "inner intuition" in play here brings the world – and not just the objects in it – to intuition. Hegel attempted to present the various kinds of world-view in his lectures on aesthetics. Thus prior to all conceptual–scientific knowledge, the way in which we look upon the world, and upon our whole being-in-the-world, takes shape in art.

We can see now the positive significance of taking vividness as our starting point: it saved us from the temptation of introducing here the concept of sensible intuition and thus the abstract epistemological opposition of intuition and understanding. It allows us to look instead at these modes of intuiting, and hence at the formative processes that shape them. In other words, we were able to look instead at the productivity of imagination and its interplay with understanding. Now surely the real intention of Kant's grounding of aesthetics is to dissolve the subordination of art to conceptual knowledge without at the same time eliminating the significant relation of art to conceptual understanding. Yet there is an undeniable weakness in Kant's distinction between artistic and natural beauty: in the case of art, according to Kant, the "free" play of imagination is related to the "given concept." Artistic beauty is not "free," but "dependent" beauty. Here Kant falls into the false alternative of an art that represents an object and a nature that does not, instead of understanding freedom from the representational (that is, from the "concept" of an object) as an immanent variation within creative art itself, with its own peculiar relation to truth. The existence of the classical music of his time alone could have saved Kant from this one-sidedness.[14]

Nevertheless, Kant defines genius and spirit "in their aesthetic significance" as the ability to present aesthetic ideas (*CJ*, § 49, p. 157). No doubt this concept of the "aesthetic idea" is much too oriented toward its opposite, the rational idea, and above all remains much too bound to the concept of an object, which the idea is said to "enlarge" (leaving something of a trace in Kant's doctrine of the attributes) (*CJ*, § 49, p. 158). One must nonetheless say that the concept of the aesthetic idea correctly formulates something even independently of such a relation to the object. Although an idea is not a concept, it is nevertheless something in whose direction we must look, even if no determinate concept of an object is presented through the idea. In this case, all talk about the "enlarging" of a given concept becomes meaningless.

It seems to me that here – rather than in a return to the judgment of taste – lies the real task of carrying Kant's philosophical achievement further and liberating his insight from the fetters of the opposition of intuition and concept. It is with Kant's introduction of the concept of genius that we first have anything to do with art in such a way that it is not already viewed from the standpoint of taste. On the one hand, to the extent that for Kant, genius consists in "discovering ideas for a given concept" (*CJ*, § 49, p. 160), we can trace the distorting influence of Kant's theoretical paradigm and its constriction of artistic experience. On the other hand, Kant eludes this restriction when he sees that the faculty of genius resides in "seizing the quickly passing play of imagination and unifying it in a concept (which is even on that account original and at the same time discloses a new rule . . .) that can be communicated without any constraint of rules"(*CJ*, § 49, p. 161). Here the concept is actually not "given," but is "original." This has a twofold significance: it is not itself an imitation, and although it can set itself up as a model, we cannot use this model as a "new rule" ourselves without falling back into mere imitation. This "concept" is ultimately the unity of intuition itself, an original mode of intuition that the work of art "discloses."

The situation is much the same when Kant assigns poetic art to the highest rank because it "sets the imagination free" (*CJ*, § 53, p. 170). Even there, to be sure, he immediately adds, "within the limits of a given concept." However, when one looks more closely, this cannot mean that the concept is merely "enlarged" by being raised to an aesthetic idea, since poetry "plays with appearance." It allows the mind to "feel its free, spontaneous . . . power" and to "observe nature as phenomenon, in accordance with aspects which it does not present in experience for either sense or understanding" (*CJ,* § 53, p. 171). Not even for the understanding! If nature, as phenomenon, is used here "as a sort of schema for the supersensible," it recalls the feeling of the sublime. For there too it is a question of the relation to the ideas of reason and not to the understanding. That, however, still means that poetry is not bound by the limits of a given concept, but instead points beyond the realm of the concept, and hence beyond the realm of the understanding. Certainly this does not mean that the free play of imagination is a stream of association. The freedom of imagination, which belongs to it by definition, is genuinely bound by the fact that imagination must "harmonize" with "knowledge in general" in spite of its free play. "With knowledge in general" means "with reference to the understanding in order to harmonize with its concepts in general (without any determination of them)" (*CJ,* § 26, p. 94). The phrase "without determination" seems to be an entirely appropriate description of the play with appearance, considering that imagination produces inner intuition without presupposing the determinacy of a given concept, and considering that it does not merely follow vague associations (as may arise in regard to natural beauty), but really "gives rise to thought." What Kant here describes from the side of the subject as the achievement of aesthetic judgment, of genius and spirit, can be formulated from the other side as the intuition of the world that every work of art presents. This act of intuiting is not limited by any determinate object given in intuition. The image built up in the inner act of intuiting lets us look out beyond everything that is given in experience. Kant's phrase, "the beautiful representation of a thing" (*CJ,* § 48, p. 154), is therefore too narrow to express this.

In this context, we must constantly return to Kant's remarkable seventeenth section, "On the Ideal of the Beautiful." There the concept of natural beauty, to which Kant grants priority in the context of the analytic of taste, seems imperceptibly to pass over into art. Kant is not content to treat the concept of the idea as a model of taste, but rather assumes an ideal of beauty as something we "strive to produce in ourselves." In any event, this ideal could be understood as a presentation in imagination that serves the judgment of something in nature or art. Presentation is here not simply in ac-

cordance with the judgment of taste, as when the normal idea of
beauty talks of a presentation as having "followed the rules." It is
presentation as art. Even the ideal of beauty, which Kant recognizes
"solely in human form" because it is capable of being an "expression of the moral," turns out in the end to be a task for the artist that
"requires a union of pure ideas of reason with great power of
imagination even in the one who wishes to judge it, still more in the
one who wishes to present it." And he concludes "that the judgment
in accordance with such a standard can never be purely aesthetic"
(*CJ*, § 17, p. 72).

It seems that whether we are talking of nature or art, satisfaction
in the beautiful here commands "a great interest" in equal measure
and, in both cases, entirely without "sensible charm." Is this a moral
interest (such as natural beauty is capable of awakening [*CJ*, § 42])?
Or is it an artistic interest (which of course would also be a moral
interest, and not just an aesthetic one)? Should the approach to the
ideal of beauty be experienced in a beautiful person whom we
actually encounter, or in an artistic representation of such a person?
The context of this argument and its conclusion at bottom only permits the latter "under the condition of a determinate concept" (as
the heading to Section 16 has it). However, this concept of the ideal
of a beautiful human being is a unique one inasmuch as it expresses
the moral dimension, rather than the perfection of an object. Do we
not find ourselves moving here into an entirely new dimension
where the sole conditioning factor is not a determinate concept, but
rather the very concept of humanity itself or, as Kant puts it, its
"supersensible substrate," its "transcendental freedom"? And is not
art really defined by the fact that, whatever may be presented in it,
humanity encounters itself?

If this is the case, then we can incorporate the aesthetic of the sublime into the theory of art, in a way Kant did not fully accomplish
himself. It is indeed true that the feeling of the sublime is first
encountered from the standpoint of taste and treated solely as the
sublimity of nature (which can itself also be represented in art).
Nevertheless, sublimity points clearly beyond the standpoint of
taste. The question is whether the transition from the standpoint of
taste to that of genius is not prepared for by the sublime, and particularly the dynamically sublime in nature, in which the "supersensible" vocation of humanity is experienced.[15]

This is consistent with Kant's claim that "the sublime in nature is only improperly so-called" and that "the deduction of the judgment of taste [is only] the judgment concerning the beauty of natural things" (*CJ*, § 30, pp. 121–2). In any event, Kant here is not yet talking about works of art. But since we must look upon the whole of nature as we do the sublime in nature – that is, as the occasion for the elevation of the mind to its supersensible vocation – and since we thus experience a satisfaction that elevates us beyond the unpleasant experience of our insignificance and powerlessness, we are then fulfilled by an intellectual interest. And this, in turn, is related to intellectual interest in the beautiful, which inspires the work of art as a product of genius. Of course, this interest in art does not present that aspect of formlessness and immeasurability offered by the sublime in nature, which excites a paradoxical pleasure in something unpleasant. And yet, it is also not the mere pleasantness of the "form of the object" that allows us to find the work of art "beautiful." What pleases only in this fashion is dismissed in the judgment of art as "merely decorative."

On the contrary, when the product of genius "elevates" us, it is always connected with "transcendental freedom," as Kant would say. That the work of art not only pleases but "elevates" us, clearly includes the fact that it excites not only pleasure but also displeasure. This is not just occasionally so, as with the explicit presentation of the sublime in art, in great tragedy for instance. No, the true work of art does not blend neatly into the context of life as mere decoration, but stands out in its own right, and hence always presents itself as something of a provocation. It does not merely please, it almost forces us to dwell upon it, issuing the challenge "to let it please us." Heidegger has spoken of the impact that art makes on us.[16] In fact, the world appears different when we look at it through the eyes of the work. We may well be inclined to find Kant's concepts narrow and restricting, particularly his concept of genius, with its roots in a concept of nature that is ultimately grounded in a theology of creation. But that is exactly what makes his analysis of the feeling of the sublime so interesting. For here the "standpoint of taste" is necessarily surpassed. This happens when the task of grasping the immense in an intuition or of fathoming the overwhelming and facing up to it, fails. Thereupon we become aware of our "supersensible" vocation. Is not the intuition, to which the imagination seeks to elevate itself in the act of intuiting the work of art, of a similar immensity (and a similar overwhelming power) insofar as it cannot

be expounded by concepts? The agreement of the faculties of
knowledge with "knowledge in general," which, for Kant, characterizes aesthetic experience, acquires indeed a specific determinacy
of its own in the case of art. Yet that agreement is not achieved in a
"concept," but rather in a stream of inner intuitions in which the
view of the world, to which any given work of art forces us, is
built up.

In retrospect, despite differences of time, taste, conceptuality,
and approach to problems separating Kant and ourselves, his contribution to the clarification of things appears to be truly relevant in
one respect. This is in his development of the temporal structure that
belongs to the concept of intuition. Of course, he did not really util-
ize it in his theory of art. In the *Critique of Pure Reason* we find the
famous remark:

> Psychologists have hitherto failed to realize that imagination is
> a necessary ingredient of perception itself. This is due partly to
> the fact that this faculty has been limited to reproduction,
> partly to the belief that the senses not only supply impressions,
> but also combine them so as to generate images of objects. For
> that purpose, something more than the mere receptivity of
> impressions is undoubtedly required, namely, a function for
> the synthesis of them (A 120n).

The synthesis of imagination, which according to Kant constitutes
the unity of "apprehension," certainly remains tied to the givenness
of objects in the manifold of sensations. Nevertheless, the play of
syntheses must be understood as something performed in a temporal
series, as a "reading" – just as the temporal structure of the synthesis
of "apperception" has been clarified by Husserl's phenomenological
analysis. After all, the special case of the mathematically sublime
already pointed in this direction. For the temporal form that the
"free play" of productive imagination eminently possesses, also
comes to acquire a fundamental significance for the theory of art.
From this perspective, the role of intuition in this domain can be
divested of its dogmatic character. That, however, involves overcoming a certain traditional one-sidedness in the theory of art: it
means abolishing the preeminence accorded to the visual arts over
the art of poetry in aesthetic concept formation. I would not say,
with Manfred Frank,[17] that intuition is sublated in metaphor. It is, I
would say, formed anew through metaphor. For the theory of

metaphor, Kant's remark in Section 59 seems to me most profound: that metaphor at bottom makes no comparison of content, but rather undertakes the "transference of reflection upon an object of intuition to a quite different concept to which perhaps an intuition can never directly correspond" (*CJ*, § 59, p. 198). Does not the poet do that with every word? The poet suspends every direct correspondence and thereby awakens intuition.

It sounds almost paradoxical when Hegel begins from the immediate and therefore sensible knowledge of art, speaks of the unity of the concept in its universality with individual appearance, but then continues: "Now, of course, this unity is accomplished in art, not just in sensible externality, but also in the element of representation, especially in poetry."[18] Hegel, of course, knows very well that in poetry, "every content is grasped in an immediate way and is brought to representation." In art, it is never a question of "isolated sensible existents which, taken by themselves, do not grant an intuition of the spiritual." In fact, the methodological pre-eminence that thus belongs to poetry over all the other arts – and that by no means diminishes their rank or human significance – lies simply in the decisive way in which poetry takes its stand upon the "intuition of the spiritual."[19]

Notes

EDITOR'S INTRODUCTION

1 M. Heidegger, "The Origin of the Work of Art," trans. by A. Hofstadter, *Poetry, Language, Thought* (New York: Harper & Row, 1971). Henceforth this work will be referred to as *"PLT."*

2 The phrase is from Hölderlin's poem "Bread and Wine." I attempt to elucidate Heidegger's dialogue with Hölderlin in the third chapter of *The Question of Language in Heidegger's History of Being* (New Jersey: Humanities, and London: Macmillan, 1985).

3 M. Merleau-Ponty, "Eye and Mind" in *The Primacy of Perception and Other Essays,* ed. by J.M. Edie (Evanston, IL: Northwestern University Press, 1964).

4 *The Will to Power,* trans. by W. Kaufmann and R.J. Hollingdale (New York: Random House, 1967), p. 261, No. 466.

5 *Truth and Method,* trans. by W. Glen-Doepel (London: Sheed & Ward, 1975), Part One. Henceforth this work will be referred to as *"TM".*

6 Gadamer confirmed this in a letter he wrote to Leo Strauss. "Correspondence concerning *Wahrheit und Methode," The Independent Journal of Philosophy,* II, 1978, pp. 5–12.

7 *TM,* p. 112. See also W. Pannenberg, *Theology and the Philosophy of Science* (Philadelphia: Westminster, 1976), p. 169n.

8 M. Heidegger, *Nietzsche, Vol. 1: The Will to Power as Art,* trans. by D.F. Krell (New York: Harper & Row, 1979), p. 80. Henceforth this work will be referred to as *"Nietzsche."*

9 G.F. Hegel, *Aesthetics,* Vol. I, trans. by T.M. Knox (London: Oxford University Press, 1975), p. 11. This passage is discussed by Heidegger in the Epilogue to "The Origin of the Work of Art," *PLT,* pp. 79–81.

10 H.-G. Gadamer, "On the Problematic Character of Aesthetic Consciousness," trans. by E. Kelly, *Graduate Faculty Philosophy Journal,* IX, No. 1 (1982), p. 33.

11 This point of view may help to explain Gadamer's somewhat shocking judgment in "On the Contribution of Poetry to the Search for Truth" that there is no real drama in the Christian period.

12   The first essay in this volume, "The Festive Character of Theater," which predates *Truth and Method* by six years, already shows Gadamer's preoccupation with the theme of continuity in change. But I would suggest that it is in the essays "The Speechless Image" and especially "Art and Imitation" that the historical continuity of art takes over as the central theme.

13   R. Bernasconi, "Bridging the Abyss: Heidegger and Gadamer," *Research in Phenomenology,* XVI (1986). I also try there to break free of seeing the question as simply one of continuity versus discontinuity, which is ultimately too simplistic a way of formulating the problem.

14   Gadamer invariably refers "pure poetry" to Mallarmé. So far as I am aware, the exact phrase appears in Mallarmé only once (*Correspondance 1862 –71* [Paris: Gallimard, 1959], p. 105) though he does write also of the "pure work," a phrase Gadamer uses on one occasion to refer to aesthetic differentiation (*TM,* 76). The phrase "pure poetry" can be traced beyond Mallarmé to Poe and Baudelaire, who used the phrase once and four times respectively (D.J. Mossop, *Pure Poetry* [London: Oxford University Press, 1971], p. 82). It was perhaps Valéry who was most effective in popularizing the idea of pure poetry and he did so with constant reference to Mallarmé. Surprisingly, Gadamer does not quote the central passage of *Un coup de des,* where Mallarmé himself insists on continuity: "I shall nevertheless have outlined, rather than the first draft, a 'state' of the attached Poem such as does not totally break with tradition" (*The Poems,* trans. by K. Bosley [Harmondsworth, Middlesex: Penguin, 1977], p. 257).

15   This suggests the possibility of a challenging comparison with Derrida who offers a reading of Mallarmé's *Mimique* in "The double session," in *Dissemination,* trans. by B. Johnson (Chicago: University of Chicago Press, 1981).

PART I

The relevance of the beautiful

1   H.-G. Gadamer, "Plato and the Poets" in *Dialogue and Dialectic,* trans. by P. Christopher Smith (New Haven: Yale University Press, 1980), pp. 39–72.

2   G.W.F. Hegel, *Aesthetics,* Vol. I, trans. by T.M. Knox (London: Oxford University Press, 1975), p. 11. Cf. H.-G. Gadamer, "Hegel and the Heidelberg Romantics," Hegels Dialectik (Tübingen: J.C.B. Mohr, 1971), pp. 80–81, and above all the essay "Art and Philosophy Today" by Dieter Henrich in *New Perspectives in German Literary Criticism,* ed. by R.E.

Amacher and V. Lange (Princeton, New Jersey: Princeton University Press, 1979), pp 107–133. Henrich's essay first appeared in *Immanente Asthetik – Asthetische Reflexion*, ed. by W. Iser (Munich: Wilhelm Fink, 1966) and is discussed by Gadamer in his review of that volume reprinted in *Kleine Schriften*, Vol. IV (Tübingen: J.C.B. Mohr, 1977), pp. 249–255.

3   See H.-G. Gadamer "Karl Immermanns 'Chiliastische Sonnette'" in *Kleine Schriften*, Vol. IV (Tübingen: J.C.B. Mohr, 1967), pp. 136–147. – Ed.

4   Cf. Gottfried Boehm, *Studien zur Perspektivität. Philosophie und Kunst in der Frühen Neuzeit* (Heidelberg: C. Winter, 1969).

5   Cf. H.-G. Gadamer, "Verstummen die Dichter?" in *Zeitwende. Die neue Furche*, V (1970). Reprinted in *Poetica* (Frankfurt: Insel, 1977), pp. 103–118.

6   Cf. Reinhardt Koselleck, "Historia magistra vitae," in *Natur und Geschichte. Karl Löwith zum 70 Gerburtstag*, ed. by Hermann Braun and Manfred Riedel (Stuttgart: Kohlhammer, 1967), pp. 196–219. [The painting, sometimes also called "Alexander's Victory" or "The Battle of Arbela," dates from 1529 and may be found in the Alte Pinakothek in Munich. – Ed.]

7   Cf. *Phaedrus* 265 d and also *Truth and Method*, trans. by W. Glen-Doepel (London: Sheed & Ward, 1975), p. 331. – Ed.

8   *Metaphysics*, 6.1.1025b 18-21.

9   Plato, *Republic*, 601 d-e.

10   *Cratylus*, 390 b-c. – Ed.

11   *Poetics*, 1451 b 5.

12   *Phaedrus*, 246 seq.. – Ed.

13   *Phaedrus*, 250d. Cf. *Truth and Method*, pp. 437-9 – Ed.

14   A. Baumgarten, *Aesthetica*, Sec. I (Hildesham: Georg Olms, 1961), p. 1. – Ed.

15   Cf. Alfred Baeumler, *Kants Kritik der Urteilskraft, ihre Geschichte und Systematik*, Vol. I, Introduction (Halle: Max Niemeyer, 1923).

16   Baumgarten, *Aesthetica*, Sec. 1, p. 1.

17   For more on the ideas of the image and the original, see H.-G. Gadamer, *Truth and Method*, pp. 119 seq.

18   There is no ready translation for the word *Anbild*, but the word "insight" may serve if heard in an original sense. – Ed.

19   I. Kant, *Critique of Judgment*, trans. by J.H. Bernard (New York: Hafner, 1951), Sec. 22, p. 76.

20   Cf. H.-G. Gadamer, *Truth and Method*, p. 46. – Ed.

21   *Musée imaginaire*. André Malraux used the phrase "Museum Without Walls" as the title for the first part of *The Psychology of Art*, trans. by S. Gilbert (New York: Pantheon, 1949–51). That work appeared later in a revised version as *The Voices of Silence*, trans. by S. Gilbert, (New York: Doubleday, 1953). Yet another version appeared in 1965 and was translated

two years later by S. Gilbert and F. Price under the title *Museum Without Walls* (London: Secker & Warburg, 1967). – Ed.

22 Kant, *Critique of Judgment*, Sec. 5, pp. 44–45. – Ed.

23 *Ibid.*, Sec. 22, pp 76–77 and Sec. 40., pp. 135–138.

24 *Ibid.*, Sec. 51, p. 167. – Ed.

25 *Ibid.*, Sec. 9, p. 54. – Ed.

26 Cf. H.-G. Gadamer, *Truth and Method*, pp. 39ff.

27 Cf. Max Kommerell, *Lessing und Aristoteles. Untersuchung uber die Theorie der Tragedie* (Frankfurt: Klostermann, 1957), pp. 10–11, 236–238.

28 Kant, *Critique of Judgment*, Sec. 49, p. 162. – Ed.

29 *Ibid.*, p. 160 – Ed.

30 *Ibid.*, Sec. 48, p. 154 – Ed.

→ 31 Johann Huizinga, *Homo Ludens* (London: Paladin, 1970) and Romano Guardini, *The Spirit of the Liturgy*, trans. by Ada Lane (London: Sheed & Ward, 1930). – Ed.

32 Aristotle, *De Anima* 1.3 and 1.4.405b33–408a 34. – Ed.

33 Kant, *Critique of Judgment*, Sec. 14, pp. 59–61.

34 Roman Ingarden, *The Literary Work of Art*, trans. by George G. Grabowicz (Evanston: Northwestern University Press, 1973).

35 Fyodor Dostoevsky, *The Brothers Karamazov*, trans. by D. Magarshack (Harmondsworth, Middlesex: Penguin, 1958), Volume I, Book Five, Chapter 7, p. 329. – Ed.

36 Richard Hamann, *Ästhetik* (Leipzig: B.G. Teubner, 1911).

37 H.-G. Gadamer, *Truth and Method*, pp. 105ff.

38 Titian, "Charles V on Horseback at the Battle of Muhlberg," 1548, Prado Museum, Madrid. – Ed.

39 Kant, *Critique of Judgment*, Sec. 23, pp. 82–85. – Ed.

40 See for example Hegel's journal of his trip in the Berner Oberland during July and August of 1796. *Frühe Schriften*, Vol. I (Frankfurt: Suhrkamp, 1971), pp. 616–617. – Ed.

41 Hegel, *Aesthetics*, pp. 1–2.

42 Theodor W. Adorno has fully described this indeterminacy of reference in his *Aesthetic Theory*, trans. by C. Lenhardt (London: Routledge & Kegan Paul, 1984).

43 *Symposium*, 191d. – Ed.

44 Hegel, *Aesthetics*, p. 111. – Ed.

45 The *Ge-* prefix of the word *Gebilde*, here translated as "creation," indicates a gathering. Gadamer, in a phrase omitted from the translation, illustrates this by referring us to the German word *Gebirg*, which means a mountain range. – Ed.

46 Walter Benjamin, "The Work of Art in the Age of Mechanical Reproduction," *Illuminations*, trans. by H. Zohn (London: Fontana, 1973), pp. 219–253.

47 Martin Heidegger, "The Origin of the Work of Art," trans. by A. Hofstadter, *Poetry, Language, Thought* (New York: Harper & Row, 1971), pp. 50–72.

48 Rainer Maria Rilke, "Duino Elegies" VII, *The Selected Poetry of Rainer Maria Rilke*, trans. by Stephen Mitchell, (New York: Random House, 1982), p. 189.

49 Rilke, "Archaic Torso of Apollo," *Ibid.*, p. 61.

50 Heidegger, *Poetry, Language, Thought*, p. 66.

51 Cf. Herman Koller, *Die Mimesis in der Antike. Nachahmung, Darstellung, Ausdruck* (Bern: Francke, 1954) (Dissertationes Bernenses Series 1, 5).

52 Walter F. Otto, *Dionysius. Myth and Culture*, trans. by Robert B. Palmer (Bloomington: Indiana University Press, 1965).

53 Karl Kerényi, "Vom Wesen des Festes," *Gesammelte Werke*, Vol. VII, *Antike Religion* (Munich: Albert Langen and Georg Müller, 1971).

54 H.-G. Gadamer, "Concerning Empty and Ful-filled Time," trans. by R. Phillip O'Hara, *Martin Heidegger in Europe and America*, ed. by E.G. Ballard and C.E. Scott (The Hague: Martinus Nijhoff, 1973), pp. 77–89.

55 Gadamer cites Kant's discussion in his Introduction to the *Critique of Judgment*. The actual phrase does not seem to appear until the main body of the text at pp. 62, 78, and 144. – Ed.

56 Aristotle, *Nicomachean Ethics*, 1106b9.

57 Cf. Richard Hönigswald, "Vom Wesen des Rhythmus," *Die Grundlagen der Denkpsychologie. Studen und Analysen* (Leipzig and Berlin, B.G. Teubner, 1925).

58 An allusion to the second stanza of Hölderlin's "Bread and Wine." – Ed.

PART II – ESSAYS

1. The festive character of theater

1 Cf. Walter Otto's important introduction to his book *Dionysos*, trans. by Robert B. Palmer (Bloomington: Indiana University Press, 1965).

2 "Komodie," *Prosa*, IV, ed. by Herbert Steiner (Frankfurt: S. Fischer, 1955), p. 95. The quoted sentence, which opens Hugo von Hofmannsthal's 1922 essay, derives almost word for word from a letter written to him by Rudolf Borchardt on 23 July 1911, see Hofmannsthal and Borchardt, *Briefwechsel*, ed. by Marie Luise Borchardt and Herbert Steiner (Frankfurt: S. Fischer, 1954), pp. 52–53 – Ed.

3 Friedrich Schiller, "Ueber das gegenwärtige Teutsche Theater," *Sämtliche Werke*, V (Munich: Artemis & Winkler, 1975), p. 88 – Ed.

4   Friedrich Schiller, "The Stage Considered as a Moral Institution" in *An Anthology for Our Time*, trans. by Jane Bannard Greene (New York: Frederick Ungar, 1959), pp. 262–283 – Ed.

5   Rilke, "The Fourth Duino Elegy," *The Selected Poetry of Rainer Maria Rilke*, ed. and trans. by Stephen Mitchell (New York: Random House, 1982), p. 187. – Ed.

2. Composition and interpretation

1   The reader is referred to Roman Ingarden's important book, *The Literary Work of Art* (Evanston: Northwestern University Press, 1973) for further discussion of the questions raised here.

2   Paul Valéry, "Poetry and Abstract Thought," *The Art of Poetry*, trans. by D. Folliot (London: Routledge & Kegan Paul, 1958), p. 56 – Ed.

3   Ernst Jünger, "Epigramme" (1934), *Werke*, Vol. VIII; Essays, Vol. IV (Stuttgart: Ernst Klett, 1963), p. 654 – Ed.

4   Goethe's letter to Carl Ernst Schubarth of April 2, 1818, *Goethes Briefe*, Vol. III, "Hamburger Ausgabe," ed. by Bodo Morawe (Hamburg: Christian Wegner, 1965), p. 426. Cf. Gadamer's *Truth and Method*, trans. by W. Glen-Doepel (London: Sheed & Ward, 1975), p. 69. – Ed.

5   On the concept of gesture, see Chapter 3, "Image and Gesture."

6   Rainer Maria Rilke, *Sonnets to Orpheus*, trans. by J.B. Leishman (London: Hogarth Press, 1967), Part One, No. 3, p. 39. – Ed.

7   *Theogony*, lines 26–28. – Ed.

8   The line is to be found only in the second version of Hölderlin's poem, "Mnemosyne." *Gedichte nach 1800*, "Stuttgarter Hölderlin Ausgabe," Vol. II., 1, ed. by Friederich Beissner (Stuttgart: Kohlhammer, 1951), p. 195 – Ed.

3. Image and gesture

1   Cf. the essays on Hölderlin and Goethe in H.-G. Gadamer, *Kleine Schriften*, Vol. II (Tübingen: J.C.B. Mohr, 1967). – Ed.

2   Walter F. Otto, *The Homeric Gods* (New York: Pantheon, 1954). – Ed.

3   Cf. the contributions of Bruno Snell, as well as Albin Lesky's *Göttlichen und menschliche Motivation im homerischen Epos*, Sitzungsberichte der Heidelberger Akademie der Wissenschaften (Heidelberg: Carl Winter, 1961).

4   Rainer Maria Rilke, *Sonnets to Orpheus*, trans. by J.B. Leishman (London: Hogarth Press, 1967), Part 1, No. XII, p. 57. – Ed.

5   J.W. Goethe, *Iphigenia in Tauris*, Act 1, Scene 1, in *Dramatic Works*, trans. by Anna Swanwick and Goetz von Berlichingen (London: Henry G. Bohn, 1850), p. 155. – Ed.

6   Cf. my essay on Werner Scholz's watercolors, "Die Mythologie der Griechen" in the *Frankfurter Allgemeine Zeitung*, No. 130, 1955.

4. The speechless image

1 *Phaedrus* 265d. – Ed.

2 In his book *Zeit-bilder* (Frankfurt am Main: Athenäum, 1960), Arnold Gehlen has pointed out the mute quality of modern art. Cf. "Begriffene Malerei?", my critique of his interesting book, which is reprinted in *Kleine Schriften II* (Tübingen, J.C.B. Mohr, 1967), pp. 218–226.

3 As has been shown recently again by Ewald M. Vetter, *Die Maus auf dem Gebetbuch,* Ruperto-Carola (Mitteilungen des Vereins der Freunde der Studenten der Universität Heidelberg), 36, 1964, pp. 99–108.

4 Translated from the Dutch. Jan Davidsz. de Heem, "Bunch of Flowers in a Glass Vase With Crucifix and Skull," Alte Pinakothek, Munich. – Ed.

5 Cf. the instructive exposition by Charles Sterling, *La nature morte de l'Antiquité a nos jours* (Paris: P. Tisné, 1959).

6 Rainer Maria Rilke, *Sonnets to Orpheus,* trans. by J.B. Leishman (London: Hogarth Press, 1967), Part 1, No. xviii, p. 69. – Ed.

7 In my essay on Goethe's unfinished poems in *Kleine Schriften,* Vol. II (pp. 105–135), I have pursued this question with reference to a particular example.

8 *The Diaries of Paul Klee (1898-1918)* (Berkeley: University of California Press, 1964), Entry number 961, p. 318.

9 *Nicomachean Ethics,* 1106b9. – Ed.

5. Art and imitation

1 As Arnold Gehlen does; see H.-G. Gadamer, "Begriffene Malerei? Zu A. Gehlen: Zeit-Bilder," *Kleine Schriften II* (Tübingen: J.C.B. Mohr, 1967), pp. 218-226. [The book by Daniel-Henry Kahnweiler that Gadamer mentions is *Juan Gris, His Life and Work,* trans. by Douglas Cooper, new enlarged edition, London: Thames & Hudson, 1969. – Ed.]

2 Aristotle, *Poetics* 1451a37. – Ed.

3 Cf. the instructive little book by Enrico Fubini, *L'estetica musicale dal Settecento a oggi* (Turin: G. Einaudi, 1964).

4 Heinrich Wöfflin, "Ueber das Rechts und Links im Bilde," *Gedanken zur Kuntsgeschichte* (Basle: Benno Schwabe, 1941), pp. 82–96. – Ed.

5 Cf. Picasso's critical remarks on the later work of Juan Gris in Kahnweiler. ["Picasso said to me one day – and he meant it as a criticism – that, in his opinion, Gris, if he had lived, would have tended to make his pictures more and more legible. I am sure that Picasso was right, but at the same time I cannot agree with him in disparaging this tendency in Gris." Kahnweiler, *Juan Gris,* p. 134. – Ed.]

6 Cf. Walter Bröker, "Was bedeutet die abstrakte Kunst?" *Kant-Studien,* 48 (1956/57), pp. 485–501.

7 I. Kant, *Critique of Judgment,* trans. by J. H. Bernard (New York: Hefner, 1951), Sec. 9. – Ed.

8 *Ibid*, p. 167f. – Ed.

9 *Poetics* 1448b5. – Ed.

10 *Republic* 597e. – Ed.

11 *Metaphysics* 1.6.987b. – Ed.

12 *Republic* 424d. – Ed.

6. *On the contribution of poetry to the search for truth*

1 *Dichtung und Wahrheit* was originally only the subtitle of Goethe's autobiography. It first appeared as *Aus meinem Leben*. It is published in English translation as *The Autobiography of Johann Wolfgang von Goethe*, trans. by John Oxenford (Chicago: University of Chicago Press, 1974). – Ed.

2 *Herodotus*, Loeb Classics, trans. by A.D. Godley (Cambridge, Massachusetts: Harvard University Press, 1975), Book II, 53, p. 341. – Ed.

3 "The idea of Christian tragedy presents a special problem, since in the light of divine salvation history, the values of happiness and misfortune that are constitutive of the tragic action no longer determine human destiny." *Truth and Method*, trans. by W. Glen-Doepel (London: Sheed & Ward, 1975), p. 116. – Ed.

4 M. Heidegger, "On the Essence of Truth," *Basic Writings*, ed. by D.F. Krell (New York: Harper & Row, 1977), pp. 119, 127. – Ed.

5 The phrase *Es stehet geschrieben* – and variations upon it – is prominent in Luther's translation of the New Testament and also occurs, though less consistently, in his translation of the Old Testament. It corresponds to the phrase "it is written" as found throughout the authorized version of the Bible. – Ed.

6 "It was impossible to say whether the fit had come on him when he was descending the steps, so that he must have fallen down at once unconscious, or whether it had been brought on as a result of the shock." Fyodor Dostoevsky, *The Brothers Karamazov*, trans. by D. Magarshack (Harmondsworth, Middlesex: Penguin, 1958), Volume I, Book Five, Chapter 7, p. 329. – Ed.

7 Aristotle, *De Interpretatione* 17a18. – Ed.

8 E. Husserl, *Ideas Pertaining to a Pure Phenomenology and to a Phenomenological Philosophy*, trans. by F. Kersten (The Hague: Nijhoff, 1982), Book I, Section 111, pp. 260–262. – Ed.

9 Friedrich Hölderlin, "Wie wenn am Feiertage . . . " Translations of the poem may be found in *Selected Poems*, trans. by. J.B. Leishman (London: Hogarth, 1944), pp. 101–105 and *Poems and Extracts*, trans. by Michael Hamburger (London: Routledge & Kegan Paul, 1966), pp. 373–377. – Ed.

10 *Grenzsituation* was a favorite term of Karl Jaspers. See his *Philosophy*, Vol. II, trans. by E.B. Ashton (Chicago: University of Chicago Press, 1970), pp. 177–222. – Ed.

11 G.W.F. Hegel, *Aesthetics,* Vol. II, trans. by T.M. Knox (London: Oxford University Press, 1975), p. 1048. – Ed.

7. Poetry and mimesis

1 G.W.F. Hegel, *Aesthetics,* Vol. I, trans. by T.M. Knox (London: Oxford University Press, 1975), p. 11. – Ed.

2 Aristotle, *Poetics* 1448b6. – Ed.

3 *Ibid.,* 1448b17. – Ed.

4 Plato, *Timaeus* 48e-49a. – Ed.

5 *Poetics* 1451b1. – Ed.

6 Plato, *Philebus* 49d-50b. – Ed.

7 H.-G. Gadamer, *Truth and Method,* trans. by W. Glen-Doepel (London: Sheed & Ward, 1975), pp. 105ff.

8. The play of art

1 *Poetics* 1451b5-7. – Ed.

2 *Beyond Good and Evil,* trans. by Walter Kaufmann (New York: Random House, 1966), Sec. 94, p. 83 – Ed.

9. Philosophy and poetry

1 *Republic,* Book X, 607b. – Ed.

2 Paul Valéry, "Poetry and Abstract Thought," *The Art of Poetry,* trans. by D. Folliot (London: Routledge & Kegan Paul, 1958), p. 56. – Ed.

3 *Phaedrus,* 274c-277a. – Ed.

4 G.W.F. Hegel, *Phenomenology of Spirit,* trans. by A.V. Miller (London: Oxford University Press, 1977), p. 35. – Ed.

5 Cf. Edmund Husserl, *Ideas Pertaining to a Pure Phenomenology and to a Phenomenological Philosophy,* First Book (The Hague: Martinus Nijhoff, 1982), trans. by F. Kersten, Sec. 70, p. 160 and Sec. 112, pp. 262-3. See also Oskar Becker, "Von der Hinfälligkeit des Schönen, und der Abenteuerlichkeit des Künstlers," *Festschrift für Edmund Husserl zum 70 Geburtstag* (Halle: Max Niemeyer, 1929), p. 36nl. – Ed.

6 The frescoes are by the seventeenth-century painter Andrea Pozzo and show the triumph of Saint Ignatius. – Ed.

7 M. Heidegger, "The Origin of the Work of Art," trans. by A. Hofstadter, *Poetry, Language, Thought* (New York: Harper & Row, 1971), p. 46. – Ed.

8 *Metabasis eis allo genos.* This Aristotelian phrase for illegitimate passage beyond boundaries may be found, for example, at *De Caelo* I, 1, 268b1. – Ed.

9 E.g. "On the Process of the Poetic Mind," trans. by Ralph Read III, *German Romantic Criticism,* ed. by A. Leslie Willson (New York: Continuum, 1982) p. 235. – Ed.

10 G.W.F. Hegel, *Science of Logic,* trans. by A.V. Miller (London: George Allen & Unwin, 1969), p. 90. For Hegel's classic discussion of the speculative proposition, see *Phenomenology of Spirit,* pp. 36–41. – Ed.

11 *Phaedo,* 99e. – Ed.

12 *Republic,* 511c.

13 *Phenomenology of Spirit,* p. 77. – Ed.

14 *Posterior Analytics,* II, 100b5-17. – Ed.

15 *Phenomenology of Spirit,* pp. 142–143 – Ed.

16 *Topics,* VI, 139a27-30. – Ed.

17 Both senses of the Greek word *horos* – the ordinary sense of "boundary," as well as the sense of "definition" that it has for Aristotle in his logical treatises – are taken into account by Hegel in his discussion of "the limit" in the *Science of Logic,* pp. 122–129. – Ed.

10. Aesthetic and religious experience

1 F. Schleiermacher, "The Academy Addresses of 1829: On the concept of Hermeneutics, with reference to F.A. Wolf's Instructions and Ast's Textbook," *Hermeneutics: The Handwritten Manuscripts,* trans. by J. Duke and J. Forstman (Missoula, Montana: Scholars Press, 1977), p. 182. – Ed.

2 See page 178, n5. – Ed.

3 Hesiod, *Theogony,* lines 26-28. – Ed.

4 Goethe's letter to Carl Ernst Schubarth of April 2, 1818. – Ed.

5 Fragment 93 (Diels). – Ed.

APPENDIX

Intuition and vividness

1 Daniel L. Tate, the translator of this essay, would like to thank his wife, Karen Robbins, for her assistance in preparing the translation. The words of the German title, *"Anschauung und Anschaulichkeit,"* are closely related, as they are not in the English equivalents chosen for them here, "intuition" and "vividness," respectively. *Anschauen* has been translated as "act of intuiting" or "intuiting," and *anschaulich* as "vivid". – Ed.

2 A. Baumgarten, *Aesthetica* (Hildesheim: Georg Olms, 1961), Sec. 1, p. 1. – Ed.

3 I. Kant, *Critique of Judgment,* trans. by J.H. Bernard (New York: Hafner, 1951), Sec. 49, p. 157. Henceforth this work will be referred to as *CJ*. – Ed.

4 Cf. I. Kant, *Critique of Pure Reason,* trans. by N. Kemp Smith (London: Macmillan, 1929), p. 165, B 151. – Ed.

5 Hegel sent the poem to Hölderlin, dated August 1796. A translation by Clark Butler and Christiane Seiler may be found in *Hegel: The Letters* (Bloomington: Indiana University Press, 1984), pp. 46–7 – Ed.

6 I. Kant, "On the Form and Principles of the Sensible and Intelligible World" (Inaugural Dissertation, 1770), *Selected Pre-Critical Writings,* trans. by G.B. Kerferd and D.E. Walford (Manchester: Manchester University Press, 1968). – Ed.

7 E. Husserl, *Ideas Pertaining to a Pure Phenomenology and to a Phenomenological Philosophy,* First Book, trans. by F. Kersten (The Hague: Martinus Nijhoff, 1982), Sec. 43, p. 93. – Ed.

8 *De Anima,* 418a22-23 and 425a25-26. – Ed.

9 *Metaphysics* 9.10.1051b32. *Innesein,* here rendered "noetic grasp," is Gadamer's translation of Aristotle's *noein.* For a discussion of this translation, cf. H.-G. Gadamer, "Uber das Göttliche im frühen Denken der Greichen," *Kleine Schriften III* (Tübingen: J.C.B. Mohr, 1972), p. 78. – Translator's note.

10 For example, *Politics,* 1279b15. – Ed.

11 *Epibole* appears in the surviving texts of Epicurus on a number of occasions. *Athroa epibole* is found only once. "Epistula ad Herodotum," 35, 9, *Opere,* ed. by Graziano Arrighetti (Turin: Giulio Einaudi, 1960), p. 35. In Plotinus the phrase takes on almost a technical status and comes to mean a "unified intuition." See *Ennead,* IV, 4, 1. – Ed.

12 "Again you fill bush and vale hushed with luminous mist." – Goethe, *An den Mond.* – Ed.

13 The word *Weltanschauung* is encountered in this original sense in Kant himself when he speaks of the infinite as the Noumenon "which admits of no intuition, but which yet serves as the substrate for the intuition of the world as a mere phenomenon" *(Critique of Judgment,* Sec. 26, p. 93). Of course here, as with Schleiermacher and Hegel, we must not introduce our own well-worn concept of world-view. I would like to point out that the particular concept of "world-view" with which we are familiar is more of a perspective than a collection of views.

14 Compare Adolf Nowack's account of the role of compositional technique in Viennese composers which brings the autonomy of the musical work of art to fulfillment: "Anschauung als musikalischer Kategorie," *Neue Hefte für Philosophie,* 18/19 (1980), pp. 103–117.

15 This was first brought out in Johann H. Trede's 1965 dissertation, *Die Differenz von theoretischem und praktischem Vernunftgebrauch und dessen Einheit innerhalb der "Kritik der Urteilskraft"* (Heidelberg, 1969).

16 M. Heidegger, "The Origin of the Work of Art," trans. by A. Hofstadter, *Poetry, Language, Thought* (New York: Harper & Row, 1971), p. 65. – Ed.

17 M. Frank, "Die Aufhebung der Anschauung im Spiel der Metapher," *Neue Hefte für Philosophie,* 18/19 (1980), pp. 58–78.

18 G.W.F. Hegel, *Aesthetics,* Vol. I, trans. by T.M. Knox (London: Oxford University Press, 1975), p. 101.

19 *Ibid,* p. 102.

Gadamer's works in English translation

"Articulating Transcendence," *The Beginning and the Beyond,* ed. by Fred Lawrence; Chico, Calif: Scholars Press, 1984, pp. 1–12.

"Being, Spirit, God," trans. by S. Davis, in *Heidegger Memorial Lectures,* ed. by W. Marx; Pittsburgh: Duquesne University Press, 1982, pp. 55–74.

"A Classical Text – A Hermeneutic Challenge," trans. by F. Lawrence, *Revue de l'Université d'Ottawa,* 1981, pp. 637–642

"Concerning Empty and Ful-filled Time," trans. by R.P. O'Hara, in *Martin Heidegger in Europe and America,* ed. by E.G. Ballard and C.E. Scott; The Hague: Martinus Nijhoff, 1973, pp. 77–89.

"The Continuity of History and the Existential Moment," trans. by Thomas Wren, *Philosophy Today,* Vol. 16, 1972, pp. 230–240.

"Correspondence Concerning *Wahrheit und Methode*" (with Leo Strauss), *The Independent Journal of Philosophy,* Vol. 2, 1978, pp. 5 – 12.

"Culture and Words – from the Point of View of Philosophy," *Universitas,* Vol. 24, 1982, pp. 179–188.

Dialogue and Dialectic, trans. by P. Christopher Smith; New Haven: Yale University Press, 1980.

"The Drama of Zarathustra," trans. by Z. Adamczewski, in *The Great Year of Zarathustra (1881–1981),* ed. by D. Goicoechea; Lanham: University Press of America, 1983, pp. 339–369.

"The Eminent Text and its Truth," trans. by Geoffrey Waite, *Bulletin of the Midwest Modern Language Association,* 1980, Vol. 13, pp. 3–10.

"Gadamer on Strauss: An Interview," *Interpretation,* Vol. 12, No. 1, 1984, pp. 1–13.

Hegel's Dialectic, trans. by P. Christopher Smith; New Haven: Yale University Press, 1976.

"Heidegger and the History of Philosophy," trans. by Karen Campbell, *The Monist* Vol. 64, No. 4, October 1981, pp. 434–444.

"Heidegger's Paths," trans. by C. Kayser and G. Stack, *Philosophical Exchange*, Vol. 2, Summer 1979, pp. 80–91.

"Hermeneutics and Social Science," *Cultural Hermeneutics*, 2, 1975, pp. 307–316. Also "Summation," pp. 329–330, and "Response," p. 357.

"The Hermeneutics of Suspicion," in *Hermeneutics, Questions and Prospects*, ed. by Gary Shapiro and Alan Sica; Amherst: University of Massachusetts Press, 1984, pp. 54–65.

"Historical Transformations of Reason," in *Rationality Today*, ed. by T. Geraets; Ottawa: University of Ottawa Press, 1979, pp. 3–14.

"History of Science and Practical Philosophy" (Review of J. Mittelstrass' "Neuzeit und Aufklarung"), *Contemporary German Philosophy*, Vol. 3; Philadelphia: Pennsylvania State University Press, 1983, pp. 307–13.

The Idea of the Good in Platonic-Aristotelian Philosophy, trans. by P. Christopher Smith; New Haven: Yale University Press, 1986.

Lectures on Philosophical Hermeneutics, Pretoria: Universiteit van Pretoria, 1982.

"Letter by Professor Hans-Georg Gadamer," in Richard J. Bernstein, *Beyond Objectivism and Relativism;* Oxford: Basil Blackwell, 1983, pp. 261–265.

"Natural Science and Hermeneutics: The Concept of Nature in Ancient Philosophy," trans. by Kathleen Wright, *Proceedings of the Boston Area Colloquium in Ancient Philosophy*, ed. by John Cleary, vol. 1, 1986, pp. 53–75.

"Notes on Planning for the Future," *Daedalus*, Spring 1966, pp. 572–589.

"On Man's Natural Inclination towards Philosophy," *Universitas*, Vol. 15, No. 1, 1973, pp. 31–40.

"On the Problematic Character of Aesthetic Consciousness," trans. by E. Kelly, *Graduate Faculty Philosophy Journal*, Vol. 9, No. 1, Winter 1982, pp. 31–40.

Philosophical Apprenticeships, trans. by Robert R. Sullivan; Cambridge, Massachusetts: MIT Press, 1985. Includes "On the Origins of Philosophical Hermeneutics."

Philosophical Hermeneutics, trans. by D.E. Linge; Berkeley: University of California Press, 1976.

"Philosophy and Literature," trans. by Anthony J. Steinbeck, *Man and World*, Vol. 18, 1985, pp. 241–259.

"Plato and Heidegger," trans. by I. Sprung, in *The Question of Being*, ed. by M. Sprung; Philadelphia: Pennsylvania State University Press, 1978, pp. 45–83.

"Plato's Parmenides and its Influence," *Dionysius*, Vol. 7, 1983, pp. 3–16.

"The Power of Reason," trans. by H. W. Johnstone, *Man and World*, Vol. 3, February 1970, pp. 5–15.

"Practical Philosophy as a Model of the Human Sciences," *Research in Phenomenology*, Vol. IX, 1979, pp. 74–85.

"The Problem of Historical Consciousness," trans. by J.L. Close, *Graduate Faculty Philosophy Journal*, Vol. 5, No. 1, Fall 1975, pp. 1–51.

"The Problem of Language in Schleiermacher's Hermeneutic," trans. by D.E. Linge, *Journal for Theology and the Church*, Vol. 7, pp. 68–95.

Reason in the Age of Science, trans. by F.G. Lawrence; Cambridge, Massachusetts: MIT Press, 1981.

"Religion and Religiosity in Socrates," trans. by Richard Velkley, *Proceedings of the Boston Area Colloquium in Ancient Philosophy*, ed. by John Cleary, vol. 1, 1986, pp. 53–75.

"Religious and Poetical Speaking," in *Myth, Symbol and Reality*, ed. by A.M. Olson; Notre Dame, Ind.: University of Notre Dame Press, 1980, pp. 86–98.

"The Religious Dimension in Heidegger," in *Transcendence and the Sacred*, ed. by Alan M. Olson and Leroy S. Rouner; Notre Dame, Ind.: University of Notre Dame Press, 1981, pp. 193–207.

"Rhetoric, Hermeneutics and the Critique of Ideology: Metacritical Comments on *Truth and Method*," trans. by Jerry Dibble, *The Hermeneutics Reader*, ed. by Kurt Mueller-Vollmer; Oxford: Blackwell, 1985, pp. 274–292. (A translation of this essay by G.B. Hess and R.E. Palmer is to be found in *Philosophical Hermeneutics* under the title "On the Scope and Function of Hermeneutical Reflection.")

"Science and the Public," trans. by M. Clarkson, *Universitas*, Vol. 23, No. 3, 1981, pp. 161–168.

"Theory, Technology, Practice: The Task of the Science of Man," trans. by H. Brotz, *Social Research*, Vol. 44, No. 3, Autumn 1977, pp. 529–561.

Truth and Method, trans. by W. Glen-Doepel; London: Sheed & Ward, 1975.

"The Western View of the Inner Experience of Time and the Limits of Thought," *Time and the Philosophers;* Paris: UNESCO, 1977, pp. 33–48.

Index